# THREE CENTURIES
## OF
# AMERICAN DEMOCRACY

BY
WILLIAM MacDONALD, LL.D.
SOMETIME PROFESSOR OF AMERICAN HISTORY
IN BROWN UNIVERSITY

NEW YORK
HENRY HOLT AND COMPANY
1923

4-23-65

# PREFACE

I HAVE had particularly in mind, in writing this book, the very large number of persons who want to know the main facts and the formative influences in the growth of the United States as a democratic nation, but who nevertheless have no time to read elaborate narratives or to study a series of books on special periods or topics. I hope, however, that the book may also prove useful to students and teachers as a summary narrative around which the details of lectures or comprehensive reading can be grouped.

The references to authorities are intended, like the text, primarily for the general reader who may wish to pursue the subject further in books that are most worth while. So many elaborate bibliographies of American history are now available that anyone who desires to follow any particular topic to its limits can easily find guidance, while the systematic student will naturally enlarge his bibliography according to his needs or the library resources at his command.

I can acknowledge only in a general way, but at the same time with sincere appreciation, my indebtedness to the long list of scholars, many of them my valued associates and friends, whose labors have made so much of American history an open book to whomsoever will read. I must pay particular hom-age, however, to the late Professor William A. Dunning and Professor John W. Burgess of Columbia University, who more than any others have placed the constitutional aspects of the Civil War and the Reconstruction period in their true light, and whose views at a number of points will be found reproduced in these pages.

WILLIAM MacDONALD

January, 1923.

# CONTENTS

# THREE CENTURIES OF AMERICAN DEMOCRACY

## CHAPTER I

## THE CENTURIES OF BEGINNINGS

THE United States is often spoken of as preeminently a country of rapid growth. Only in comparison with Europe, however, where civilization had reached a high development centuries before the existence of the American continent was known, or with China and India, where culture was a well-developed plant ages before European civilization had wholly broken with barbarism, is America a young country. Between the first voyage of Columbus and the Declaration of Independence nearly three hundred years elapsed, and the Declaration of Independence is now almost a century and a half behind us. The establishment of the elements of European civilization in North America was accomplished only by long and devious efforts, with steps often halting and always slow, while the imposing political structure which the United States presents today has been the arduous achievement of four generations.

The discovery of a New World at the end of the fifteenth century, only forty years after the invention of printing, was one of a succession of events which completed the historical transition from the later middle ages to early modern times. Preceded as it was by a series of geographical discoveries which had revealed the general form of the African continent, and by an eager study of geography which rapidly dispelled many older notions regarding the shape and size of the globe, the discovery of extensive land areas to the west took its place at first with the other discoveries that were being made, and years passed before the importance of what had been found was generally appreciated. Even after the existence of two great continents and numerous adjacent islands had been definitely established, and map makers had drawn in crude outline the form of the American Atlantic coast, only three European states, Spain, France, and England, interested themselves in the new discoveries and for more than a century Spain alone attempted permanent occupation. The importance of America, either as a field for European colonization or as an element in the spread of political influence, dawned but slowly upon the consciousness of Europe.

It is interesting to note that the colonizing efforts of Spain, the nation which until the end of the sixteenth century took the lead in American discovery and settlement, were directed throughout to regions whose influence upon the development of the United States has been relatively slight. The theory of colonization which England in time came to follow, namely, the transfer over seas of a population which should reproduce in the colony something of the social and political life of the mother country and work its way to eventual self-support, found no illustration in Spain. To Spain the American colonies meant a rich revenue with which to support dynastic and political ambitions at home, and revenue and control rather than general economic or social development were the chief aims. Spain found what it wanted in the native states of the west coast of South America and in Mexico, where in each case the native population was virtually enslaved for the exploitation of the mines and a few natural products.

By the time of the American revolution Spain was in control of all of South America except Brazil, which a papal bull had allotted to Portugal, of Central America and Mexico, of the peninsula of Florida and the Gulf coasts of the present States of Alabama, Mississippi, Louisiana, and Texas, and of the Pacific coast as far north as San Francisco, this latter point having been reached in the year in which the Declaration of Independence was issued. In none of these regions, however, was there a veritable Spanish civilization, none had any considerable Spanish population, and in none had the general economic development of the country been systematically undertaken either by the government or by the inhabitants. The records of the labors and journeys of missionary priests and soldier adventurers are still fascinating reading, and the old Spanish missions of California still recall the days when church and state made common cause for the advancement of the kingdom of God and the king; but the American colonies of Spain were only outposts of Spanish political influence, occupied territories held rigorously in subjection and mercilessly exploited, foreign areas which Spain had appropriated in the days of its greatness and which it long clung to in its decay.

France, a century behind Spain in American colonization save for one or two unimportant essays, pursued in general the same unenlightened policy. Until the defeat of the Spanish armada, in 1588, destroyed the naval power of Spain and in consequence weakened its hold upon its colonies, no nation ventured seriously to interfere with its activities in the regions which it had occupied. French adventurers turned to the north, explored the Gulf of St. Lawrence, followed the St. Lawrence river to its source in the Great Lakes, traversed the lakes and charted their limits, found the headwaters of the Mississippi, and pursued the Father of Waters to the Gulf and paddled their canoes the length of the Ohio, the Illinois, and other tributary streams. From Quebec, the seat of French power in America, traders and priests made long and hazardous journeys into the interior, fraternized with the Indians when tribes were not hostile, exchanged European goods, firearms, and brandy for furs, and cultivated regard for the French people and respect for the French king. By the middle of the eighteenth century the whole northern half of the continent east of the Rocky Mountains and a large part of the Mississippi valley were in French hands, and the colony of New France was the proudest appanage of the French crown. A century and a half of romantic effort, however, had brought no considerable French population to New France, the economic foundations of a permanent society had not been laid, food and other articles of common use had still in part to be brought from France, and the fur trade, the one remunerative venture, had begun to show decline. There was little assurance that French colonial power in North America would long continue even if political events in Europe had not conspired to overthrow it.

With the exception of California and the States of the southwest, no important traces of either French or Spanish colonization survive in the United States. Even in Canada the use of the French language continued only within the limits of the ancient province of Quebec or here and there among fur traders and Indians, French law and customs exercised no permanent influence outside of the zone of French occupation except in Louisiana, and the Catholic faith found small tolerance in any English colony except Maryland and was long regarded with aversion in many American States. Almost the only surviving evidences of Spanish occupation, aside from the missions, in the southwest and California are the old Spanish land grants, the basis of land titles in much of the territory which once belonged to Spain, and the use of a corrupt speech, partly Spanish and partly Mexican, among certain classes of the population. The colonies which declared their independence, took the name of the United States of America, and fought to a successful issue a war of revolution were overwhelmingly English in race, language, law, social institutions, and habits of thought.

The period of English colonization which begins with the successful establishment of an English settlement in Virginia extends over a hundred and twenty-five years. The motives of colonization were various. The influx of gold and silver from the mines of Mexico and Peru, continuing with little interruption until the latter part of the sixteenth cenury, had profoundly affected economic life in Europe, made possible an increasing substitution of money exchange for barter, facilitated international trade, and supported the armies upon which the power of Spain largely rested. With the rapid decline of Spain after 1588 rival nations sought in America, although not in the Spanish colonies, the same wealth which had made Spain great. England, at last a sea power, reached out for colonies in a half-conscious search for imperial control, and with the further hope of finding markets for its goods and profits for its capital and its ships. Religious difficulties, fruits of the Protestant revolt which had separated England from Rome and given it a national church, led the members of more than one dissenting or proscribed sect to seek in America the freedom of faith and practice which was denied to them at home. To not a few Englishmen colonization appealed as a romantic adventure, a new knight errantry in which gentlemen and commoners might hope to win distinction at the same time that they recouped their fortunes or rehabilitated their reputations.

Colonization, however, was expensive, and the English crown under James I and his successors was poor. The spread of English influence beyond seas must be accomplished by private effort if it was to be accomplished at all. Resort was had, accordingly, to chartered companies and huge land grants to individuals or groups of proprietors. The Virginia company, chartered in 1606 and twice reorganized, succeeded after several years of painful effort in establishing a permanent colony in the James river region; but the cultivation of tobacco, made possible on a large scale by the gradual introduction of Negro slave labor, proved profitable, and by 1621, when the charter of the company was withdrawn and the colony reverted to the crown, the success of the Virginia experiment was assured. The Maryland colony, based upon a charter granted to Lord Baltimore in 1628, was more wisely and generously managed and prospered from the start, while the freedom of conscience which was extended to Catholics gave both the colony and its founder an honorable place in the history of religious liberty. Neither Virginia nor Maryland, however, was a source of financial profit to its founders, neither ever attracted any large emigration from England, and for many years the growth of population and trade was small.

The desire for religious liberty which led Lord Baltimore, with the help of royal connivance, to open the Maryland colony to Catholics turned the eyes of English Protestant dissenters also toward America. The first attempt at colonization, that of the Separatists or Pilgrims at Plymouth, was pitifully weak, for the supporting sect was small and without financial resource, and no Protestant body in England had charity for any other. Labors and privations as great as those which had been undergone in Virginia marked the first years of the Plymouth settlement, and the little colony never succeeded in obtaining a charter or an assured legal status.

The Massachusetts colony, on the other hand, represented a large and well-managed effort of the powerful Puritan body in England to set up in America a Puritan commonwealth. Organized in form as a trading company with a royal charter, and with a vast grant of territory far beyond any possibility of immediate settlement, the Massachusetts company was in fact a close corporation controlled by Puritans and in close touch, until the Puritan period in England came to an end, with the Puritan body and its leaders at home. Firmly and arbitrarily ruled by its Calvinist clergy and a few secular leaders, the colony ruthlessly repressed religious and political dissent, destroyed with barbaric cruelty the power of some of the Indian tribes, dominated the neighboring colonies of Connecticut and Rhode Island, spread its lines of control into New Hampshire and Maine, and for fifty years stoutly resisted every effort of the crown to call it to account or to interfere with the conduct of its affairs. Population grew, settlements multiplied, trade increased, and the level of individual prosperity was high. Alone among all the colonies that England has had Massachusetts was governed by a sect, and it was in the colony in which religion was long the greatest single force in public life that the spirit of political independence was most pronounced and the later struggle for independence most aggressive and unrelenting.

Dissenters were akin, however, in little save dissent, and the religious intolerance and arbitrary political methods of the Massachusetts Puritans caused more than one group to seek freedom elsewhere. A violent theological controversy sent Wheelwright and a few followers to Exeter, where they founded a settlement which later grew into the colony of New Hampshire. Another group, followers of Mrs. Ann Hutchinson, a strong-minded woman who had been adjudged a dangerous heretic, established themselves on the island of Rhode Island; while still another group of religious and social libertarians, led by Roger Williams, settled at Providence. The colony of Rhode Island, organized as such under a royal charter in 1663, represented the union of four different settlements, Newport, Providence, Portsmouth, and Warwick, each of which had its own particular reasons for regarding Massachusetts with distrust. A less aggressive body of dissenters, headed by Thomas Hooker, quietly withdrew to the fertile valley of the Connecticut, and a party of emigrants from England who had expected to settle in Massachusetts, but who were deterred by the heresy controversies which they found there upon their arrival, moved on to New Haven. In 1665 a royal charter merged New Haven and the river towns in the colony of Connecticut. A few straggling settlements in Maine, eventually absorbed by Massachusetts, completed the English occupation of New England.

The downfall of the Puritan commonwealth and Cromwellian protectorate in England and the restoration of Charles II, in 1660, brought a renewal of interest in colonization. The charters of Connecticut and Rhode Island, far more liberal from the standpoint of popular government than any previous charters had been, were a rebuke to the oligarchical spirit of Puritanism and an important step in the direction of a divorce of religion from politics. Charles had many political debts to pay, however, and the American continent, most of whose eastern half had already been claimed in one way or another for the English crown notwithstanding the French occupation of the interior, was a welcome resource. A Dutch colony in New York, the only attempt of The Netherlands at colonization in North America, was taken as spoils in a war with the Dutch and given to the king's brother, the Duke of York. Lord

Carteret, a royal favorite, received a grant of New Jersey, and a group of titled proprietors headed by Lord Shaftesbury obtained a grant of Carolina for which John Locke, the English philosopher, drafted a feudal constitution. The colonizing work of the seventeenth century was completed in 1681 when William Penn, the most prominent representative of the Quaker sect in England, was made lord proprietor of Pennsylvania. The Pennsylvania colony was the first English enterprise to attract a German population, and the absorption of some small Swedish settlements in Delaware presently made it even more cosmopolitan.

There was little in all this to suggest the ultimate emergence of a great nation. The English colonies, scattered along the Atlantic coast from Maine to Carolina and with their settlements everywhere easily accessible from the sea, were hemmed in between the ocean which separated them from England and an untrodden wilderness stretching no one knew how far to the west. The conquest of the country meant the levelling of primeval forests, the slow clearing of the land, and the defeat or subjugation of Indian tribes which in the centre and north long remained hostile. There was no important emigration from Europe, save to Pennsylvania, after 1640, and while the abundance of free land and a healthy climate made America a place of opportunity for those who could support the rigors of a primitive and laborious life, there was no apparent promise of a large population for many generations to come. With the abatement of religious bitterness in England and the waning of the early spirit of adventure the infant settlements were left to grow in numbers mainly by the slow process of natural increase, and to depend upon themselves for the financial resources necessary for the development of their economic life. None of the colonies was financially profitable to the companies or individuals who initiated them, and in none was prosperity due to English financial aid.

The spirit of union, too, was lacking. Each colony was a separate political entity, owing allegiance to the mother country but politically in no way bound to regard its neighbors. Virginia had nothing in common with New York or New Jersey, and Quaker Pennsylvania had small inducement to cultivate the friendship of Puritan New England. Physical communication was difficult except by sea. The Carolina settlements, separated by a wilderness from Virginia and Maryland, saw more of the English colonists in the island of Barbados, from which the early Carolina population had been in part recruited, than they did of their neighbors to the north, and another stretch of wilderness separated Virginia and Maryland from Pennsylvania. Only in New England, where distances were small and the towns of one colony touched those of another, was colonial union natural or practicable. A New England Confederation, formed in 1643 primarily for joint defence against the Indians, held the germ of intercolonial unity; but the domineering attitude of Massachusetts bred discontent in Connecticut and Rhode Island, the foundations of genuine political accord in general matters were not laid, and with the collapse of the Indian resistance the Confederation first declined and then ceased to exist. Not until the later French and Indian wars did the northern colonies again make serious attempts to act together, and the temporary unions which were then formed were for military purposes only.

Economic and social conditions, also, made for sectional diversity and separateness rather than for unity. The dominating class of landed proprietors in Virginia, Maryland, and Carolina, at one in origin and social sympathy with the Cavaliers and country gentlemen of England, preferred country life to life in towns and were averse to manual labor or personal participation in trade; and the plantation system of farming, with its staple crops of tobacco and rice marketed through agents in England, and its slave labor which climatic conditions seemed to ordain as the only form of labor possible, coincided with their tastes. Most of the southern planters who were church members, except the declining Catholic minority in Maryland, were adherents of the Church of England, and the theological controversies which were long the meat and drink of the Puritans suggested to Episcopalians only a fierce and half-successful attempt to destroy the crown and set up a Calvinist theocracy.

In New England, on the other hand, where the Church of England was nonexistent and where Puritanism left an indelible mark, the primary physical conditions were different. The climate was rigorous, the soil possessed by nature only moderate fertility, the rivers were not navigable far from the sea although good harbors were numerous, and the Indians were long a menace. Physical conditions, accordingly, dictated the location of the first settlements on the coast rather than in the interior, drew the population together in small compact communities, and reduced individual land holdings to comparatively small areas which a single family, working without the aid of either slave or hired labor, could clear and cultivate. In place of staple crops for export there was diversified production almost wholly for local consumption. Every advance of settlement into the Indian wilderness was a hazardous venture, and for a hundred and thirty years after colonization began the frontier settlers were exposed to attack. Puritan faith and practice, moreover, with their emphasis upon personal conduct and weekly religious instruction, accorded better with town life than with life in the country. The town, accordingly, became the political unit throughout New England, whereas in the south the political unit was the plantation or the county. Even in Rhode Island, an alien region of dissent so far as Puritanism was concerned, the organization of social life was essentially the same as in Massachusetts and Connecticut.

On the other hand, with all their local differences and insularities the English colonies nevertheless possessed important fundamental characteristics out of which unity might grow. The prevailing language was everywhere English. The use of Dutch in New York had begun to decline even before the colony passed into English control, and the corrupt dialect which the Pennsylvania Germans developed did not spread beyond that colony and was localized even there. Every colony had English law as the basis of its jurisprudence, and the procedure of the colonial assemblies was modelled upon that of the House of Commons. Every colony looked to England as the protecting mother, and the claims of allegiance were not disputed, except in Massachusetts, even when quarrels with the crown became most acute. Some trade went on from colony to colony, and colonial-built vessels carried lumber and fish from New England to the south, tobacco and rice from the southern colonies to England, rum to the West Indies and Africa, and Negro slaves from Africa to the plantation colonies.

Certain political resemblances, also, prepared the way for common political action later. Whatever the original legal organization of the colony, whether a chartered company as in Virginia and Massachusetts, a grant to one or more proprietors as in Maryland, Carolina, and Pennsylvania, or something resembling an incorporation of the whole people as in Connecticut and Rhode Island, time and circumstances had developed forms of government which were in the main similar from colony to colony and which in practice gave to each colony a virtually complete control of its own internal affairs. Every colony had a legislative house the members of which were elected by the freemen, or legal voters, and an upper house or council which exercised executive powers and in some cases shared in those of legislation. The governors, appointed by the crown in Virginia after 1621 and by the proprietors where proprietary control continued, were in New England chosen by the freemen, but whether elected or appointed the governor was the head of the colonial executive and the responsible director of colonial defence. The needs of local government were met by the organization of towns and counties, a system of courts with final appeal to the king in council was gradually evolved, and local and colonial taxes were voted, assessed, and collected.

Strictly speaking, however, no colony except Carolina possessed a constitution, and the elaborate feudal constitution of Carolina was not in fact applied. The colonial charters, framed with the approval of the law officers of the crown and granted in the king's name, were grants of territory and privilege and as such were naturally the fundamental bases of colonial rights; but they did not spring from the people themselves, they were not subject to amendment by the people or by the colonial governments, and they might at any time be taken away for cause by the royal authority which had granted them. From a constitutional standpoint a colonial charter resembled far more

a modern municipal charter, in which are embodied
the privileges and duties to which the municipality is
subject and beyond which it cannot go, than a modern
State constitution. The innumerable controversies
which developed with proprietors or crown over
charter rights, however, and the disposition of the
colonies to insist upon the most favorable interpretation of their claims which the charter provisions would
bear had the effect of giving to a charter something
of the character of a fundamental law, and prepared
the way for the devotion to the idea of a written
constitution which is specially characteristic of the
United States.

Some of the early grants of territory, made at a
time when the form and size of the continent were
unknown, appear grotesque. The Massachusetts,
Virginia, and Carolina grants, for example, ran " from
sea to sea," the notion that the South sea or Pacific
ocean was to be found at least as near as the Mississippi long persisting among political geographers.
The Pennsylvania and Maryland grants overlapped,
the boundaries between Connecticut and Rhode
Island and between Connecticut and New York were
long in dispute, and the aggressive colony of Massachusetts fought hard for the extension of its frontiers
into Rhode Island on the south and into New Hampshire and Maine on the north. No serious attempts
were anywhere made, however, to settle the far interior, and most of the vast region west of the Appalachian mountains eventually reverted to the crown.

The English claims to territory did not go undisputed. Spain, firmly planted in Mexico and Cuba and with its territory encircling the Gulf of Mexico, was a barrier in the way of expansion to the south, and north of Mexico was slowly conquering the southwest and the Pacific coast. France, unsuccessful as a colonizer so far as the establishment of large permanent settlements was concerned, but zealous and aggressive when the acquisition of territory and political influence was the prize, laid claim by right of discovery, exploration, and occupation to the entire Mississippi valley and the region tributary to the Great Lakes and the St. Lawrence, drew its boundaries so as to include about half of the present State of Maine, and dreamed of a mighty effort which should crowd the English into the sea and win North America for the French crown.

Perhaps France could never in any case have realized its romantic hopes even had the French and English colonies been left to settle the matter for themselves, but the shattering of its dream was the result of events in Europe to which the struggles of French and English in America were only incidental accompaniments. The accession of William and Mary as joint sovereigns, in 1689, marked the end of the attempt which Charles II and James II had persistently made, the former more or less secretly and the latter openly, to restore Catholicism in England. Charles was dead, James was a fugitive in France. Between William of Orange, who before

his accession to the English throne had been the foremost leader of political Protestantism in Europe, and
Louis XIV of France, the most powerful and dazzling
representative of political Catholicism, there had long
been relentless hostility, and the main interest of
William in the English crown was the added opportunity which it gave him to safeguard and advance
the interests of Protestantism against the schemes of
the French king. Beyond the question of religion,
however, far more a force in international politics in
the seventeenth and eighteenth centuries than it has
been at any time since, was the yet larger question of
political control in Europe and throughout the world.
When, in 1763, the power of France was broken and
the world predominance of England was assured,
Europe and America had been for nearly seventy-five
years involved in war.

The four successive intercolonial wars in America
which fill most of the period between 1689 and 1763,
and which were commonly referred to in the English
colonies as the French and Indian wars, were in
essence only the American phases of wars between
England and France in Europe. Colonial possessions, more and more regarded as potential resources
of wealth as well as undoubted resources of political
prestige, were prizes to be fought for, and when
France and England went to war in Europe the
French and English colonies went to war in America.
Until the Seven Years' war (1756–1763) only the
northern English colonies were particularly affected,

for French occupation of the Ohio valley had been too slight to permit the French to take the offensive there or to make their presence a menace. In the north, on the other hand, where the French had the advantage of position and could rest on the defensive if they chose, the frontiers of New England and New York lay open to attack, and it was along this exposed frontier that the French in Canada, reinforced by Indian allies, struck repeated blows and carried death, plunder, and devastation far and wide.

The first three wars, the last of which ended in 1748, made comparatively little impression upon the French position. The vast territory of New France remained essentially intact. A new English colony, Georgia, fruit of the philanthropic interest of Oglethorpe in debtors and men who had failed in life, had been planted between South Carolina and Florida in part as a further protection against Spanish invasion, but the other English settlements still hugged the coast and the frontier was everywhere in peril. The island of Cape Breton with its fortress of Louisburg had been taken from the French by siege only to be restored to them by treaty. No other successful attempt had yet been made to attack Canada by sea, and the colonies had been left to rely mainly upon themselves for troops, munitions, and supplies. Internally, however, New France was weaker than the English knew. Its population was hopelessly outnumbered by the population of the English colonies, its fur trade was profitless, its political administration was inefficient and corrupt, and communication with France depended far less upon French war vessels in the Gulf of St. Lawrence than upon the inactivity of the English fleet at sea.

The Seven Years' war which was to see the downfall of French power in America began irregularly in the colonies two years before war was formally declared in Europe. The opening campaigns were disastrous for the English. Braddock met defeat in an attempt to reach the Ohio, and efforts to penetrate Canada by way of Lake Champlain and the valley of the Mohawk were frustrated by dissentions, bad management, delays, and French adroitness. Nova Scotia and Cape Breton were presently taken by the English, however, some thousands of the French population of Nova Scotia being harshly deported to the English colonies, and the way was prepared for a combined attack upon Quebec and Montreal by land and sea. In 1759 an English force under Wolfe took Quebec, and the next year New France surrendered to Amherst. The rich possessions of France in India had already passed into English hands, and the colonial power of France was for the time being destroyed.

The downfall of New France was a victory for the English colonies aided by English subsidies, English troops, and the English navy, and in the laurels of victory both the mother country and the colonies were entitled to share. It was not a victory of a better theory of empire over an inferior one, nor of a nation with a healthy civilization over a nation whose civilization was unsound. It was a victory of superior numbers, superior resources, and wiser planning. While to England, however, the overthrow of the French power in America was of small importance in comparison with the humiliation of France by the establishment of English supremacy in Europe, to the colonies the intercolonial wars were an experience of far-reaching value. War had enforced the need of colonial unity. It had familiarized the colonists with military operations on a considerable scale, and the experience stood them in good stead when, a dozen years later, the war of revolution broke. The defeat of the French not only freed the frontier from danger of further attack, but also opened the door to the extension of settlement westward as population grew. With the obstacle of New France removed the building of a great colonial dependency could go on unchecked. The immediate future of the American continent north of the Spanish possessions was now in English hands.

By the peace of Paris, concluded in 1763, France ceded to England all French territory on the mainland of North America, while Spain, which had joined in the war, ceded Florida and a narrow strip of territory on the Gulf of Mexico as far west as the Mississippi. The entire eastern half of the continent, from the Mississippi to the Atlantic and from the Gulf of Mexico to the Arctic ocean, thus passed under English control. A royal proclamation, issued shortly after the peace, provided for the administration of the newly-acquired territory. Three governments were created: Quebec, comprising in general the parts of Canada which depended upon the St. Lawrence and the Great Lakes; East Florida, practically coextensive with the present State of Florida; and West Florida, comprising the extreme southern parts of what are now the States of Alabama, Mississippi, and Louisiana as far as the Mississippi delta. The region between Quebec and the Floridas and west of the Appalachians as far as the Mississippi was left without organization, and the governors of the English colonies were forbidden to make any grants of land in the region without special authorization. By drawing a demarcation line along the Appalachian watershed which separates the streams flowing into the Atlantic from those which belong to the Mississippi river system, and setting off the territory west of the line as a region apart, the proclamation in effect fixed the western boundaries of the older colonies and put an end to their old claims to indefinite extension westward.

The Paris settlement was not wholly satisfactory to the older colonies. The guaranty of the continuance of French law and the Catholic faith which Amherst had given when New France surrendered, and which was confirmed by the peace, was viewed with apprehension in Puritan Massachusetts and Connecticut. The abridgment of the western land claims was unpalatable to every colony whose claims were affected, and while the royal proclamation had perforce to be acquiesced in for the moment, no colony abandoned its claims and several of them, notably Virginia, revived them after the Revolution to the temporary embarrassment of the national government.

As a whole, however, the territorial arrangements of 1763 excited little general interest. There were other concerns of more immediate appeal. War debts were heavy notwithstanding English aid, the paper currency was depreciated and the volume of specie small, and taxation was burdensome. The first charter of Massachusetts had been taken away in 1684, and the new charter of 1691, under which the governor was appointed by the crown, had been followed by renewed quarrels in which governors and people were about equally at fault. The royal governors of New York were in many instances incompetent or corrupt, and heated controversies with the assembly and the people regularly recurred. North Carolina, separated from South Carolina early in the eighteenth century, long remained a weak and backward colony in comparison with its southern neighbor, and the new colony of Georgia showed little strength until after the Revolution.

Yet the colonies on the whole were prosperous. Population was growing, intercolonial and over seas trade was expanding, and the beginnings of manufactures were to be discerned. American-built vessels were readily sold in Europe, and Virginia tobacco,

South Carolina rice, wheat from Pennsylvania, and timber, naval stores, fish, and rum from New England were increasingly in demand. Intellectual interests; too, narrow as their horizon undoubtedly was, had not been wholly neglected. The colleges of Harvard, Yale, and William and Mary were leading the way to higher education, the study of law was zealously pursued, a few libraries had been accumulated, and the writings and scientific discoveries of Benjamin Franklin had made his name familiar to European scholars. The hold of Puritanism had been greatly weakened by the spread of a liberal theological movement, and a series of preaching tours by George Whitfield, which extended to all the colonies, strengthened the trend to religious tolerance. A few colonial newspapers had sprung up, the colonial press turned out a swelling stream of pamphlets and books, and a postal system operated regularly between Boston and Philadelphia and irregularly from Philadelphia to Virginia and the south. Political discussion, although often envenomed by personalities, was on the whole serious, and practical experience in colonial assemblies and town or county meetings accorded an invaluable training for the treatment of larger general affairs when the day of union should arrive. It was a primitive, simple, healthy, conventional, hard-working, but forward-looking America which emerged from the intercolonial wars to face the grave issue of independence.

## CHAPTER II

## THROUGH REVOLUTION TO INDEPENDENCE

THE revolt of the English colonies in America against British control which broke out suddenly soon after the peace of Paris, and which in a little more than a decade developed into open revolution and a war for independence, was primarily occasioned by an attempt of the British government to tax the colonies for the purpose of meeting a part of the increasing cost of colonial administration. To the colonial protest against taxation, however, was joined a protest against a system of trade regulation which for more than a century had been imposed by Great Britain, and the enforcement of which, albeit irregular and often negligent, had long been a source of irritation and complaint. Whether the trade restrictions alone would ultimately have provoked a revolution may well be doubted, for the system was far less burdensome in fact than it was in form; but the announcement of a purpose to enforce the trade laws in connection with the project of taxation made a combination of grievances too weighty to be borne.

As early as 1649 Parliament had attempted to regulate the trade of the colonies for the special bene-

fit of British merchants and ship owners, and from
1660 a long series of statutes had sought to exclude
foreigners from the colonial trade, to insure the
marketing of all important colonial products in England or in other English colonies, and to make England the door through which foreign goods destined
for the colonies must pass. Colonial and British
vessels were, to be sure, put upon the same footing
so far as trade with the colonies was concerned, and
the purpose of the statutes was undoubtedly to encourage colonial trade rather than to check its
development; but the denial of the right to buy or
sell directly in foreign ports placed the colonial merchant and ship owner at the mercy of English ship-
builders and traders, and deprived the colonies of the
benefits of foreign competition either in prices or in
transportation rates.

The restrictions which the acts of navigation and
trade sought to impose were met in America for many
years by more or less open disregard and by systematic evasion. Smuggling was widely practiced and
generally condoned, and the bribery of customs officials and even of royal governors took on the character of a system. As a matter of fact, accordingly,
the statutes, while increasingly elaborate and detailed
as the system grew, interfered but little with colonial
prosperity, and the protests of English merchants and
shippers at the practical failure of a system which
had been created for their benefit did not avail to
secure even a moderate enforcement. It was clear

to the colonists, however, that with as yet no colonial manufactures of importance and a disposition in England to restrict the few that had been established, and consequently with a permanent adverse balance of trade which must be settled in specie, exclusion from foreign markets save through the gateway of England entailed a continual drain of specie and increasing economic servitude to England; and against the restrictive system, once the enforcement of the acts seemed likely to be taken seriously in hand, America was prepared to make vigorous protest.

The Seven Years' war left Great Britain with a heavy debt, a depleted treasury, and an unprecedented burden of taxation. It seemed to the Grenville ministry only proper that the colonies, freed by the war from any further danger from the French and with their own war expenditures in part reimbursed by grants from the British treasury, should pay some portion at least of the imperial cost of colonial administration. Apparently the ministry would have been satisfied if the amounts required could have been furnished by the colonies themselves through taxes imposed by the colonial assemblies, but the assemblies had long been prone to use the power of the purse as a lever for coercing governors and other representatives of the crown, quarrels and delays over salaries and other charges had been frequent, and even with a willing spirit the amounts obtainable through assembly grants would probably be irregular and would almost certainly be insufficient.

Accordingly, with some hesitation and apprehension, resort was had to direct taxation. An elaborate scheme of stamp duties, applicable to legal documents and certain classes of printed matter and similar in all essential respects to a system long in operation in England, was prepared, but the action of Parliament was delayed for a year in order that the colonial assemblies might, if they chose, propose some satisfactory alternative through which the desired revenue could be obtained. The assemblies were agreed only in objecting to the tax, and accordingly in March, 1765, the Stamp Act became law. The attention of the ministry having in the meantime been drawn to the great extent of colonial smuggling, the provisions of an act imposing heavy duties upon sugar and molasses, which had been allowed to lapse, were revived and extended, and preparations were made for a rigorous enforcement of the trade laws.

The Stamp Act encountered forcible resistance in the colonies. Stamp distributors were mobbed or intimidated, stamps and stamped paper were destroyed, and only in the Carolinas and Georgia were the requirements of the act observed. A colonial congress, meeting at New York, adopted resolutions protesting against the claim of right to tax the colonies without their consent. Four months after the act was to have gone into effect it was repealed, the repeal being accompanied, however, by a resolution asserting the constitutional right of Parliament to tax

the colonies in all cases whatsoever — a declaration
which would have been ominous had there been any
real likelihood of translating it into a permanent
policy.  The attempt to enforce the trade laws proved
to be extremely costly, but naval vessels with revenue jurisdiction continued to patrol the coast notwithstanding that smuggling still went on.  In 1767,
with a new ministry, a new revenue scheme of indirect
taxation through customs duties was elaborated, and
writs of assistance authorized revenue officers to
search for and seize smuggled goods.  The anticipated revenue, however, was not obtained, and frequent collisions with customs officers kept alive the
fires of revolt.

It was reasonably clear that America could not be
made to pay taxes of any kind for the support of the
British colonial establishment, and that the enforcement of the revenue laws involved an expense out
of all proportion to the revenue collected.  It was
equally clear that the relations between the colonists
and British officials were becoming dangerously
strained and that the authority of the crown was
being openly defied.  Not all of the colonies, however, were equally aggressive in their opposition.
Down almost to the outbreak of war the leadership
of colonial resistance lay with Massachusetts and
Virginia, and while Connecticut, Rhode Island, and
New York followed willingly where others led the
way, neither New Jersey, Pennsylvania, nor Maryland showed equal energy in resisting the crown

demands, and the Carolinas and Georgia followed Virginia only afar off. Had the British ministry comprehended the real situation it might very possibly have divided the colonies by concessions or special treatment, and checked the growth of the movement for independence before the movement had become strong.

The task of raising the controversy from the narrow plane of economic grievance to the broader field of constitutional right was assumed by Massachusetts. The Puritan colony was well fitted for the work. Almost from the beginning of its existence it had stubbornly resisted every attempt of the crown to interfere with its affairs, and had boldly claimed rights and privileges under its charters which neither the first nor the second charter had apparently intended to grant. In the new controversy which had now opened the arguments drawn from the restrictive effect of the trade laws were urged with all the force and ingenuity that they would bear, but the attempt to raise a revenue by taxation was met by the contention that, among Englishmen, there could be no taxation without representation. That the American colonies were not represented in Parliament even indirectly could not be questioned; that they could in practice be represented, in view of the distance which separated them from England, was more than doubtful; and if they could not enjoy the privilege of representation which the British constitution enshrined, they were by that fact freed from any obligation to pay taxes save such only as their own elected assemblies imposed. And since taxation without representation was unconstitutional, taxation without representation was tyranny, and tyranny might properly be resisted by force.

Such was the argument which Samuel Adams and other revolutionary leaders in Massachusetts developed, and which in time, with far-reaching inferences and applications, twelve other continental colonies came to accept. Only slowly, however, did the logic of Adams and his followers win its way. Many members of the aristocratic and official classes, many professional men and large landowners, and an appreciable percentage of the rank and file either rejected the argument altogether as leading straight to revolution and independence, or gave it only a half-hearted assent, or surrendered at last to the inevitable only when the patriot party, admirably organized and wholly uncompromising, resorted to coercion. The revolution which made the United States an independent nation was undoubtedly in its inception the work of a small minority, and the partisans of England who were forcibly suppressed or harshly expelled numbered some of the wealthiest and most influential men whom colonial life had produced; but the minority had laid hold of the great ideas of nationality and independence which the conservative opposition did not share, and with those ideas the minority carried the day.

To the growth of the spirit of resistance and independence which the revenue schemes aroused, British colonial policy made a substantial contribution. The colonial theory which regarded the colonies as fields for economic exploitation, and measured the strength of empire by the area to which imperial rule extended rather than by the happiness and prosperity of the people, was not English in origin, for the same theory had obtained throughout in Spain and France; and the restrictions which England had imposed upon colonial shipping and trade were no more unenlightened than was the economic policy of the eighteenth century generally. The attempt to tax the colonies directly, however, in addition to taxing them indirectly through the control of their most lucrative trade, was a grave political blunder all the more serious because the constitutional issue involved was easily to be perceived; and constitutional struggles had more than once brought revolution in England itself. It was long the fashion to blame the king, George III, for the loss of the American colonies, and the baneful influence of the royal personality was unquestionably great and compelling; but the statesmen who scrambled and bribed for office under George III showed little more practical wisdom than did the king when the American colonies were concerned. Neither Whigs nor Tories, the two great parties of the day, were deeply troubled about the constitutional rights of Englishmen, and no strong, clear voice save that of Edmund Burke was long heard in opposition. Later generations, more liberal and intelligent, were

to see in the struggle against absolutism in America
an important phase of the still longer struggle against
a similar policy in the mother country, but the full
significance of the contest was not appreciated until
after a vast colonial domain in America had been lost.

Multiplying incidents showed better than argument
the inflammable state of colonial public opinion. A
street fight with British troops at Boston in March,
1775, magnified by history into a massacre, evidenced
the hatred which the British uniform excited. In
1772 the British sloop-of-war *Gaspee,* engaged in
enforcing the customs laws, was burned by Rhode
Island men in Narragansett bay. Associations whose
members pledged themselves not to import or use
British goods were formed, and when the ministry,
seeking to make a test case as well as to help the
East India Company out of financial embarrassment,
reduced to a low point the colonial duties on tea, the
people of Boston threw the consignments of tea into
the harbor and tea ships arriving in other colonies
were sent back or their cargoes impounded. Colonial
newspapers published long discussions of colonial
rights, revolutionary pamphlets multiplied, and patriotic clergy spoke out.

It was not in the British temper to yield to opposition without a struggle, and a policy of open coercion was now inaugurated. Massachusetts was
obviously the chief offender, and that colony was
singled out for punishment. In 1774 the port of
Boston was closed to commerce except in food, the

embargo to remain in force until satisfaction was accorded to the East India Company for its tea, town meetings were forbidden, and the choice of members of the colonial council was placed under the control of the royal governor. A parliamentary statute, applicable to all the colonies, authorized the trial in England or in another colony of persons charged with offences under the revenue laws, colonial juries being notoriously unwilling to convict even in the face of indubitable evidence. Boston passed under martial law, General Gage arrived as military governor, and the military and naval forces in America were strengthened.

The open resort to coercion was the one thing needed to unite the colonies. From New Hampshire to Georgia the people rallied to the support of Massachusetts and the relief of the embargoed inhabitants of Boston. A Continental Congress framed a forcible but dignified statement of colonial rights, and adopted articles of association which looked to complete commercial nonintercourse with Great Britain and the encouragement of American industries. Secret committees of correspondence kept the several colonies informed of British plans and proceedings, committees of public safety collected arms and organized military drill, and available stores of munitions and military supplies were carefully listed. When in April, 1775, a British force from Boston, attempting to destroy some military stores at Lexington and Concord, met stubborn resistance and was driven back in ignominious retreat, the time for argument had passed and the war of revolution had begun.

Not as yet, however, was it a war for independence. The second Continental Congress, which in 1775 assumed the direction of colonial resistance and governed by general consent until it was replaced by the Congress of the Confederation in 1781, appointed George Washington commander-in-chief of the forces of the United Colonies, planned military operations on a comprehensive scale, wrestled with problems of finance, authorized one colony after another to resist the crown, and opened to trade all American ports; but it also framed a " declaration of the causes and necessity of taking up arms " which explicitly repudiated the idea of independence and asserted that forcible resistance had been resorted to only because the rights of the colonies were endangered. It was the logic of events, enforced by the practical arguments of a small minority who had caught the vision of nationality and were determined at all hazards to make it a reality, that turned the war from the narrow confines of organized resistance to the large ground of a war for independence. That independence was inevitable once open warfare had begun is today easily to be perceived, but nearly fifteen months elapsed after the fighting at Lexington and Concord before the great Declaration made the United States an independent nation.

The British defeat of April 19, 1775, was followed by the investment of Boston by irregular colonial forces, the nucleus of the American army of which Washington shortly took command. Royal governors were driven out, assemblies which had been prorogued or dissolved were reconvened and popular governments restored, and forts and munitions were seized. Thousands of loyalists, willing to oppose the mother country by peaceful means but unwilling to oppose it by force, sought in England or Nova Scotia new homes in place of those which they were constrained, not always gently, to abandon. An ambitious attempt under Benedict Arnold to capture Quebec failed disastrously, but the hope of conquering Canada, whose inhabitants showed no desire to join the English colonies in revolt, continued to be cherished. In March, 1776, the British were forced to abandon Boston, and the British headquarters were transferred to New York, thereafter throughout the war in British hands. The strategical importance of the Hudson river, separating New England from the middle and southern colonies and opening access to Canada by way of Lake Champlain and the Mohawk valley, made the New York region the key to the military situation; and the success of Washington in maintaining himself on the Hudson, keeping open land communication with New England, and preventing the successful invasion of the colonies from the north was one of the great causes of ultimate victory for the American arms.

The response of the British ministry to colonial protest and resistance was a combined offer of the sword and the olive branch. A royal proclamation declared the colonies to be in rebellion, an act of Parliament interdicted all trade, and more troops were sent. With these coercive measures went the announcement that the right to impose taxes in the colonies would not be exercised provided the colonial assemblies would themselves undertake to make provision for the support of the British administration. In terms the concession might mean much or little, but there was no confidence in America in the good faith of either the king or his minister, Lord North, and the reply of the Continental Congress was a stinging rejection of the offer. No other reply could well have been made even if confidence had been great, for the signature of John Hancock, president of the Congress, to the Declaration of Independence was only a few hours old when the answer was given.

The Declaration of Independence, in the main the work of Thomas Jefferson, combined with rare skill and effectiveness a theory of government and a statement of grievances. The theory of a free state, grounded in a divine order of human equality, subsisting under forms of government sanctioned by the consent of the governed, operating for the maintenance of human rights, and subject to change through revolution when the government ceased to serve the ends for which it had been created, was of a piece with the political philosophy which the writings of Rousseau immortalized, but it was also, although with different phraseology, the essential foundation of

English political theory and practice. No modern state has made its entrance into the family of nations with a more noble statement of doctrine than that which the United States adopted as the basis of its faith, none has more solidly buttressed its programme of independent action with a convincing specification of grievances. The long indictment of the king and Parliament which the Declaration contains swept the field of British injustice and misconduct, and left no other possible conclusion than that the colonies had become absolved from further allegiance to the British crown and were entitled to live henceforth as free and independent states. Here and there an earnest patriot drew back from this last irrevocable step, but the overwhelming majority of what was now to become the American people approved. From the fourth of July, 1776, there was no longer a group of American colonies but an American nation.

Independence had been proclaimed, but the declaration had still to be made good. More than five years of dreary and desperate war, illumined on only two occasions by decisive successes, were to pass before the preliminaries of a victorious peace could be signed. The brilliant campaigns of Washington in New Jersey, while they revealed to the world a master of strategy, did not shake the hold of the British upon New York, and the " rebel capital " of Philadelphia passed easily into British hands when the British were ready to take it. The defeat of Burgoyne and the capitulation of his army, however, in October, 1777, put an end to all danger of further invasion from Canada and brought to the United States the active aid of France. South of Virginia, where early grievances against Great Britain had been less serious and where enthusiasm for the war was in consequence less sustained than in New England and the middle States, the British for a time overran the country, but the persistent and skilful fighting of Nathanael Greene and his associates eventually drove Cornwallis from the interior of North and South Carolina to the coast and ended the possibility of dismembering the union by cutting off the Carolinas and Georgia. On the sea American losses were heavy, but American naval vessels and privateers terrorized British commerce even in British waters and bred respect for American seamanship and daring.

The alliance with France, cemented by political and commercial treaties in 1778, was of inestimable importance to the United States. Everything that was chivalrous and romantic in the French temperament had been stirred by the spectacle of a group of struggling colonies resisting British domination and boldly asserting their right to independence, and the Declaration of Independence made a profound impression in a country in which the seeds of a yet greater revolution were already ripening. It was to the lasting credit of Franklin, for ten years a colonial agent in England before the war and now the American diplomatic representative in France, that he should from the first have gauged with precision the temper of the French people, and he used all the resources of his extraordinary personal popularity and consummate diplomatic skill to win France to the American cause. Official French support for the United States was not, of course, wholly disinterested. There was still the memory of a New France that had been lost, there was still the age-long antipathy to England and English policy which waited only a favorable moment for revenge; and while the recovery of New France was a hope too shadowy even for a dream, the loss by Great Britain of its colonial possessions in America would be a blow to British imperial prestige which France might help to strike and from which it might expect to reap advantage.

The opportunity came with the defeat of Burgoyne at Saratoga, and in February, 1778, the treaties of alliance and commerce were signed. From a political point of view the terms were exacting for the United States, because France, foreseeing that an open alliance with America meant a renewal of war with England, insisted that in the making of peace between the United States and Great Britain the interests of France should be consulted. The United States, in other words, was not at liberty to make peace alone. But the conclusion of an alliance meant also French troops and French naval forces in America, much needed supplies of war material, and loans, in addition to formal recognition as a nation, and the price was not too high. Moreover, the widening of the field of war, dividing British forces and multiplying

British efforts, was reasonably likely to work to the supreme advantage of the United States if another victory like that over Burgoyne could be obtained.

The victory came at Yorktown in October, 1781, through the combined efforts of the Americans and the French. The British forces under Cornwallis, escaping northward from the Carolinas and counting upon aid from Clinton at New York, were caught in the Yorktown peninsula by the armies of Washington and Rochambeau which had hurried from the north, and surrendered. The war for independence was over. Couriers carried the good news from town to town and from State to State, night watchmen echoed the joyful tidings as they made their rounds, and bonfires, parades, and church services voiced the gratitude of a people whose anxious hopes had been long deferred. The ministry of Lord North fell, and the demand for peace which had been growing in England ever since the signature of the French alliance needed no further arguments to enforce it. In September, 1782, a preliminary peace was signed. A year elapsed before the terms of peace with France and Spain, both of which nations were now parties to the war, could be arranged; then in September, 1783, a definitive treaty in terms identical with those of the preliminary treaty of the previous year ended the state of war. The Declaration of Independence issued more than seven years before had been made good, and the United States took its unquestioned place among the nations.

In the discussion of the terms of ultimate peace which had gone on in Congress ever since the alliance with France, the question of how much territory should be claimed had naturally played an important part. The early hope of conquering Canada had been abandoned, but there were still many who desired to include within the boundaries of the United States all British territory at least as far north as the St. Lawrence. This ambition was wisely laid aside. The French population of Quebec had no grievances against the British crown, it was guaranteed the use of the French language and French law and the free exercise of the Catholic faith, and its incorporation in the new United States would have introduced an alien element not easily to be assimilated. The settled portion of French-speaking Canada, accordingly, remained in British hands. West of the point, in the northern part of the State of New York, at which the boundary line cut the St. Lawrence the line followed the middle course of the river and Lakes Ontario, Erie, and Huron to a point on the western side of Lake Superior, and thence to the source of the Mississippi, incorrectly supposed at that time to rise in the Lake of the Woods. The western boundary was the Mississippi, while the southern boundary was the provinces of East and West Florida, which at the close of the war were retroceded by Great Britain to Spain. All of the region west of the original thirteen States, which by the royal proclamation of 1763 had been detached from the coast colonies and left without

political  organization,  thus  passed  to  the  United
States.

The war had been a bold adventure, and almost to
the end defeat seemed often more imminent than
victory.  It is clear that Great Britain persistently
underestimated the magnitude of its military task,
and that more troops and better leadership might
have crushed American resistance beyond reasonable
hope of early resurrection.  The larger proportion of
the British forces were always available for a single
engagement or campaign, and the task of Washington, with widely scattered contingents less in numbers by a fourth than those of his opponent, was to
avoid operations in which his army would certainly
be crushed and at the same time keep the field.
Nearly one-half of the American land forces were
furnished by New England, but the difficulties of
recruiting increased as the war dragged on and short
term enlistments and desertion were a constant menace.  Arms, munitions, clothing, food, and supplies
of all kinds were pitifully deficient, and the sufferings
of the American troops in the memorable winter at
Valley Forge were only a more striking example of
privations which were endured by all the American
forces throughout the period of the war.

Economically, the war exacted a heavy toll.
Manufacturing was in its infancy when the war began,
and supplies of the most common and necessary
articles were speedily drained.  Foreign and coast-
wise commerce was all but destroyed, and the few

staples upon which the colonies had depended for purchase of European goods remained unsold. So far as the civil population was concerned there was at no time any serious lack of food, but the depreciated paper currency issued by Congress and the States, practically worthless by the end of the war, paralyzed trade and made the provisioning of the army difficult and irregular. The attempts of Congress, none of them more than temporizing devices, to deal with the pressing problems of finance and trade achieved no important result, and the country drifted into bankruptcy beyond the power of either the nation or the States to prevent it. Far the larger part of the loans which France extended took the form of supplies rather than money, and almost the only specie in circulation was that which the British shrewdly dispensed in purchasing food. Fortunately for the future there was little devastation of the country, and few scars of war remained to tell where the armies had fought.

The war bore with unequal weight upon the different sections of the country. New England saw few important military operations after the British evacuation of Boston. New York City, on the other hand, was occupied by the British until the conclusion of peace, and Washington's most difficult and brilliant operations were carried on in New Jersey and near Philadelphia. Virginia saw no fighting of importance after the opening of hostilities until the siege of Yorktown, notwithstanding that for two years

British and American forces were pursuing one another back and forth across the Carolinas. When, following the surrender of Burgoyne, the British turned their attention to the south, it was apparently with the hope of detaching the southern States from the rest of the country and holding them for the crown either by conquest or by conciliation. That the effort failed was due to the prompt action of the patriot party, which at the very beginning of the war had crushed a loyalist rising in western North Carolina, and which now met the campaigns of Cornwallis and the raids of Tarleton with the guerilla tactics of Marion, Sumter, and Pickens reinforced by the able generalship of Greene. " United we stand, divided we fall " had been an early colonial motto, and the underlying spirit of union, albeit very unequally developed in different States and sections, was sufficient even under the severest stress of war to defeat the plans for disrupting the nation.

No story of the American revolution would be complete which did not take account of the great personalities which the more than sixteen years of continuous struggle brought to the front. To Samuel Adams of Massachusetts, more than to any other one man, belongs the honor of seeing from the beginning the inevitable connection between open resistance and independence; and to the achievement of independence and the rejection of every offer of compromise he devoted himself with unrelenting zeal. No other Massachusetts leader stands out so prominently in the first ten years, but the constitutional arguments of John Adams, elaborated in pamphlets and newspaper articles, carried weight with many thoughtful patriots to whom oratory and agitation made less convincing appeal, and stamp their author as one of the great constitutional statesmen of the revolutionary period. A somewhat similar matching of personalities was to be found in Virginia, where the fiery speeches of Patrick Henry were balanced by the dignified but powerful writings of Jefferson. The state papers and controversial articles which flowed from the pen of John Dickinson of Pennsylvania were so numerous and important as to earn for their author the title of " the penman of the revolution," and although, when the Declaration of Independence was adopted, Dickinson drew back at the thought of an irrevocable break with the crown, he nevertheless accepted the decision of Congress and the people and entered the patriot army as a common soldier.

The greatest of Pennsylvanians and the peer of American diplomatists, Franklin, served the colonies faithfully in England until the approaching rupture dictated his withdrawal, took the leading part in negotiating the treaties which brought France to the American side and the treaties with Great Britain which ended the war, and lived to put his name to the Constitution of the United States. The impressive figure of John Rutledge, combining in himself for more than two years all the powers of government of South Carolina while Greene and the partisan leaders fought the British until Cornwallis withdrew, is one to which historians have yet to do full justice. The popular writings of Thomas Paine, reaching ears which were dull to formal argument, lent a weight which more sober leaders gladly recognized.

The overshadowing personality of Washington had more than military greatness to give it distinction. It fell to Washington, first as commander-in-chief responsible to Congress and later as military head with virtually dictatorial powers, to deal with Congress and the country as well as with the army; and his wisdom, patience, and hope, sorely tried as they were by the incompetence of politicians and the intrigues of his own military subordinates, stand out boldly even in the days of deepest gloom. The military success which came to him after years of desperate struggle would of itself have sufficed to make him a national hero, but it was the dignity and nobility of his character combined with his abilities as a general which marked him even during the war as the most representative American. It is said that John Adams, who as a member of Congress proposed the choice of Washington as commander-in-chief, was shrewdly of the opinion that a Virginian and an Episcopalian as commander of a New England army of dissenters would make for colonial unity; but whatever the opinion of the candidate on that question, it is certain that neither during the war nor afterwards as president was Washington regarded as the representative of anything less than the whole United States.

The one hundred and seventy years which intervened between the first charter of Virginia and the Declaration of Independence had transformed thirteen independent colonies into States and bound the States together in a nation. The sharp conflicts which had ended in separation had not greatly changed the essentially English character of the American people, for America was still English in habits of thought as well as in its fundamental political and legal institutions, and the resentment and bitterness which the war evoked did not long survive the conclusion of peace. The way was open now, however, for the development of practices, institutions, and ideals which should be distinctively American. The immediate outlook for success was not encouraging, for the treasury was empty, industry was prostrate, and the structure of national government was upon the point of falling to pieces. Few nations have begun their careers with greater burdens than those which in 1783 rested upon the United States. It was for the men who had organized the country for independence and war to show that they could now organize it for nationality and peace. If that great step could be successfully taken the future of the new American nation was assured.

## CHAPTER III

## FRAMING A NATIONAL CONSTITUTION

No sooner was the Declaration of Independence adopted than the Continental Congress turned its attention to the preparation of a national constitution. The informal union of the States which had taken the name of the United States of America rested as yet only upon general consent, and the Congress which had assumed the direction of affairs had only a precarious and undefined authority. If the States which collectively had declared their independence were to receive recognition as a nation, capable of making war and concluding peace, of conferring and maintaining rights of citizenship, and of exercising the powers and enjoying the privileges which international law accorded to sovereign nations, it was necessary that the powers of the national government should be defined and the relations between the nation and the States regulated. English precedent would have dictated the formation of a constitution partly written and partly the creation of precedent, in which case the Declaration of Independence would have been only one of numerous constitutional documents. The controversy over taxation and representation, however, the peculiar importance which in a number of colonies had been attached to the charters or proprietary grants, and the inclination early shown by States to draw up constitutions for themselves, combined to dictate a national constitution which should be written. Only in this way, it was believed, would the independent powers of the States be preserved and the limits of national authority established. It was a novel idea for which the practice of nations afforded no conclusive precedent, but it accorded with the American temperament and seemed likely to meet, better than any other method, the existing conditions.

The committee to which the matter was referred was industrious, and within a few weeks after the adoption of the Declaration of Independence a draft form of Articles of Confederation was reported to Congress. The engrossing preoccupations of war, on the other hand, delayed consideration, and it was not until November, 1777, some fifteen months after the draft was reported, that the document received congressional approval. The States, whose acceptance was necessary before the Articles could become effective, took their time, and a controversy over claims to western lands in which Virginia, which had asserted a preposterous claim under one of its ancient charters to the region of the Ohio valley and about the Great Lakes, refused to yield unless other States would surrender their claims, threatened for a time to defeat the scheme. Only in March, 1781, more than three years and three months after the Articles had been approved by Congress, was the ratification of the last

State received. Almost every political, social, and military condition which existed when the draft was first presented had changed by the time the first constitution of the United States became operative.

The Articles of Confederation provided for a national government in which legislative and executive powers, the latter only rudimentary, were vested in a Congress the members of which were designated by the State legislatures, the number of representatives being not less than two nor more than seven as each State might choose, but each State having one vote. The powers conferred upon Congress and the limitations imposed upon the States were similar, so far as they went, to the powers and limitations set forth later in the Constitution of 1787, but neither directly nor indirectly was Congress vested with power to enforce its decisions, nor could any State be compelled to observe the restrictions which the Articles laid down. With the exception of an unwieldy system of arbitration courts for the settlement of controversies over land grants a judicial department was lacking, and there was no recognition of a " supreme law of the land " which the present Constitution accords to acts of Congress, treaties, and the Constitution itself. The only financial resource of the national government was requisitions apportioned among the States, but while the States were of course morally bound to pay the requisitions, Congress was financially helpless if payment failed or was refused.

The defects of the Articles of Confederation, obvious enough in the light of the more perfect Constitution which replaced the Articles, were bound in the long run to prove fatal, but the narrowness of political vision with which the statesmen who framed the document have often been charged should not be over-emphasized. There were serious obstacles in the way of constructing any scheme of national government at all. A union composed of thirteen States, no one of which had any organic political connection with any other and each of which regarded itself as independent and sovereign, must in the nature of things be a federal union; and a federal union, if it was to be successful, presupposed not only a just and workable distribution of duties and privileges between the States on the one hand and the national government on the other, but also an assured protection of the States against the encroachment of the nation and power in the national government to enforce and maintain the rights conferred upon it. It was precisely at these elementary but vital points that the Articles of Confederation were inherently defective, but the defects were due to the suspicions and jealousies of the States and their unwillingness to accept a central authority rather than to the short-sightedness and political inexperience of the Congress which framed the plan. In the then state of public opinion independence was one thing and nationality another, and the States which individually or in informal co-operation had pressed the controversy with Great Britain and taken up arms in defence of their rights had yet to learn that only through organic union could they insure for themselves or for their posterity a common defence or a general welfare.

Throughout nearly the entire period of the war, accordingly, the United States continued to lack a national government legally constituted. The Continental Congress which organized American resistance, concluded an alliance with France, pledged the faith of the nation for the repayment of foreign loans, and wrestled with the all but insoluble problem of revenue was indeed a government *de facto,* and its acts, though often questioned and still more often ignored, were nevertheless to be looked upon as grounded in general consent; but it was not a government *de jure,* and the long interval which elapsed between the adoption of the Articles of Confederation by Congress and their acceptance by the States made the eventual transition from revolutionary to constitutional government far more a matter of form than of practical substance.

At the beginning of March, 1781, the Articles having at last been ratified, the Continental Congress, which during the larger part of the war had sat at Philadelphia, quietly transformed itself into the Congress of the Confederation. In October came the surrender of Cornwallis at Yorktown, and before another year had passed the preliminary treaty of peace had ended the war. Aside from the conclusion of peace, in regard to whose terms there was frequent debate, the most pressing issue was that of revenue.  So much of the army as did not melt away was disbanded, and Washington took leave of his officers, surrendered his commission to Congress, and retired to his seat at Mount Vernon.  But the army was unpaid, the national government was bankrupt, the national and State currency retained only a shadow of value, and every State was heavily in debt.  Washington, in a circular letter to the governors, urged the necessity of establishing public credit and paying the revolutionary debts, but the counsel was not easily to be acted upon in a country from which specie had almost disappeared from circulation and domestic industry and foreign trade were stagnant.  There were still staple products to export, but the British trade laws, which in spite of their restrictions had given America a privileged market in Great Britain and the British West Indies, now operated to exclude American products as those of a foreign country or to burden them with heavy duties; and the absence of a commercial treaty with Great Britain to supplement the political treaty of peace left American commerce to seek its markets in other parts of the world or else to risk the evasion of the British trade laws by the old device of smuggling.

The eight years during which the Articles of Confederation remained nominally in force are a gloomy record of desperate and ineffectual attempts on the part of Congress to obtain a revenue.  The response of the States to requisitions grew more and more lax, and by 1786 all hope of further returns from that source had disappeared. A natural source of revenue, that of customs duties, could be made available only with the consent of all the States, and two urgent requests for authority to levy such duties were negatived, one by the refusal of Rhode Island, the other by the opposition of New York. The western lands, the claims to which had been ceded to the United States and which were held as public domain, were vaguely regarded as a potential source of wealth from which the national debt might eventually be paid; but although the survey of the lands and the acquisition of the Indian titles was begun, no appreciable returns from sales were received until years after the Constitution was adopted, and the public lands never yielded in revenue as much as they had cost.

Within the States, also, social order was disrupted and the authority of government was in peril. As happens in every war some fortunes had been made by speculation, but the people as a whole were poor, taxes were heavy, efforts of creditors to press their claims in court were a grievance hard to bear, and farm products could not be sold. Even with the best of public spirit the requisitions of Congress could with difficulty have been paid because of the lack of specie and the worthless condition of the currency, and with little money for any purpose the States naturally looked first to their own needs rather than to those of the nation. There were alarming symptoms of insurrection, and when in 1786–87 an armed revolt against the State government broke out in Massachusetts and only with difficulty was suppressed, it was clear that events were moving toward a crisis. Massachusetts had appealed to Congress for aid, but there was no national army adequate for the emergency and Congress doubted its own constitutional authority to act. If a formidable revolt against government could develop in Massachusetts, admittedly one of the strongest States in the Union, what might not insurrection accomplish in a weaker State with a national government impotent?

It was evident that the Articles of Confederation must be revised. The question of revenue and debt could not be much longer postponed, and the States must be guarantied protection against domestic violence in case their own powers were insufficient. A conference at Annapolis, Maryland, called nominally to consider a commercial dispute between Maryland and Virginia involving jurisdiction over the waters of Chesapeake bay, could find no way of permanently settling either that or any other controversy between States so long as the Articles remained in force. The obstacles to revision were serious, for the Articles themselves could be amended only with the unanimous consent of the States, and the same particularistic spirit which had twice defeated the attempt to secure an independent national revenue could be counted upon to oppose changes which, if they were to meet the existing difficulties, would certainly deprive the States of some of their powers. Washington and other political leaders, however, had for some time been corresponding on the subject, and with this preparation and the added influence of the Annapolis convention Congress took the bold step of calling for a convention to revise the Articles and " adapt them to the exigencies of the union."

The Constitutional Convention assembled in May, 1787, at Philadelphia. It was a notable body, representative of the best intelligence, the widest political experience, and the most devoted public spirit of the States. The choice of Washington as president of the Convention, while it removed him from the floor, insured a dignified and serious conduct of business and at the same time left him free to exercise his influence personally with members. The proceedings went on behind closed doors, the journal recorded action and not debate, and the public knew nothing of the proposals submitted or the controversies engendered until, after more than four months of labor, the new Constitution was transmitted to Congress for submission by that body to the States.

It was well, perhaps, that the proceedings were secret, for acute and fundamental divergencies of opinion developed from the first. The Convention had been called to revise the Articles of Confederation, and any amendments which it proposed would require the approval of all the States. But it was early perceived that a mere revision of the Articles, remedying a defect here and supplying an omission there, would not meet the existing crisis. It was the

Articles themselves that were at fault.  A government without an independent revenue or power to enforce its votes could never be a workable institution, and neither of these indispensable attributes could be grafted upon the Articles without changing fundamentally the essential character of the document and creating a wholly new relationship between the nation and the States.  Was the Convention at liberty to frame a new system under the guise of amending the Articles, and, if it was, would its work have to go for naught unless every State approved?  In view of the attitude of Rhode Island and New York toward the two revenue proposals which Congress had made, and of the suggestive fact that Rhode Island, alone among the States, had failed to send any delegates to the Convention, no member of the Convention would have been willing to affirm that any amendment that might be framed would receive the assent of all the States.

When the Convention, convinced that a new federal government must somehow be constructed, turned to that task it met other serious difficulties.  How, for example, was the relative influence of large and small States in the new national legislature to be adjusted? In the Congress of the Confederation each State, irrespective of the number of delegates which it chose to send, had one vote.  If that system were continued the large States, less numerous at the time than the small ones, might at any time find themselves out-voted, and the majority of population and wealth in the country would thus be subjected to the will of a minority merely because the minority happened to represent a greater number of organized commonwealths. On the other hand, if the voting power of the States were to be made proportionate to their population, the minority of large States would enjoy a complete and permanent control and the views of the small States could be disregarded at will. The problem of how to connect representation and voting with population was further complicated by the existence in five southern States of a considerable population of Negro slaves. If the slave population were deducted and only whites were counted, these five States would be automatically reduced to relative unimportance in the national legislature; while if slaves were counted the southern whites, who save in rare instances alone enjoyed political rights, would have a political weight out of all proportion to their numbers.

The rival economic interests and contrasted social conditions of the several States provoked still other controversies. In those States in which, as in Massachusetts, Connecticut, New York, and Pennsylvania, manufactures were developing and interest in foreign trade was keen, traders and manufacturers wanted a strong national government which should encourage industry and trade by imposing discriminating tariff duties and restrictive navigation laws as an offset to the hostile commercial policy of Great Britain. The agricultural interests, on the other hand, strong in all the States and predominant in the South, feared lest protective tariffs and restrictive trade laws should operate to raise the prices of manufactured goods without any corresponding increase in the prices of agricultural products in either home or foreign markets.    In the States in which Negro slavery no longer existed or had become of no importance the conflict between aristocratic and democratic theories of government was already going on; and although the influence of the aristocratic classes had been much weakened by the expulsion of loyalists during the Revolution, the wage-earning population of the larger towns and many small farmers and merchants looked with distrust upon any government, State or national, in which wealthy landowners and representatives of a few old families were in control.    Many members were opposed to Negro slavery, and others were anxious to abolish the African slave trade even though slavery itself was not disturbed.

These were some of the problems of a national legislature.    The question of a national executive, while apparently regarded as less fundamental, was not easily settled.    A New York delegate, Alexander Hamilton, later the organizer of the national finances and the consummate expounder of foundation theories of American constitutional law, frankly wished for a strong executive with powers akin to those of the British crown.    At the other extreme were members who would have put the executive power in the hands of a committee or commission and subjected it closely to the legislature. An executive elected for seven years, an executive ineligible for re-election whatever the length of the term, an executive chosen by Congress, were among the proposals submitted. The question of a national judiciary, a department of government which was lacking under the Articles, seems to have given less trouble than either the legislature or the executive, possibly because there was little reason to anticipate that national courts would be of much importance; but the related question of how best to make national laws and obligations binding upon a State without something like physical coercion at the hands of Congress and the executive was not easily settled.

Only with sharp differences of opinion, and a near approach to rupture which led Franklin to suggest that the proceedings of the Convention be opened with prayer, were the divergent views of States, sections, and classes finally compromised. In the Constitution as at last adopted the existing Congress of one house, with each State possessing one vote, was replaced by a Congress of two houses, the upper house, or Senate, composed of two members from each State and the lower house, or House of Representatives, made up of members whose number varied with the population of the States, each member of either house having one vote. The question of slaves was compromised by counting three-fifths of the slave population for purposes of representation in the House of Representatives. The interests of the small States were safeguarded by giving to the States equal representation in the Senate and requiring the assent of both houses to every act of legislation; the interests of the large States were protected by reserving to the House of Representatives the right of originating bills for raising revenue; and the desires of those who wished for commercial retaliation against Great Britain were satisfied by giving to Congress the right to regulate commerce with foreign nations and between the States. To the Senate, which was thought of as a body having somewhat the character of an executive council notwithstanding its legislative functions, was reserved the right of approving treaties and confirming executive appointments, but in most other respects the powers of the two houses of Congress were equal save in respect of money bills.

The executive authority was vested in a president, chosen for four years not by the people, or by Congress, or by the State legislatures, but by electors equal in number to the senators and representatives to which each State was entitled, and selected for the purpose in any manner that a State might think best to adopt. On the question of the eligibility of the president for a second or third term the Constitution was silent, and the only suggestion of a cabinet was a reference to " heads of executive departments " whose opinions the president might require in writing. A vice-president, chosen in substantially the same manner as the president and for the same term, was designated as the presiding officer of the Senate, but no share in the executive power was assigned to him, and no provision was made for the choice of another vice-president in case the elected vice-president, through the death, resignation, removal, or disability of the president, became president. Between the president and Congress, on the other hand, a certain connection was established by provisions impowering the president to suggest desirable legislation and giving him a qualified veto upon bills or resolutions which the two houses might pass.

The federal judicial system, as a whole the most novel feature of the Constitution in comparison with the Articles of Confederation, comprised a Supreme Court and such lesser courts as Congress might from time to time create. The judges of all the courts, appointed by the president with the approval of the Senate, were protected against political interference by a tenure of office during good behavior — an English definition which meant in practice tenure for life — and a guaranty that their salaries should not be reduced during their terms of service. The jurisdiction of the federal courts was carefully guarded, but the all-important supremacy of federal law was insured by the provision that the Constitution, the laws of Congress, and treaties should be " the supreme law of the land," binding upon officials and courts of the States as well as upon those of the nation. With federal law directly applicable to individuals throughout the United States, devices for coercing a State in case of neglect or disobedience became unnecessary except in the event of open rebellion, and of open rebellion the Convention was not called upon to think.

The powers which the new Constitution granted to Congress insured to the federal government an independent revenue, the control of the post office and of interstate and foreign commerce, the sole right to coin money, and complete authority in international relations. The admission of new States to the Union, together with the administration of federal territory not yet organized, was also vested in Congress. With the grant of power, however, went the imposition of obligations, one of the most important obligations being that which bound the United States to guarantee to every State a republican form of government, to protect a State against invasion, and to aid in the suppression of domestic violence if requested to do so by the State legislature or executive. Domestic risings such as had lately threatened the government of Massachusetts, if they occurred again, would have now to reckon with a federal government constitutionally impowered to interfere.

The fact that the Constitution of 1787 has never been revised as a whole, and that amendments of its specific provisions have for more than one hundred and thirty years been regarded as sufficient to adapt it to the needs of a growing nation, has been in large measure responsible for the " worship of the Constitution " which foreign critics have often noted as an American political trait. Historically considered, however, the Constitution had both virtues and defects. The virtues were many and great. The Constitution replaced a loose, primitive, and hopelessly inadequate scheme of federal government with a firmly-knit, highly-organized, and practically effective plan. It gave an equitable voice in national affairs to States which differed widely in population and economic condition, preserved to the States the control of their domestic affairs at the same time that it merged their common interests in the larger general welfare of the nation, and conferred upon the federal government the powers necessary to effective existence without thereby making the federal government absolute. It created executive and judicial departments, and defined the limits of their powers and of those of the legislature at the same time that it provided for the co-operation of Congress, the president, and the courts in the joint work of government. Not the least of its virtues was that it was brief and concise, drawing broad lines and framing fundamental definitions. Its provisions were definite enough to sustain all the powers granted, flexible enough to admit of application to changing social conditions, and open to amendment whenever three-fourths of the States could agree upon a change. It was essentially a practical document, drawn up by practical men to meet a practical need, and the fact that it has worked in the main as it was expected to work notwithstanding the vast social changes which have since taken place is a tribute to the political wisdom of the statesmen who laboriously hammered it into shape.

The defects of the Constitution were chiefly such as time alone could show. The overpowering personality of Washington, marking him out beyond cavil as the first president under the new scheme, apparently blinded the eyes of the Convention to the inherent weakness and possible mischief of an electoral procedure under which a majority of the whole number of electors, with no opportunity for joint consultation, must nevertheless agree upon the same candidate if the choice of a president was not to be thrown into the House of Representatives. The growth of political parties and elaborate party organizations was not foreseen, and the Constitution in fact contains no allusion to parties, candidates, or platforms. Few persons anticipated the admission to the Union of a long series of new States, none foresaw the extension of American territory to the Pacific, Alaska, and the islands of the sea. The growth of great business corporations, the struggles of capital and labor, and a host of economic and social problems now regarded as of national rather than State concern, and in the face of which the ancient Constitution has sometimes been subjected to grave strain, were all in the future. It was the Constitution rather than the nation which in 1787 led the way, but it is easy to see that the growth of the nation has today left the Constitution somewhat behind.

The fundamental weakness of the Constitution,

viewed from the standpoint of European rather than American political development, lies in the absence of provisions for direct popular initiative and control in federal affairs. The English theory of responsible government, under which the direction of national policy is vested in a ministry which represents the party majority for the time being in the popular branch of the legislature, finds no illustration in the American Constitution of 1787. Instead, the Constitution prescribes fixed chronological terms of six years and two years respectively for senators and representatives, and creates an executive head who is not responsible to Congress, performs none of the functions of a prime minister, and only indirectly can control or direct legislative action. The membership of the House of Representatives is renewed as a whole every two years. The members of the first Senate were divided by the Constitution into three classes elected for two, four, and six years respectively, so that while the maximum term is six years, in practice the renewal of one-third of the membership of the Senate coincides with the biennial renewal of the entire membership of the House. A change of public sentiment which showed itself in a complete alteration of the party complexion of the House could not, accordingly, affect more than one-third of the Senate, while the four-year term of the president overlaps two full terms of the House and is itself overlapped by the full term of the Senate. There is no way in which members of the House can be called to account by their constituents before the expiration of the chronological period of two years, and the Senate, prior to the adoption of a recent amendment, was removed from direct popular control by the fact that its members were chosen by the State legislatures.

The reason for the adoption of this rigid system instead of a system generally spoken of as popular or responsible were mainly two. The first was the absence as yet of national political parties organized for the support of national policies. The beginnings of American parties date only from the submission of the Constitution of 1787 to the States for ratification, and the first national elections were those for which the Constitution itself provided. Neither nominating conventions nor formal platforms were to appear for more than forty years. To have constructed a national government which embodied the principles of ministerial responsibility and control such as in theory, although at the time very little in practice, prevailed in England would have been to frame a constitution for political conditions which did not yet exist.

The second reason was the underlying fear which a majority of the Convention felt of too great popular control. No State as yet had universal manhood suffrage, and the connection between voting and property holding was everywhere recognized as one rightly to be maintained. The system of so-called " checks and balances " which set the Senate over against the House of Representatives, the executive against the Congress, and the States against the federal government, while primarily intended to preserve the States, the nation, and the several departments of the government from encroachment one upon the other, operated equally to make the federal government secure against sudden or radical changes of public opinion; and such security the Convention obviously tried to attain. The new frame of government did indeed insure government by the people, but " the people " were long to be regarded not as the whole nation taken together and governing directly through elected representatives, but rather as a select minority fitted by education, property, and social position for the high duties of voting and the special privilege of holding office. The growth of democracy waited upon the growth of nationality.

A comparison of the texts of the Articles of Confederation and the Constitution shows many similarities of phrase, and a number of the provisions of the earlier document were transferred bodily to the later instrument. Only a liberal use of language, however, could regard the Constitution as a revision of the Articles, and the procedure which the Convention agreed upon for the adoption of the Constitution by the States was as revolutionary as was the other action taken. The Articles, it will be remembered, could be amended only with the consent of all the States. There was only too much reason to fear that some of the States would object, and the Constitution

itself accordingly provided that ratification by conventions in nine States should be sufficient to put
the Constitution into effect for those nine. What
would happen if the States which refused or neglected
to ratify should insist upon their rights under the
Articles was not clear, but it was apparently assumed
that if nine States accepted the Constitution the
superiority of the new system would eventually win
the adhesion of the others. The Constitution was
accordingly transmitted to Congress with the request
that it be submitted to the States for ratification by
conventions in accordance with its terms.

The submission of the Constitution to the States
made public for the first time the text of the document, and within and without the State conventions
party lines speedily formed. Innumerable objections
to details were of course raised, but the objection
that the Convention had exceeded its authority in
framing a new constitution instead of revising an old
one had weight with those only who enjoyed splitting
technical hairs. The most fundamental criticism had
to do with the essential nature of the new federal
scheme, and in particular with the mutual relations
of nation and States. The champions of the Constitution, taking the name of Federalists, while insist-
ing that a new government would be useless unless
it was strong where the Confederation was weak, took
pains to point out that the proposed federal government would possess only such powers as the States
delegated to it, and that whatever was not granted

was to be understood as withheld. The national government must be independent and efficient, otherwise it would not long endure, but there was no danger, it was urged, that the States would be reduced to inferiority, because the control of their own domestic affairs and large powers of government generally would still rest with them. Accordingly the omission of a bill of rights, the absence of which provoked immediate and general criticism, was not important because none of the personal privileges and immunities which the traditional bill of rights embodied was affected by any of the powers given by the Constitution to the federal government.

The argument was satisfactory to those who wanted a strong central government, able to deal with finance and trade and capable of inspiring respect among the nations. It was not at all convincing to the Anti-Federalists, who dreaded the encroachment of a strong federal authority and preferred to trust the States rather than the nation. Patrick Henry warned the Virginia convention of the anticipated danger, and further pointed out that, once in the new union, no State could withdraw. The difference between the Federalists and the Anti-Federalists at this stage should be correctly understood. No one wished to perpetuate the weaknesses of the Confederation; no one desired a national government which could not command respect. To the Federalists, however, the hope of developing a strong nation lay in the creation of a strong centralized government, while to the Anti-

Federalists such a hope seemed most likely to be realized by preserving a high degree of State independence and reducing the powers of the national government to the lowest practicable terms. Over these two divergent points of view American political parties were to fight their battles for more than seventy years.

Happily for the nation the victory lay with the Federalists. On December 7, 1787, Delaware ratified the Constitution, and on June 21, 1788, the affirmative vote of New Hampshire brought the number of ratifying States to the prescribed nine. In Delaware, New Jersey, and Georgia acceptance had been unanimous, and the majorities in Pennsylvania, Connecticut, Maryland, and South Carolina were large. In Massachusetts, on the other hand, where opposition was curiously strong, ratification was secured only by the close vote of 187 to 168, and the vote in New Hampshire stood 57 to 46. With the ratification of New Hampshire, the ninth State, the Constitution was technically in force. Two of the most important States, however, Virginia and New York, had not yet ratified, and without their support the union would fail. Fortunately the question did not come to an issue, the ratification of Virginia following only four days after that of New Hampshire, while New York ratified in July. In each of these States the margin of assent was slight, the vote of Virginia standing 89 to 79 and that of New York 30 to 28. In North Carolina and Rhode Island political controversies long prevented ratification, and neither of these States was represented in the new union until some time after the new federal government had been put into operation.

More than forty years later, in the great debate in the Senate between Webster and Hayne, the question was raised as to who ratified the Constitution. Webster, expounding a large nationalist view, insisted that ratification, although in form the work of State conventions, was in fact the solemn act of the people of the whole United States, and that the States as such were not parties to the agreement. Hayne, who was supporting the attempt of South Carolina to nullify an act of Congress so far as the territory and people of that State were concerned, insisted that ratification was the work of the States, and that " the people of the United States " was a meaningless phrase since the only " people " in 1787–88 was the people of the several States. The letter of the Constitution sustained the argument of Hayne, but the theory of Webster, embodied in the constitutional law of the United States, was the theory of nationality and the only one upon which the nation could oppose disunion. Four years of civil war, however, were necessary before the old theory of State rights was finally disposed of and the national theory of the Constitution established.

One notable piece of legislation, profoundly affecting the future of the United States, had come from Congress during the sessions of the Constitutional

Convention.  In July, 1787, an ordinance had been passed for the organization and government of the territory of the United States northwest of the Ohio river.  A provisional government under a governor and council was provided for, but whenever any portion of the territory attained a population of sixty thousand it was to be entitled to admission to the Union as a State on a footing of equality with the other States.  Not less than three nor more than five States were to be formed out of the region, and in each of them slavery was to be prohibited.  The ordinance marked the beginning of the system of territorial government which existed until comparatively recent years, and the present States of Ohio, Indiana, Illinois, Michigan, and Wisconsin have the ordinance of 1787 as a part of their fundamental law. Provisional governments, not as yet recognized by Congress, had already been set up in Vermont and Kentucky, and settlement was spreading into Tennessee, so that with the prospect of a State government in Ohio the thirteen original States seemed likely in a few years to have their number increased to at least sixteen or seventeen.  It was with this modest expansion in mind that the Constitutional Convention gave to Congress the right to admit new States, but with the proviso that no new State should be formed out of another State or by uniting two or more States or parts of States without the consent of the States concerned as well as of Congress.

As soon as the adoption of the Constitution by the

ratification of eleven States was assured, Congress took the necessary steps to put the new government into operation. The first Wednesday of January, 1789, was designated as the date for the choice of presidential electors, the first Wednesday of February as the date at which the electors should meet and cast their votes for president and vice-president, and the first Wednesday in March as the date for the inauguration of the new government. In the absence of party organizations and nominating machinery the system of independent and isolated selection which the Constitution had provided was left to work out such results as it might. That the scheme did not break down completely at the start was due solely to the general expectation that Washington would be the first president, and the electors met that expectation by making him their unanimous choice. With regard to the vice-presidency, on the other hand, there was no such unanimity, and the choice of John Adams, while representing the largest number of votes cast for any candidate except Washington, represented also a minority of the whole number of votes cast. Until 1804, however, the Constitution required a majority vote only in the case of the president, the vice-president being chosen by a plurality.

Pending the selection of a site for a national capital it had been agreed that the new government should be inaugurated at New York. The journey of Washington from Mount Vernon was a triumphal progress,

towns and States vying with one another in doing
honor to the first citizen of the reorganized republic.
But difficulties of communication and travel, together
with the dilatory habits which the lax times of the
Confederation had encouraged, made the new Congress late in assembling, and it was several weeks
before the two houses were able to organize. In an
impressive ceremony of inauguration, delayed until
April 30, Washington took the oath of office, read a
brief address, and the first presidential administration
began. For his services as commander-in-chief during the Revolution Washington had declined to accept
compensation, asking only that his necessary expenses
be reimbursed, and he now followed the same course
as president.

With the inauguration of the new government
under the Constitution the Congress of the Confederation, which for some weeks before had held no
sessions, ceased to have a legal existence. There
were none to mourn its going, but its record, weak
indeed in comparison with that of the powerful body
to which it gave place, had not been without honor.
It had made the peace which recognized the independence of the United States. It had held the
nation together in the face of bankruptcy, economic
prostration, and social confusion. It had provided a
governmental organization for the western territory
and paved the way for the admission of new States.
It had summoned the Constitutional Convention and
directed the transition from the old government to

the new.   Its weakness was the weakness of the loose
confederated system under which it worked — a system which magnified the States at the expense of the
nation and exposed the national government to vexa-
tious obstruction.   That the Congress could have
done much better few would now care to affirm; that
it did as well as it did was to its credit.

With a scheme of government indefinitely superior
to that which it had hitherto possessed and with a
president who commanded universal affection and
respect, the Republic passed into a new stage of its
career.   There remained the task of organizing the
system which the Constitution outlined, of binding
the States together in a new loyalty, and of making
the United States a nation in fact as well as in name.

# CHAPTER IV

## THE ORGANIZATION OF GOVERNMENT AND POLITICS

THE United States of 1789 occupied a continental area considerably less than one-third of that to which the republic, exclusive of Alaska, now extends. The population, slightly less than four million in 1790, the first census year, had already begun an irregular movement westward, but four-fifths of the population was still to be found within a comparatively short distance of the Atlantic. There were as yet few large towns, the most important being Boston, New York, Philadelphia, and Charleston. To the north lay the British possessions in Canada, to the south the Spanish provinces of East and West Florida barred access to the Gulf of Mexico save by way of the Mississippi, and the vast region west of the Mississippi also belonged to Spain. The treaty of peace with Great Britain had proclaimed freedom of navigation on the Mississippi and its tributaries, but Spain held the mouth of the river and New Orleans, and it was some years before unimpeded access to the gulf was secured. The boundary line between the American and British possessions, defined in terms by the peace treaty, had not yet been run, and more than fifty years were to pass before the last remnants of boundary controversy disappeared.

The political subdivisions of the United States comprised the thirteen original States and the Northwest Territory. Vermont, which had maintained an independent political organization since the Revolution, was ready for admission as a State as soon as the opposition of New York and New Hampshire, which between them claimed jurisdiction over the region, should be withdrawn. The District of Maine, substantially identical in area with the present State, was a part of Massachusetts, although separated from Massachusetts proper by the intervening State of New Hampshire. The admission of Kentucky awaited the consent of North Carolina, which had not yet ratified the Constitution but which asserted a shadowy jurisdiction over the Kentucky settlements; and the admission of three, four, or five States out of the Northwest Territory had already been promised whenever the requirement of the ordinance of 1787 regarding population should be met. A region not exceeding ten miles square, the location of which had not yet been determined, to be acquired by cession on the part of one or more States, had been assigned by the Constitution to the exclusive jurisdiction of Congress as the seat of the national government.

Each of the States had an organized government based upon a written constitution. The State constitutions differed widely in form and content, and in Connecticut and Rhode Island the colonial charters of the previous century, amended by substituting the authority of the State for that of the crown, continued to serve for many years the purpose of constitutions. In every State, however, legislative, executive, and judicial powers were more or less clearly separated, State officers and members of the legislature were elected for short terms, and appropriate forms of local government served local needs. In New England, where compact settlements were numerous, the local government was the town; in the more sparsely settled South, the county; while in the middle Atlantic States the two forms were variously combined. City government was still in its infancy, but a few communities had special forms of municipal organization. A property qualification for voting and holding office was practically universal, and the percentage of voters to population was from two to five times less than the present average.

The Congress which assembled in March and April, 1789, faced a colossal task. There was a written Constitution to interpret and a national government to organize. All of the debts which the Congress of the Confederation had contracted and all of the other engagements which it had entered into were by the Constitution made binding upon the new government, but almost the only action of the earlier Congress which could be called legislation was the ordinance of 1787, which the new Congress promptly confirmed. A department of foreign affairs, a department of war, a finance department, and an office of postmaster general had been created under the Confederation, but with these exceptions there was hardly the intimation of a federal administrative system to be taken over. The new congressional system of two houses bore little resemblance to the previous system of a single chamber, while for the organization of the federal courts there were no federal precedents whatever. For all practical purposes the work of organization had to be begun at the foundation.

The Federalist and Anti-Federalist parties which had been formed while the Constitution was before the States for ratification continued into the constitutional period, but with important changes in character and purpose. The Federalists, who had championed the Constitution when it was submitted and later had won the battle in the State conventions, had succeeded in winning all the seats in the Senate and more than four-fifths of the seats in the House of Representatives, and the Federalist majority now set itself to organize a strong national government based upon a liberal interpretation of the constitutional provisions. The Anti-Federalists, with opposition to the Constitution no longer an issue, found their platform in a strict construction of the Constitution and a limitation of the powers of the federal government to the authority clearly granted. The marked legal character which American political debate exhibited for nearly a century was the direct result of these early party differences.

The position of Washington was peculiar. His

political sympathies were with the Federalists, and his appointments to office as a whole favored that party. On the other hand the presidency, as he conceived it, was essentially a nonpartisan office, far more akin to the constitutional position of the crown in Great Britain than to that of presidential party leadership at the present time. When, accordingly, Congress shortly created the executive offices of secretary of foreign affairs (soon changed to secretary of state), secretary of the treasury, and secretary of war (including for several years the navy), together with the office of attorney general, Washington apportioned the appointments equally between Federalists and Anti-Federalists. The first secretary of state, Jefferson, was the intellectual leader and presently the controlling political head of the Anti-Federalists, and the first attorney general, Edmund Randolph of Virginia, was of the same party. The secretaryship of the treasury, on the other hand, far more important at the moment than the portfolio of foreign affairs, was given to Alexander Hamilton of New York, the intellectual leader of the Federalists, and another Federalist, General Henry Knox of Massachusetts, was made secretary of war. It did not escape notice that two of the four secretaries were from the same State as the president, and that the important State of Pennsylvania had been passed over.

The practice which Washington early adopted of calling for the opinions of these heads of departments, not merely upon subjects " relating to the duties of their respective offices" as the Constitution prescribes, but upon questions of general policy as well, created the cabinet. The name, borrowed from England, was a misnomer, for the heads of the American executive departments were not ministers in the English sense, they were not responsible to Congress for the tenure of their offices, and neither collectively nor in conjunction with the president were they charged by the Constitution or by Congress with formulating or directing government policy. They were only chief clerks, holding office at the discretion of the president and subject to his control. Washington felt the need of advice, however, and consulted his cabinet frequently, and the anomalous and peculiarly American institution continued notwithstanding that a number of presidents made but little use of it.

The energy and sagacity with which Congress addressed itself to the organization of the federal system make the years of Washington's first administration among the most notable in the history of the nation. A long series of statutes, many of whose provisions are still in force, provided for the work of the executive departments, the army and navy, and the post office, established a decimal system of coinage, gave legal protection to authors and inventors in copyrights and patents, established rules for the naturalization of foreigners and the registration of shipping, and provided for the survey and sale of public lands. A protective tariff act levied discriminating duties on a considerable list of imported articles with the avowed purpose of encouraging American manufactures. The great judiciary act of 1789 created a federal district court for each State, grouped the States in three circuits over whose courts the justices of the Supreme Court were to preside, and regulated the jurisdiction and procedure of the courts and the process of appeal from a lower court to a higher. As the United States, being a government of delegated powers, had no common law such as each of the States had inherited from England, there could be no common law offences against the nation, and an act was accordingly passed defining certain crimes against the United States and providing for their punishment.

Washington was free to try the experiment of a bipartisan cabinet, but political partisanship and personal rivalries could not long be kept out of Congress when great questions of national policy were at stake. The first great controversy, destined to have a profound influence for many years upon the course of party development, arose over the question of the national debt. Hamilton, who as secretary of the treasury had been called upon by the House of Representatives to submit a plan, proposed a funding scheme under which not only the federal debt, accrued interest as well as principal and domestic indebtedness equally with foreign loans, but also the Revolutionary debts of the States should all be assumed by the United States as a funded or consolidated national debt. The total amount of this indebtedness was about eighty million dollars, of which approximately twenty-five million dollars represented the debts of the States. The existing paper currency was so nearly worthless that no attempt was made to redeem it, but provision was made for receiving the paper money in payment of subscriptions to the proposed new loan for which the funding scheme called.

Immediate and violent opposition to the plan appeared both in Congress and in the country. The aggregate of the proposed debt, it was declared, was appalling and the amount could never be paid. The principal and interest of the foreign loans must presumably be paid in full if embarrassing complications abroad were to be avoided, but why pay interest upon interest by turning the arrears of interest upon both foreign and domestic debt into a new principal? Hamilton had proposed to assume the old debt at its face value, but all of the old issues of certificates were heavily depreciated, and much of the debt was notoriously held by speculators who had bought at a ruinously low figure on the chance of a rise. It would be a gross injustice, the opponents of the plan insisted, to reward speculators who had taken a gambling chance, and neglect the original holders of the debt who, perhaps from sheer necessity, had parted with their investment at a loss. The opposition to the proposed assumption of the State debts was particularly violent. Not all of the States were equally in debt; some had already paid a part of their indebtedness, and reimbursement would be a gift out of hand; others had paid nothing, and to them reimbursement would be equivalent to approval of their neglect. It was intimated that Hamilton and his friends were in league with the speculators and the monied classes, and the presentation of the report was declared to have started numerous agents on their travels in search of debt holders who would sell.

Hamilton had anticipated most of the objections, and the arguments with which he combatted them were a lesson in ethics quite as much as in public finance. The foundation of national credit, he pointed out, was good faith, and good faith implied a scrupulous performance of engagements in accordance with their terms. A certificate of national indebtedness was a promise on the part of the government to pay to the holder the full amount for which the certificate called, and the holder, whether or not he was the original purchaser, should be taught that the promise of the government was good. If, accordingly, the original owner had parted with his certificate for less than its face value with interest, his loss was a proper penalty for his want of faith in the government; while as for the present holder who had bought the certificate at a discount, his position was identical with that of the original purchaser so far as the obligation of the government to pay the full amount called for was concerned. The arrears of interest were as much an obligation as the principal, but since under the circumstances the entire arrearage could not well be paid at once any more than could the entire principal of the debt, the only just method was to treat it as a part of the new principal. As for the debts of the States, they equally with the national debt were the price of liberty, and the nation which had won its independence because of what the States had done ought now to assume the State debts as a common charge.

The argument could not be answered, but a political bargain was nevertheless necessary to carry the funding bill through Congress. The question of the location of the national capital had aroused keen rivalry between States and sections, and the general understanding that Washington and Jefferson favored the selection of a site on the Potomac, the title to which Virginia and Maryland were prepared to cede, met with strong opposition in the middle States and New England. Jefferson, on the other hand, together with many members of Congress from the South, was bitterly opposed to the funding plan, and the opposition votes seemed likely to be sufficient to defeat the bill. Hamilton, who had the support of the northern Federalists, saved his scheme by an agreement with Jefferson under which, in return for enough southern votes to insure the passage of the bill, northern members agreed to the location of the capital on the Potomac. The funding bill became law, the new loan was promptly subscribed, and the crucial question of the debt ceased to be either a danger or an anxiety.

The funding of the debt was only a part of Hamilton's far-reaching plan. Financial machinery was still lacking, and the federal mint, whose only output for some time was copper cents, could not meet the imperative need for a national currency. Hamilton accordingly proposed the incorporation of a national bank. The bank, comparable in its organization to the Bank of England rather than to the present national banks, was to be a private corporation twenty per cent. of whose capital of ten million dollars was to be subscribed by the United States, with a corresponding representation of the government on the board of directors and close government supervision of operations. The bank was to act as the fiscal agency of the government and serve as the repository of government funds, in return for which services it was to have the privilege of issuing paper currency which the government agreed to receive so long as the notes circulated at par. The charter of the bank was to run for twenty years, and during that time no other similar institution was to be created.

The proposal of a bank precipitated another violent debate in which Jefferson, chagrined at his own share in the success of the funding scheme and now openly in opposition to the great secretary, took a leading part. It was insisted that the bank was a monopoly, that it would be able to coerce the States, and that nowhere in the Constitution was authority for the creation of a bank or any other kind of corporation to be found. The constitutional objection, raised at

a time when the supreme court had as yet rendered
no important decisions, went to the roots of the
theory of the national government. There was no
question but that the Constitution contained no reference to corporations or to banks; and if the Constitution represented a specific grant of power, and if
what was not clearly granted was to be understood as
withheld, on what ground could an action to which
the Constitution made neither direct nor indirect
allusion be sustained?

There were Federalist votes enough to pass the
bank bill, but Washington, moved by the violent
attacks in Congress and himself apparently somewhat
in doubt, called for the written opinions of his
cabinet before affixing his signature. The opinion of
Jefferson, to which that of Randolph, the attorney
general, was merely supplementary, developed con-
cisely the strict construction view of the Constitution
with which he and his political followers were thereafter to be identified. To Jefferson the question was
solely one of constitutional authority. Whether or
not a bank was a useful thing he did not discuss, for
the reason that, under his strict interpretation of the
Constitution, the federal government was limited to
things that were necessary; and since a bank, however useful or convenient, was obviously not necessary, the government was debarred from creating such
an institution. " Necessary," in the sense in which
the word is used in the Constitution, meant indispensable or unavoidable; to interpret the word in the

sense of convenient or useful would open the door to an extension of federal power whose limits no one could foresee.

The opinion of Hamilton, prepared with Jefferson's opinion before him, is the first great exposition of the legal theory of the American Constitution and the basis of the position taken years later by the Supreme Court. To Jefferson's theory of strict or literal interpretation Hamilton opposed the doctrine of implied or resulting powers. It is true that the Constitution is a grant of powers and that what is not granted is withheld, but how much is granted and how much is withheld is a question of fact whose answer must take account, not merely of the text of the Constitution, but of the nature of government in general and of the aims which the government of the United States was created to serve. Every grant of power to a government carries with it, by necessary implication, the right to employ any means that are appropriate to putting the power into effect, provided only that the means selected are not forbidden by the Constitution and, in the case of the United States, are not reserved to the States. When, accordingly, the Constitution, after enumerating at length the powers of Congress, gives to Congress the authority to make all laws " necessary and proper " to give effect to the enumerated powers, the phrase is entitled to be construed liberally; and since a national bank is not forbidden by the Constitution, infringes upon no rights of the State or of the people, and is itself a useful agency for the management of national finances, Congress is free to incorporate such an institution if it so desires.

Washington approved the bill, the bank enjoyed a successful career for the twenty years of its existence, and the notes of the bank provided a national currency which circulated at par.

The importance of the bank controversy in the development of American nationality can hardly be overestimated. The broad construction views which Hamilton and his followers expounded, while they unquestionably widened the application of the Constitution far beyond anything which the framers of the instrument probably had in mind, nevertheless gave to the federal government a range of power, a wealth of resource, and a weight of authority which the restrictive interpretation of Jefferson and the Anti-Federalists would have denied. The Jeffersonian view was in essence the theory of a loose confederation, while Hamilton's view was that of a nation. Yet for more than two generations the Jeffersonian doctrine was to continue to find able and aggressive supporters, political parties were to make strict construction the underlying basis of their programmes, and national control was to encounter resistance in the States on the ground that State rights were being infringed. It was no mere theoretical discussion among lawyers that divided States, sections, and public men into hostile camps and prepared the way for civil war. It was a profound and soul-stirring consideration of the nature of the American union, a searching inquiry into the philosophy of American political and social life, and in defense of the rival opinions thousands of good men later dared to die.

A third part of Hamilton's financial programme remained. The great measures which Congress had adopted still left the national revenue deficient, and this deficit Hamilton proposed to meet by the imposition of internal taxes on distilled spirits. The question in this case was one of policy rather than of constitutional right. Internal revenue or excise taxes were notoriously hateful, and the inquisitorial methods which had commonly been employed for their collection had provoked evasion and fraud if not open resistance. Hamilton pointed out, however, that not only were distilled liquors everywhere regarded as proper subjects of taxation, but that the inducement to fraud would be greatly lessened by a licensing system under which the producer, while subject to strict governmental supervision, would find it to his advantage to pay the tax in return for the exclusive privilege of manufacture and sale. It was apparent that, with the exception of customs duties, the available sources of federal revenue were few, and the need of revenue carried the proposal through Congress. A local insurrection in western Pennsylvania directed against the tax was later suppressed without bloodshed by an imposing display of military force, and the ability of the government to secure obedience to its laws was demonstrated.

With the submission of an elaborate report on manufactures in which the economic doctrine of protection to young industries was set forth at length, the financial work of Hamilton came to an end. He had brought order out of financial chaos, given the nation a revenue, laid the foundations of American constitutional law, and framed for the Federalists a political theory and a programme; and the great work which he accomplished still, in its principles, survives.

More than two hundred amendments to the Constitution had been proposed by the ratifying conventions of the States, and there was general agreement that a bill of rights ought to be incorporated in the document. James Madison of Virginia, who had been a member of the constitutional convention and later had been elected to the House of Representatives, took the lead in urging amendment. One of the first acts of Congress, accordingly, was to frame out of the numerous proposals twelve amendments, ten of which were ratified by the State legislatures and became in 1791 a part of the Constitution. North Carolina ratified the Constitution before the end of 1789, and the ratification of Rhode Island followed in 1790. The next year Vermont was admitted as a State. The admission of Kentucky in 1792 and of Tennessee in 1796 brought the number of States to sixteen before the close of Washington's second administration. In 1791 the seat of the national government was transferred from New York to Philadelphia, where it remained until 1801, when it was permanently established in the District of Columbia.

Meantime the party struggles of Federalists and Anti-Federalists grew more intense. The congressional elections of 1790, while making no material change in the party complexion of the House of Representatives, reduced to a narrow margin the Federalist majority in the Senate — an indication that in some of the States Federalism was losing ground. Washington and Adams were re-elected with unimportant opposition in 1792, but the congressional elections of that year gave the Anti-Federalists, now coming to be known as Republicans, a slight majority in the House. The democratic principles of Jefferson, reinforced by the early successes of the French Revolution of 1789 and systematically spread by correspondence, private conversations, and a radical press, were making their way among the people, and although the great organizing work of the Federalists was not likely to be undone, the class spirit which that party embodied and the arrogant temper which it more and more exhibited presaged a fall.

Until 1792 the United States was happily free from foreign entanglements, but the declaration of war by France against Great Britain in that year suddenly raised the question of the position of the United States under the treaty of alliance with France. One of the provisions of the treaty of 1778 was a mutual guaranty of territorial integrity in case of attack; and if the war between Great Britain and France, although formally declared by France, was in fact a war for the defence of the French Revolution, the United States was apparently bound to side with its ally. The arrival early in 1793 of a new French minister, the Citizen Genet, eager to insure American support, precipitated a decision. The official reception of the minister would be a recognition of the revolutionary government which he represented, and such recognition would probably lead to war with England. Washington and his cabinet, however, took the ground that while Genet should be received, the war was not a war of defence, and a proclamation of American neutrality was accordingly issued. The proclamation gave deep offence to Genet, and his political intrigues and criticism of the administration, continued for several months, finally led Washington to ask for his recall. A change of government in France in the meantime would have put Genet's head in peril had he returned, and he preferred to remain in America as an exile. He married a daughter of Governor Clinton of New York, became a gentleman farmer and a promoter of agricultural societies, and died in 1836.

The controversy with Genet was followed in 1794 by the conclusion of a commercial agreement with Great Britain. No British minister had as yet been accredited to the United States, and the only diplomatic agreement between the two governments was the peace treaty of 1783. Now that Great Britain and France were at war, American commerce, already suffering somewhat from the discriminating duties and regulations of the acts of trade, was exposed to loss unless American neutrality was respected. In November, 1794, John Jay, chief justice of the Supreme Court, whom Washington had sent to England as a special envoy, succeeded in concluding a commercial treaty. The treaty was far from satisfactory in a number of respects, and the provision regarding trade with the British West Indies, a trade particularly lucrative for Americans and consequently greatly coveted, was so restrictive that the Senate, in ratifying the treaty, rejected the West Indies article. Imperfect as it was, however, the agreement was better than no treaty at all, for it at least laid a foundation for commercial relations. The House of Representatives, which under the Constitution has no voice in the ratification of treaties, but is nevertheless under obligation to vote any money for which the execution of a treaty calls, attempted to make political capital for the opposition by calling upon Washington for copies of the papers relating to the negotiations, but the request was refused and the necessary appropriations were eventually made. A British minister was presently sent to the United States, and diplomatic intercourse between the two countries ran for a time as uneventful a course as the continued wars of revolutionary France would permit.

Washington could probably have had a third term had he desired it, but his decision to retire to private

life in 1797 set the precedent which has ever since
been followed of two terms as the maximum period
of presidential office. He had not found the presidency a bed of roses. Dissensions in the cabinet had
sorely tried his patience, and partisan criticism in
Congress and in the country had proved a painful
and exasperating experience. Great as was the
personal affection which the people as a whole still
accorded to him, his political popularity had suffered
with the waning prestige of the Federalist party.
His farewell message, apparently in considerable
measure the work of Hamilton, was a legacy of wise
political counsel to the young but growing nation, and
his warning against " entangling alliances " with
foreign states strengthened a conviction which has
continued to the present time as one of the main
characteristics of American policy. At the expiration
of his term he retired to Mount Vernon, where he
died suddenly in 1799. The luster of his name has
not dimmed with the years, and the stately home
which he loved is still a pilgrims' shrine.

John Adams, upon whom the choice of the presidential electors fell, had long served the States and
the nation honorably and well. He was an able
lawyer, an experienced diplomatist, a staunch patriot,
and a statesman of ripe knowledge and high purpose.
But the qualities and tastes which in Washington
showed themselves in an impressive dignity produced
in Adams a coldness and hardness of manner which
repelled, and those of his political supporters who

most respected him felt for him little personal regard. The political position of the administration, moreover, was anomalous. The election of 1796 had given Adams seventy-one electoral votes and Jefferson sixty-eight, and as the vote of Jefferson was larger than that of any other candidate except Adams, Jefferson became vice-president. With a Federalist president and a Republican vice-president, and with the vice-president the acknowledged head of a party whose power in the country was rapidly becoming predominant, the electoral contest of 1800 was foreshadowed from the start.

The congressional elections of 1798 seemed to indicate a Federalist revival. The Republican majority in the House of Representatives was reduced and the Federalist majority in the Senate increased. In 1798 an attempt on the part of three mysterious go-betweens in France, whose names were concealed in the published diplomatic correspondence by the letters X, Y, and Z, to extort money from American envoys as the price of a new treaty with the government of the Directory, and the indignant declaration of Adams that he would never send another minister to France until he could be assured that the American representative would be received and treated in a becoming manner, caused an outburst of war fever, raised Adams for a brief moment to popularity, and in the congressional elections of that year gave the Federalists control of both branches of Congress.

It was a short-lived victory, however, for the

Republican tide could not be stayed and the days of the Federalists were numbered. Jefferson could perhaps have prevented the Federalist success of 1798 had he chosen to exert his strength, but he preferred to wait until 1800 when the presidency as well as Congress might be won. In the meantime the strongholds of Federalism were attacked on their doctrinal side. A suit against the State of Georgia, in 1793, brought in a federal court by a citizen of another State, had suddenly opened the eyes of the States to the possibility of using the federal courts to enforce the claims of private persons against sovereign States. Under pressure from the States a constitutional amendment excluding from the jurisdiction of the federal courts suits against a State by citizens of other States or of foreign countries was framed by Congress, and in 1798 became a part of the Constitution. There could be but little doubt that the Constitution as originally adopted made possible such suits as were now barred, but the adoption of the Eleventh Amendment was a clear victory for the reserved rights of the States on whose behalf Jefferson had long forcibly argued.

The theory of State rights and strict construction was further developed in the political field in two notable documents. Two sets of resolutions, one drafted by Madison and the other by Jefferson, were introduced in the assemblies of Virginia and Kentucky and with some modification were adopted. Approaching the question of the nature of the union from a different angle than that which had been taken in the controversy over the bank, the Kentucky and Virginia resolutions laid down the doctrine that the federal union was a political compact between sovereign States. To this compact each State gave its adhesion as a State, and since the powers which the Constitution conferred upon the federal government were such only as the States themselves had voluntarily granted, each State was entitled to judge for itself whether or not the compact had been observed and, if the terms had been violated, of the nature and means of redress. Precisely what, in practice, were the means at the disposition of a State for obtaining redress in case the federal compact was violated the Virginia resolutions did not make clear, but the Kentucky resolutions declared that a State might rightfully nullify within its own territory an act of the federal government which it believed the Constitution did not authorize.

This was the famous compact theory of American government which, thirty years later, Webster in his debate with Hayne vigorously opposed and to which South Carolina by an ordinance of nullification essayed to give practical application. The extent to which nullification might rightfully be carried, and the situation in which a State would find itself if the federal government refused to yield, were questions to which the resolutions afforded no satisfactory answer, but no great political wisdom was needed to perceive that nullification, if it meant anything more than formal protest, could end only in a forcible repudiation of federal authority. Moreover, if the union was a compact to which the States were severally parties, any State which felt itself aggrieved might presumably withdraw and become independent, for as between a State and the nation there naturally could be no impartial judge before whom the case might be tried. That such was the necessary outcome of the combined theories of compact and nullification, however, Jefferson and his followers did not go so far as to admit, and the dark clouds of a superficial and unworkable political doctrine, conceived in opposition to a growing national government whose unifying force able men were long eager to resist, continued to hang over the progress of the nation until the civil war cleared the air.

The State legislatures to which the Kentucky and Virginia resolutions were sent either returned guarded replies or sought to turn the argument by emphasizing the importance of the union, but the Federalist leaders nevertheless looked forward with apprehension to the presidential election of 1800. The party could do no less than support Adams for a second term, and the foreordained candidate of the Republicans was Jefferson. The electoral vote showed an unexpected result. Jefferson had received seventy-three votes; Aaron Burr of New York, a Republican aspirant for the vice-presidency and for the presidency if he could get it, had the same number; and Adams had received sixty-five. The Constitution

provided that in case of a tie vote the House of Representatives should choose the president by ballot
from the two or more candidates having the same
number of electoral votes, each State casting one ballot. The choice, accordingly, lay between Jefferson
and Burr, with the further consequence that which-
ever of the two was not chosen president would become vice-president by virtue of having, after the
choice of a president, the next highest number of
votes.

It was a bitter situation for the Federalists, for
that party was in a majority in the House, and a
Federalist House was now called upon to choose between two Republican candidates. Politically, the
only question was which of the two was the least
objectionable. Burr, a brilliant but unscrupulous
politician of questionable morals, who had long been
the leading opponent of Hamilton in New York, was
frankly regarded as dangerous. Jefferson, on the
other hand, while radically opposed to Federalist
policy at most points, was the author of the Declaration of Independence and had had practical experience of public affairs as governor of Virginia,
secretary of state, and vice-president. After long
discussion and rumors of attempted intrigue, ten
States voted for Jefferson and he was accordingly
elected. Burr, who then had the highest vote of the
remaining candidates, became vice-president. The
congressional elections had given the Republicans a
majority of more than two-thirds in the House and of

nearly one-third in the Senate, so that both the executive and the legislative departments of the government were now in the hands of the same party. The majority of the Supreme Court was Federalist, and the Federalists attempted to insure judicial protection for their policies by creating, in the last hours of the Adams administration, an additional and wholly unnecessary set of federal district courts whose judges, under the Constitution, could not be removed on political grounds. The attempt to set the courts in opposition to the rest of the government failed, however, for while the new administration could not remove the judges the same result was presently attained by abolishing the new offices.

The Republican victory in 1800 ended the importance of the Federalists as a national party. Federalist candidates for the presidency or vice-presidency continued to be voted for as late as the election of 1816, but the control of Congress was never regained. In a number of States, particularly in New England, there continued to be for some years an influential Federalist following, but the party attitude toward national issues became increasingly one of mere factional opposition, and during the war of 1812 some fragments of the party were openly disloyal. The great achievements of the party in its early years, however, endured. The Federalists had carried the Constitution to ratification in the State conventions, organized the new federal government on a broad and practical basis, championed a theory of national rights and powers which no subsequent assaults were able to overthrow, and prepared the way for general respect for the United States abroad. They had brought to the support of the government in its period of beginnings the indispensable aid of the propertied classes and placed the national finances on a solid foundation. The administrative system which they set up is identical in principle with that which obtains today, and much of the constitutional law which the federal courts expound is only the logical development of the doctrine which Hamilton, the greatest of all the Federalist statesmen, laid down.

The strength of the party was also its weakness. With all the practical ability of the Federalists in getting necessary things done, their conception of government was essentially aristocratic rather than popular. The conservative reaction which set in in Europe after the first few years of the French Revolution found its counterpart in America in the Federalist devotion to the idea of a strong and centralized government and in a profound dread of popular control. A numerous democracy comprising the whole adult manhood of the nation, free from property qualifications for voting or office holding and acting upon Congress and the president through the influence of organized public opinion, was a political conception alien to the Federalist mind. The incoming wave of Jeffersonian democracy, accordingly, could be met by the Federalists only with an instinctive resistance whose end was party collapse. They had laid the foundations and erected the super-structure, and the imposing building which they planned still stands as their monument, but the house was now to become for a time a people's house in a sense of which its Federalist builders had not dreamed.

# CHAPTER V

## DEMOCRACY AND NATIONALITY

JEFFERSON was the first great American statesman whose personal ascendancy was both complete and undivided. Hamilton, notwithstanding his intellectual power and rare political skill, shared his political influence among the Federalists with Washington and Adams, and neither in elections nor in the working out of party policy in Congress was his leadership the only force to be reckoned with. Jefferson, on the other hand, had no peers. He dominated his party from the beginning to the end of his eight years of office, and the leaders whom he drew about him only echoed his thoughts, repeated his words, and did what he desired. Jeffersonian Republicanism was more than a phrase; it represented a body of doctrine and a political programme of action of which Jefferson, far more than any of his contemporaries, was the author and the responsible exponent, and long after he had retired from office his followers continued to associate themselves with his name and to turn to him for advice. Time has modified the Jeffersonian principles and worked revolutionary changes in their application, and the Democrats who today celebrate the anniversary of Jefferson's birth are a party whose

opinions and acts Jefferson would often have viewed
with apprehension, but the commemoration is nevertheless a tribute to a statesman who fought the Federalists to defeat by the popular force of democratic
argument.

The personality of Jefferson presented striking
contradictions.  He was widely read, possessed an
omnivorous interest in science, literature, geography,
politics, and philosophical speculation, and enjoyed
a wider personal acquaintance in France and a more
intimate knowledge of French thought and social
habits than had been possessed by any other American except Franklin.  In an age when theological
opinions were prevailingly rigid and dogmatic he was
an extreme liberal, and Puritan ministers in Massachusetts did not hesitate to brand him as an atheist
and to hold his name anathema.  He possessed a
modest fortune which made him financially independent, and his life as a Virginia planter was in
most external respects like that of his neighbors.  But
he had also, to a degree quite without parallel among
American statesmen, a French love of political theory
and of theoretical consistency.  The democratic ideas
which the French Revolution embodied held for him
the only sound philosophy of government, and his
opposition to Federalism was a matter both of conscience and of intellectual conviction.

Jefferson took office under peculiarly favorable
conditions.  The overwhelming success of the Republicans in the election of 1800 had given the party a

clear working majority in the Senate and an impreg-
nable majority in the House of Representatives, and
congressional support for presidential policies was
assured.  The country was prosperous.  In most of
the States except those of the slaveholding South
manufactures were developing, and both domestic and
foreign trade were active.  The new secretary of the
treasury, Albert Gallatin of Pennsylvania, while entirely sympathetic with Jefferson's political views, was
an able financier of the Hamilton school, and the
finances of the nation were certain to have competent
management at his hands.  The census of 1800
showed a population of more than 5,300,000, an increase of over one-third since 1790.  The settled
area was expanding rapidly toward the west and by
1802 Ohio was ready for admission as a State, while
within the manufacturing States the growth of industry was drawing people from the country into the
towns and enlarging the varied interests of an urban
life.  In Europe the peace of Amiens, in 1802, ended
for a time the war which for ten years had been going
on between Great Britain and France, and gave the
harassed continent a brief breathing space before the
long struggle with Napoleon which was soon to begin.
With Europe at peace and American industry expanding the economic outlook was bright.

Jefferson was zealous for economy, and Gallatin
shared his view.  Hamilton, in submitting his funding
plan, had argued that the debt certificates or bonds,
in a country where money capital was deficient, would

serve some of the purposes of currency. Hamilton apparently regarded a public debt as a permanent charge upon which other financial transactions could be based, but to Jefferson a debt was a burden and a menace and he accordingly bent all his efforts to discharge it. By drastic economies in every direction, including the reduction of the army and navy almost to the vanishing point, the debt was reduced nearly one-half by March, 1809. The early hope of obtaining a revenue from the public lands, on the other hand, was not realized. The cost of surveying the lands was small, but a low price per acre led to large purchases by speculators and discouraged settlement, while a high price or sales only in large tracts deterred individual buyers who desired homes. No satisfactory solution of the difficulty was ever found, and although the varying prices which were adopted from time to time — for a considerable period $1.50 per acre for ordinary land in quantities not less than a quarter section, or 160 acres — aimed primarily to encourage settlement, the large grants eventually made to highways, railways, and other public objects in addition to those made to the States left a final deficit on the land account.

Jefferson was an expansionist. He believed in the West, and before the ordinance of 1787 had been adopted he had drafted a plan for the organization of the western territory and a scheme of public land survey. When, accordingly, in 1802 it became known that Spain by a secret treaty had transferred all of its vast possessions between the Mississippi river and the Rocky mountains to France, Jefferson took alarm. The hold of Spain upon New Orleans and the mouth of the Mississippi was already an obstacle to the development of commerce between the young settlements in Ohio, Kentucky, and Tennessee and the other States by way of the Gulf of Mexico; and with the province of Louisiana, as the western possessions of Spain were called, in the hands of Napoleon the facilities for the transshipment of goods at New Orleans which Spain had accorded might at any time be withdrawn. The prospect of a French colonial empire in America, moreover, filled Jefferson with so much apprehension as to lead him to declare that an alliance between the United States and Great Britain would become a necessity.

The American minister at Paris was accordingly instructed to negotiate for the purchase of so much of Louisiana as would give to the United States the control of the lower course of the Mississippi and insure unimpeded access to the gulf. Napoleon's interest in Louisiana was short-lived, and although the French foreign minister, Talleyrand, refused to part with the mouth of the river he suddenly offered to sell the whole province, and with some hesitation the offer was accepted. The purchase price, to be paid partly in money and partly by the assumption of certain claims of French subjects against the United States, was about $15,000,000.

Jefferson had fought the Bank of the United States

on the ground that neither directly nor indirectly was such an institution authorized by the Constitution, and it was even more clear that the Constitution contained no reference to the acquisition of foreign territory. Constitutional objections, however, appear to have had no weight with Jefferson so far as Louisiana was concerned, and he not only approved the treaty of purchase but continued to the end of his life to regard the acquisition of Louisiana as one of the great achievements of his career. The opposition in Congress was unimportant and in April, 1803, the treaty was ratified. The Louisiana purchase nearly doubled the area of the United States, and the nation was committed to a policy of expansion which thereafter was steadily pursued.

The interest of Jefferson in Louisiana did not date from the transfer of the province from Spain to France. Some time before the secret treaty was known in America he had proposed to Congress the dispatch of an exploring expedition which should trace the course of the Missouri river, find the headwaters of the Columbia, and follow the latter river to the Pacific. The fact that the region to be traversed belonged to another nation did not deter him, and in the message in which he communicated the suggestion to Congress he even went so far as to refer to the " declining state " of Spanish influence in the region and to the expedition itself as a " literary enterprise " to which Spain would probably not object. The Lewis and Clark expedition which set out in 1804 was the fruit of this proposal, and upon its discoveries was later based in part the claim of the United States to the Columbia river valley and the Oregon country.

The frontier population of Kentucky and Tennessee had at no time felt respect for the Spanish authority at New Orleans, and a policy of expansion favored conspiracies and plots. As far back as the beginning of Washington's second administration there had been mysterious intimations that Genet, the French minister, had in mind an attack upon Spanish power in Louisiana and West Florida and that Jefferson, then secretary of state, was not ignorant of what was going on. The recall of Genet, however, ended the matter until the project was revived by Aaron Burr. Burr, who had killed Hamilton in a duel in 1804, and in consequence had disappeared from public office at the close of his first term as vice-president, was now a disreputable figure and a desperate man. He still possessed, however, a certain underground influence which made him dangerous, and neither public odium nor poverty lessened his capacity for political intrigue. In 1806, after protracted negotiations and plottings the precise nature of which is not yet fully known, he started down the Ohio at the head of a small armed force, apparently expecting to be reinforced in Kentucky and in the recently organized Territory of Mississippi and to stir up a revolution in the southwest or in West Florida. Jefferson, who had kept himself informed of Burr's movements, waited until the expedition was well on its way; then at Natchez Burr was arrested and later was tried in Virginia for treason. The federal court was obviously hostile to Jefferson as Jefferson was to the court, but Chief Justice Marshall properly held that Burr could not lawfully be tried in Virginia for an alleged crime committed in the West, and intimated that if he were guilty of treason at all, in regard to which there was doubt, the place for the trial was Ohio, where the expedition had been organized. The case was not pressed, but the episode completed the political ruin of Burr, and the once powerful politician lived thereafter in obscurity and poverty until his death in 1818.

Jefferson's attitude toward Burr was for the moment sharply criticized. It was true that he had risked his political popularity in the Southwest by arresting Burr, and the trial was an assertion of the right of the United States under the Constitution to protect itself against treasonable conspiracy notwithstanding that the Burr expedition had much popular support. But the president had taken no steps to break up the conspiracy while the plans were being almost openly laid, and his effort to secure a conviction from the court was so apparent as to lead to the suspicion that he was seeking to crush a political opponent quite as much as to vindicate the national authority. It was once more a case, apparently, of the defect of the quality. Jefferson's belief in State rights made him in general tolerant of opposition and indifferent to intrigue, but the same temper made him merciless in punishment when his authority as president was openly defied. The episode did not permanently injure either his own popularity or that of his party. Jefferson himself had been re-elected in 1804, the congressional elections of that year and of 1806 still further reduced the dwindling Federalist minority in both houses, and the Republican position was secure. The federal and State officials in the Southwest who had refrained from breaking with Burr until they could see how the enterprise was likely to turn out hastened to wash their hands of him after his arrest, and before long the Burr conspiracy had ceased to be talked of as sober history and had become a romantic tale. The people of the Southwest, on the other hand, did not change. They cared little for Burr personally and they respected Jefferson, but they had only contempt for the Spanish rule in West Florida and were ready, when the time should come, to put an end to Spanish authority by force and carry American territory to the gulf.

In the meantime Jefferson and his party had been meeting a test of a different kind. The renewal of war in Europe under Napoleon in 1803 again exposed American commerce to attack. Napoleon was unable to cope with Great Britain on the sea, and he accordingly sought to break its power by the establishment of a " continental system " under which virtually the whole Atlantic coast of Europe was declared to be under blockade and neutral commerce with Europe or with British dependencies was subjected to search, seizure, or confiscation. The United States as a neutral power had no direct interest in the war, but although the expiration of the Jay treaty in 1806 left it once more without a commercial agreement with Great Britain, it insisted upon its right as a neutral to trade with both belligerents in goods which were not contraband of war, and denied the right of either France or Great Britain to enlarge the definition of contraband to include food and articles of common use merely because such goods might possibly serve military purposes. But if France was anxious to prevent American trade with Great Britain, Great Britain was equally determined to prevent American trade with France, and as the " continental system " stood by the end of 1806 any American vessel bound for a European port was liable to be searched or seized by a British naval vessel, at the same time that any American vessel which had been searched by a British vessel was thereby, under Napoleon's decrees, rendered liable to seizure by France. The claim which France put forward was peculiarly irritating because search and seizure could not as a rule be safely resisted by merchant vessels, and the detention of vessels and their cargoes under such circumstances appeared very much like an insult added to injury.

The position of the United States was obviously one of great difficulty. Legally, its rights as a neutral power were hardly open to serious question even though some of its claims were debatable. Under such war conditions as prevailed in Europe, on the other hand, American rights could not be maintained except by force, and force implied an efficient navy and an administration willing to use it. But the economies of Jefferson had reduced the navy to a few vessels, and any attempt to meet British and French aggression by force would not only court ignominious failure but might involve the United States in war with both of the European belligerents. Jefferson adopted a policy of systematic non-resistance. He refused to allow American naval vessels to leave port or to be put into commission, he declined to authorize the privateering which at that time was sanctioned by international law. For the defence of the coast against naval raids he relied upon gunboats, light draught vessels carrying one or two small cannon and capable of operating in shallow waters and small harbors which the deep draught British or French vessels could not enter. The gunboats, at which the Federalists jeered with delight, never rendered any appreciable service, but more than one hundred were built at the cost of Gallatin's carefully accumulated surplus. Finally, in 1806, the American ports were closed altogether to commerce by an embargo act.

The effect of the embargo was disastrous. The trade of Great Britain, against which the act was specially aimed, suffered no serious injury, but the American export trade was destroyed. Manufactures and agricultural staples could not be sold, prices declined heavily, workingmen and farm laborers were thrown out of employment, merchants sustained heavy losses or went into bankruptcy, and vessels deteriorated at their wharves. For nearly two years, however, the embargo continued; then, with the business of the country stagnant and commercial and manufacturing New England apparently on the point of revolt, the embargo act was withdrawn and an act of non-intercourse substituted. The only material difference between the two systems was in the permission which the non-intercourse act gave for the resumption of trade with either Great Britain or France in case either of those powers lifted its restrictive orders or decrees.

Jefferson's second term ended with the controversy still pending. In all probability he could have been again elected had he offered himself as a candidate, but the precedent which Washington had set could not with dignity be disregarded. Few presidential administrations are so difficult to judge impartially. A later disciple of Jefferson and an even more rigorous exponent of strict construction doctrine, John C. Calhoun of South Carolina, admitted that Jefferson did not live up to his theoretical opinions during his presidency, and the historian Hildreth acutely observes that Jefferson's political philosophy was always more negative than positive. It was his fate to come to prominence, first as author of the Declaration of Independence and later as head of the Anti-Federalists, primarily as a critic of abuses and leader of an opposition, and throughout his career his attention was centered far more upon what he regarded as excesses and usurpations of power than upon the formulation of a constructive policy. The political evils which needed to be combated always bulked larger in his mind than the good which a self-governing society might hope in practice to attain.

Once authority was in his hands, however, the inevitable demands of a growing nationality gripped his judgment and made short work of his theoretical scruples. The ostentatious simplicity which led him at the opening of his first administration to present himself without display to take the oath of office gave place within two years to an official routine which differed but little from that which had characterized the administrations of his predecessors; and his substitution of written for spoken addresses to Congress, while due in part to the fact that he was a poor speaker, strengthened rather than weakened his official influence through the power of his pen. The administrative machine which the Federalists had constructed was too efficient and too necessary to be displaced, and while most of the Federalist functionaries who were in office in 1801 had given way to Republicans by 1809 and the number of civil employés had been cut down, the everyday operations of government went on very much as before. Jefferson bought Louisiana without a shadow of direct constitutional warrant because the safety and welfare of the nation seemed to require it, and because so superb an opportunity for territorial expansion was not to be lost. He ruled his party with an iron hand, and his control of the government was far more absolute than that which Washington had ever exercised or than any succeeding president was to enjoy until the memorable days of Andrew Jackson; yet he never ceased to believe and to declare that power belonged to the people, and it does not appear that he ever thought of himself as acting in any other capacity than that of the people's chosen representative. It was the familiar case of a statesman whose theoretical views, stoutly held to throughout as matters of doctrine, bent in practice to the necessities of circumstance and the exigencies of party leadership, and the dreary episode of the embargo and non-resistance did not shake his hold upon the devotion of the people or prevent the nation from marching forward on its way.

A Twelfth Amendment to the Constitution, ratified by the States in time for use in the election of 1804, had made impossible the recurrence of such a complication as had arisen in 1800 by requiring the electors to cast two ballots, one for president and the other for vice-president, both president and vice-president being chosen by a majority of all the votes cast for the respective offices. The mantle of Jefferson descended upon Madison, the third Virginia president, who had served acceptably as secretary of state and was in full sympathy with the Jeffersonian programme. The opposition to the embargo caused the congressional elections of 1808 to show a slight

Federalist gain, but there was no sign of any real weakening of Republican control. Anything like open opposition to the federal government such as was being talked of quietly in New England was too serious a step to be taken lightly; a war policy was out of the question at the moment unless the United States wished deliberately to invite defeat, and the plight of American commerce might at any time be ended by the decisive victory of Great Britain or France in Europe. If the new administration could weather the storm Republican ascendancy might apparently long continue.

Madison, however, although the inheritor of the Jeffersonian tradition, had none of the commanding personal influence which had been Jefferson's great resource, and the progress of events carried him swiftly forward in a current whose force he could not resist and in which he was hardly free to choose his course. The Napoleonic wars, growing in magnitude and bitterness until almost every European nation was involved, had locked Great Britain and France in a life or death struggle, and no small state, least of all a small and remote neutral nation like the United States, could hope for consideration from either combatant. Small as was the United States in comparison with the European belligerents, however, it was independent, it had neutral rights to maintain and national dignity and self-respect to assert, and the drift toward war was irresistible. But against whom, if war came, should war be declared?  So far as injuries to American commerce were concerned both France and Great Britain were aggressors, for what was not seized by the one was ruthlessly appropriated by the other. Should the United States declare war against both and launch its combat against all Europe? The fact that England was the ancient enemy and France the ancient friend had some weight in determining public opinion, but war must be justified nevertheless and as between the two aggressors it was not easy to apportion guilt.

The war of 1812 has sometimes been spoken of as a second war of independence, but the resemblance to the great contest of 1775–83 is slight. Madison, in his message to Congress recommending a declaration of war against Great Britain, felt called upon to specify a number of grievances, but none of them except interference with American commerce and the impressment of American seamen by the British navy had previously been emphasized and the unfriendly conduct of France was overlooked. As a matter of fact specific grievances, irritating as they were, had much less to do with the case than the general feeling of indignation and chagrin which the long-continued aggressions of both Great Britain and France had caused, and the declaration of war was levied against the former rather than against the latter because the British navy, since Nelson had ended the sea power of France at Trafalgar in 1805, had been the chief offender. Whether or not Madison, as hostile rumor charged, consented to war as the price of a renomination, is of no great importance and there was no need of denial to disprove the tale, for Madison was too shrewd a politician and too well informed regarding public opinion not to know that the country as a whole wanted war, and that if he opposed a declaration another president would be chosen in his place.

The war was a record of almost unrelieved incompetency, unpreparedness, and failure for the United States so far as land operations went, and the land operations of the British in America brought them no glory. The naval victory of Commodore Perry on Lake Erie in September, 1813, stirred the nation to enthusiasm, but the attempt of the American forces to invade Canada was a failure notwithstanding one or two successful engagements, and the burning of the capitol building at Washington by the British in retaliation for the destruction of the parliament building at York, now Toronto, was an inglorious achievement. New England was openly opposed to the war throughout, and a convention at Hartford, Connecticut, adopted a series of resolutions demanding, among other constitutional amendments which were deemed essential, one which should take from Congress the power to declare war without the support of three-fourths of the States represented. The disheartening failures on land, however, were offset by some brilliant victories on the sea, and the small American navy, supplemented by privateers, made American skill and courage respected.

So much of Europe was at war in 1812 that the

addition of a war with the United States made little difference for the moment, and Great Britain in fact paid relatively small attention to the American campaigns until after the overthrow of Napoleon in 1814. The opinion of Wellington, whose advice was then sought, was unfavorable to the continuance of the war in America, and as the downfall of Napoleon left no reason for continuing the policy of restricting neutral commerce, no particular reason for going on with the war remained. The British orders in council affecting American trade had in fact been withdrawn shortly before Congress issued a declaration of war, but the withdrawal was not known in the United States until after hostilities had begun and the action was then too late to exert any influence.

The peace treaty, signed at Ghent on December 24, 1814, made no mention of the causes or occasion of the war and contained no renunciation by Great Britain of the commercial policy over which the war had in the main been fought. Both parties appear to have realized that the past with its irritating and grievous incidents was over, and that with the disappearance of the circumstances went also the dropping of the policy of harassing neutral trade. There was no conquered territory to change hands and the United States made no claim for damages on account of injuries to its commerce, but provision was made for settling the long-standing dispute over the northeastern boundary. Three weeks after the treaty was signed, but before the news was known in America, the one brilliant American victory of the war came with the defeat of a British army at New Orleans by General Andrew Jackson, and victory and peace were celebrated at the same time. The conclusion of a commercial treaty presently re-established commercial relations between the two nations, and controversy with Great Britain disappeared for a time from American politics.

The conclusion of peace opened a new period of enlargement for American industry. Political opposition to the Bank of the United States had been sufficient to prevent a renewal of the bank charter upon its expiration in 1811, and the United States went through the war without the aid of a fiscal agency and a stable paper currency such as the bank had provided. In 1816, however, a second bank, substantially identical in character with the earlier institution but with a capital of thirty-five million dollars instead of ten million, was chartered and the financial policy which Hamilton had inaugurated was resumed. A new tariff act of the same year imposed relatively high duties on an enlarged list of imported articles with the avowed object of encouraging and protecting American manufactures. The war itself had not been particularly expensive, but the decline of revenue during the period of the embargo had stopped the reduction of the debt, and the costs of war together with the added expenses of civil administration caused the debt to increase from $53,000,000 in 1810 to about $91,000,000 in 1820. A policy of economy and the absence of extraordinary expenditures reduced the debt by nearly one-half in the course of the next decade. Louisiana was admitted as a State in 1812, and the admission of Indiana in 1816 brought the number of States to nineteen by the close of Madison's second administration.

It was apparent that the Republican party was changing its policy, and that theories and practices which the Anti-Federalists and even Jefferson himself would have rejected were now recognized elements of the Republican programme. A Republican Congress, for example, had refused in 1811 to extend the charter of the first Bank of the United States, but it was a Republican Congress which chartered the second bank five years later. The encouragement of American manufactures by the imposition of protective tariff duties was a Federalist rather than an Anti-Federalist policy, but it was a Republican Congress that enacted the protective tariff act of 1816. Theoretically the Republicans still stood for State rights and a strict construction of the Constitution, for economy in expenditure and the reduction of the powers of the federal government to the lowest point consistent with efficient administration, but in actual practice there was little now to distinguish Republican methods at these points from those which had obtained during the years of Federalist control. The powerful influence of the Supreme Court, forced into the background under Jefferson but now asserting itself more and more as important cases multiplied, was thrown consistently upon the side of a liberal interpretation of the Constitution, and the greatest of all the chief justices, John Marshall of Virginia, whose appointment to office was one of the last acts of the Adams administration, must be counted among the foremost builders of American nationality.

Virginia has been called the mother of presidents, but in the early years of the republic the Federalist opposition referred to the succession of Virginia presidents which began with Jefferson by the less complimentary epithet of the Virginia hierarchy.  The Hartford convention of 1814 had proclaimed as one of its grievances the apparent purpose to keep the presidential succession, which already numbered Washington, Jefferson, and Madison, in the Virginia line and to make the office of secretary of state, which both Jefferson and Madison had held, a stepping-stone to the presidency.  Only once more, however, was the Virginia precedent to be observed.  James Monroe of Virginia, to whom the majority of the presidential electors gave their choice in 1816, had been secretary of state under Madison, and was the last of the presidents who had seen service in the Revolutionary war. Educated as a lawyer, he gave up the practice of the profession early in life and for a number of years before his election as president had been almost continuously in office, part of the time as American representative in France.  His political views were in general those of Jefferson, but he had no marked force of personal character, and the two great events

of his administration owed little of their importance
to his personal influence.  The absence of pronounced
political color in the president, on the other hand, was
at the moment an advantage rather than an embarrassment.   Party  lines  were  fading,  and  although  the
" era of good feeling," as the later years of Monroe's
presidency came to be called, was in reality a period
of factional struggle and uncertain groping for new
issues, there was no assured party following which
Monroe or any other president could have led.   His
all but uncontested re-election in 1820 was a tribute
which a more aggressive president could hardly have
received, and the modest dignity and urbanity with
which he filled the presidential office helped to facili-
tate the passage of the political life of the nation
from an old order to a new.

The disappearance of old party distinctions and the
temporary waning of popular interest in the legal
and constitutional aspects of public questions was
largely due to the marked changes in social and
economic conditions which the United States was
undergoing.   The first two decades of the republic
had seen the invention and development of the steamboat, the cast-iron plough, the cotton gin, the textile
carding machine, the high-pressure steam engine, and
the screw propeller; and the application of steam,
joined to rapid improvements in machinery and
mechanical processes, was working an industrial revolution whose effects were felt throughout the country.
The steamboat solved the problem of up-stream navi-

gation on the Ohio and Mississippi, opened the West to the manufactured products of the middle States and New England, and shortened by one-half the ordinary voyage to Europe.  Until 1793 the difficulty of clearing the cotton fiber of seeds and chaff had kept the cultivation of cotton at a low level in comparison with tobacco and rice, but the invention of the cotton gin in that year changed the face of southern agriculture and in a few years made cotton the king of American staples.  In the face of an expanding industrial life at once varied and profitable the old controversies over a strict or loose interpretation of the Constitution and the reserved rights of the States lost interest for the average citizen, and the people turned with a new zeal to the conquest of the western wilderness and the acquisition of wealth through manufactures and trade.

The lure of the West, strong even during the Revolution, drew the venturesome with an irresistible attraction.  A steady stream of population from the older States of the East poured into the Ohio valley, and a new frontier was hardly established before the waves of migration again pushed it forward.  One by one the Indian tribes were dispossessed and their remnants removed to the border of the Mississippi or beyond, and town and county organizations reflected the local political habits of the settlers from New England, the middle States, and Virginia and the Carolinas.  North of the Ohio river slavery had been excluded by the ordinance of 1787, and it was a free population of workers that levelled the forests, broke the prairies, and built homes, churches, and schools. Into the Atlantic coast States in turn filtered, after 1815, the first appreciable beginnings of the mighty stream of European immigration which within another generation was largely to displace native-born labor in the mills, reinforce the westward movement, and give to the United States a permanently cosmopolitan character. Census returns of population leaped from 5,300,000 in 1800 to 7,200,000 in 1810; by 1820 the figure had grown to 9,600,000. Mississippi was ready for admission in 1817 and Illinois was added the following year. In 1819, after a tedious diplomatic controversy and a period of irregular fighting hardly to be dignified by the name of war, the Spanish provinces of East and West Florida passed into the control of the United States by purchase and territorial expansion had reached the Gulf of Mexico. The admission as a State of Alabama, the gulf portion of which American forces had early invaded, followed immediately, but nearly a generation elapsed before Florida was ready for statehood.

The Florida annexation was just being completed when there burst upon the country, with a suddenness which to the aged Jefferson was as a fire bell in the night, the political issue of slavery. The Territory of Missouri, organized in 1812 with a western frontier which extended to the Rocky mountains, applied for admission as a State, and at the same time a similar application was made, with the approval of

Massachusetts, by the District of Maine. Maine, of course, would be a free State, and the House of Representatives, a majority of whose members represented States in which slavery did not exist, demanded that slavery should be excluded from Missouri. The admission of two free States, however, would destroy the balance which thus far had been maintained between free and slave States, and give the free states a permanent majority in the Senate, where the States were represented equally, as well as in the House. The Senate, its action controlled by the slavery interests, refused either to pass the Missouri bill or to admit Maine unless slavery was to be permitted in Missouri, while the House refused to vote for the admission of Missouri save as a free State, and the result was a deadlock in Congress and a controversy which shook the nation to its foundations.

The political opposition to slavery went back to the beginning of the government. The compromise in the constitutional convention by which three-fourths of the slaves were counted in reckoning the population of a State for purposes of representation in the House was a concession to the political power of the slaveholding States which the free States had been compelled reluctantly in 1787 to make. A further compromise, aimed at the African slave trade, had allowed the trade to continue for twenty years, at the end of which time Congress was empowered to prohibit it, and a prohibitory statute had been passed in 1806. At the time when the Constitution was framed slavery was relatively of small importance, and many southern slave owners shared the feeling of repugnance which the institution inspired in the North; but with the invention of the cotton gin slave labor suddenly took on a new significance for industry, and the wealth which was now being drawn from the cotton fields dulled the opposition of southern planters as well as of many northern merchants and manufacturers to the inherent evils of the system. Yet it was clear that with all its apparent prosperity the South was not sharing in the industrial development of the rest of the country, that free labor and manufactures would not go where slave labor predominated, and that the South was doomed, if it adhered to slavery, to remain a primitive agricultural section constantly declining in relative wealth and importance.

Negro slavery, in other words, was on the defensive as an economic system. To have abolished it, on the other hand, would have been to overturn the established economic and social order of the slave-holding States with no assurance that free labor, under the peculiar conditions of a hot climate, would take its place; at the same time that the political importance of the southern States, with a relatively small white population which would alone enjoy political rights, would hopelessly decline. A large part of the South seemed predestined by nature for the production of cotton, and the destruction or even the serious curtailment of one of the greatest of American industries was something not even to be threatened.

The weakness of slavery was thus also to some degree its strength. The only hope of slavery, in a nation which was developing a varied industry carried on by free labor, was in the maintenance of a balance between slave and free States in the Senate, where the equal representation of the States would be sufficient to bar hostile legislation; and the free States were certain in the long run to support such a compromise lest the entire cotton industry, production, manufacture, and export, should be put in jeopardy. Of the twenty-two States which in 1819 composed the union eleven were free and eleven were slave. The admission of Missouri with slavery, Maine being free, would maintain the sectional balance, but with slavery excluded from Missouri the control of the Senate would be lost forever. The free State membership of the House of Representatives already exceeded the slave State membership by twenty-four, and with a growth of population appreciably less in the slaveholding section than in the rest of the country there was no prospect that slavery would ever gain control of the House.

The argument was political and sectional but it was not constitutional, and if slavery was to be protected the Constitution must somehow be brought to its side. The supporters of slavery found their ground in a new development of strict construction doctrine, namely, that under the Constitution every State was entitled to maintain its own " domestic institutions " without interference by the other States or by Congress, and that the protection to which the States were constitutionally entitled extended to their labor system whether slave or free.  It was not difficult to show that the Constitution recognized slavery as existing, but whether or not the Constitution was intended to protect slavery was not so clear.  If slavery was a national institution Congress might certainly regulate or restrict it, but if it was in fact one of the " domestic " institutions over which the States were assumed to retain complete control, only great latitude of interpretation could bring it within the scope of the " general welfare " for which Congress was empowered to provide.

The controversy could not be settled on principle and it was accordingly settled by compromise.  The House of Representatives agreed to the admission of Missouri as a slave State, the Senate agreed to the admission of Maine, and the two houses joined in prohibiting forever the admission of further slave States from the Louisiana purchase north of the parallel of latitude 36′ 30″, the southern boundary of Missouri.  As the boundary between the United States and the Spanish possessions in the Southwest at that time coincided roughly with the eastern and northern boundaries of the present State of Texas and the western boundary was the Rocky mountains, it was evident that the territory which the Missouri compromise left open for the organization of slave States was very much smaller than the territory which would be free; but the disparity seemed less then

than it does now because most of the territory west
of the Mississippi and the Missouri was regarded as
permanently unfit for settlement, and for years thereafter was represented in maps as the great American
desert.

The Missouri struggle was a rude shock to the
spirit of national unity.  The growth of slavery in
one-half of the States, slowly molding economic life
and social habit into forms radically different from
those which the other States enjoyed, had suddenly
provoked a grave political crisis which had divided
the nation and in regard to which political parties
must henceforth take sides.  The controversy was
novel to many in that it seemed to present only a
fundamental issue of right or wrong, but a social
institution to which a large part of the nation was
devoted, and upon which material prosperity seemed
at the moment vitally to depend, was certain, now that
it had been put upon the defensive, to ally itself with
every national or sectional interest from which it
might hope to draw support, and to put the Union
itself in peril rather than to yield ground.  In the
presence of slavery the American nation found itself
sectional, and the fatal step of compromise taken in
1820 indicated the line which for forty years the
nation was to follow.

Thanks to the far-seeing statesmanship of John
Quincy Adams, Monroe's secretary of state, the Monroe administration won a diplomatic victory abroad
which did something to offset the rebuff which the

Missouri controversy had given to national unity at home. The attempt of Napoleon to bring Spain under the control of France had awakened a new spirit of nationality among the Spanish people, and with the failure of that attempt and the subsequent downfall of the Napoleonic power in the peninsula a succession of revolts against the reactionary Spanish crown spread throughout the colonies of Spain in America. By the beginning of Monroe's second administration every Spanish colony in Central and South America had a revolutionary government and was successfully maintaining the independence which it had declared. Under the lead of the Holy Alliance, a reactionary combination of European powers of which Metternich, the chief minister of Austria, was the moving spirit Spain was encouraged to' attempt the recovery of its colonies. The prospect of a Spanish invasion of Central and South America backed by the military resources of the Holy Alliance was a grave menace to the United States, presaging a renewal of political complications with Europe even more serious than those from which the United States had lately emerged. At the same time Russia, which already held Alaska, took occasion to assert an ill-founded claim to so much of the Pacific coast as lay between Alaska and the Oregon country, and an imperial ukase closed the region to foreign trade. If the Russian claim were allowed to go uncontested and the plans of the Holy Alliance were carried out, the United States would find itself confronted with a powerful European combination to the south and the Russian imperial government in the northwest, and the American continents would once more become a field for European exploitation.

Adams had been the principal negotiator of the treaty of Ghent, and a long official residence abroad had made him intimately aware of the political spirit of Europe. He accordingly persuaded Monroe to incorporate in his annual message to Congress in 1823 two passages which together constitute the famous Monroe doctrine. One, aimed particularly at Russia, declared that the American continents were not hereafter to be regarded as fields for colonization by any European power. The other, directed at Spain and the Holy Alliance, announced that while the policy of the United States was one of non-interference with the affairs of any European state and non-participation in European political arrangements, any attempt on the part of the allied powers to assist Spain in overthrowing the revolutionary governments which had declared their independence, and whose independence the United States had recognized, would be regarded as "the manifestation of an unfriendly disposition" toward the United States. The bold warning was sufficient, the plans of Spain and the allies were abruptly dropped, and the independence of the governments of Central and South America was assured. Negotiations with Russia had been begun before Monroe's message was delivered, and a treaty presently provided for the withdrawal of the Russian claim.

The substance of the Monroe doctrine was not new, for the policy of holding aloof from entangling alliances with Europe went back to the time of Washington and was implicit in the neutrality which had several times been proclaimed. The statements of Monroe's message, however, were the first clear enunciation of the principle as a national policy, and although time has greatly modified the position taken in 1823 and national practice has more than once seriously infringed upon it, the Monroe doctrine still remains one of the primary principles of American diplomacy so far as political relations with Europe are concerned. The declaration made clear the supremacy of the United States in American affairs, and its prompt acceptance by the European powers whose schemes it disrupted was a tribute to the moral and physical weight of the young nation. The fact that Canning, the British prime minister, who was opposed to the Holy Alliance, had suggested in 1822 a joint declaration by Great Britain and the United States against European intervention in Central and South America does not lessen the distinction of Adams's achievement, for the suggestion of Canning was declined on the same ground as that upon which the declaration of Monroe was later based, and the Monroe doctrine once it was proclaimed applied to Great Britain as well as to Spain and the allies.

Monroe was not only the last of the Virginia hierarchy but the last also of the presidents who had personally taken part in the establishment of the federal government.   Most of the statesmen of the early constitutional period were dead, a new generation with new ideas and a new spirit had come upon the stage, and there was a crude but energetic West henceforth to be reckoned with.   The transition to a new order of which Monroe had seen the beginnings had been nearly accomplished, and no prophet was needed to foretell that the new order would be very different from the old.

## CHAPTER VI

## A NEW PHASE OF DEMOCRATIC CONTROL

If birth, education, and public service could ever
of themselves suffice as a preparation for the presidency, John Quincy Adams should have been one of
the most successful of American presidents. He was
the son of John Adams. He had entered the public
service in boyhood as his father's secretary, served
with distinction as a diplomatic representative of the
United States in The Netherlands and elsewhere during some of the most exciting years of the Napoleonic
wars, concluded the peace treaty with Great Britain
at the close of the war of 1812, and after the war had
returned to the United States to become for eight
years secretary of state under Monroe. He was
widely read, possessed a greater familiarity with
European politics than any American of his day, and
was one of the few presidents who have had a practical knowledge of foreign languages. His one-time
Federalist support in New England had dropped away
when he upheld the embargo, and thereafter his political opinions became those of a moderate Republican
with whom an intense belief in American nationality
and a jealous regard for American independence and
prestige were controlling motives. No man in public

life was apparently better fitted to lead the nation in the period of political transition through which it was passing and to bridge the interval which separated the old order from the new.

Yet the four years of his presidency were for the nation a period of acrimonious political turmoil, while to Adams they brought declining official influence and personal regard and an ultimate repudiation and defeat clearly foreshadowed from the start. Trouble began with the election of 1824. Of the four candidates in the field, all nominally Republicans, Andrew Jackson of Tennessee received 99 electoral votes, Adams 84, William H. Crawford of Georgia 41, and Henry Clay of Kentucky 37. No candidate had a majority, and the election devolved for a second time upon the House of Representatives, which under the Twelfth Amendment was required to choose a president from among the three candidates having respectively the highest number of votes, each State casting one vote. Clay, accordingly, was ineligible, and the contest lay in fact between Jackson and Adams but with the supporters of Clay holding the balance in the decision. The vote of the House was delayed until February, 1825; then Clay gave his support to Adams and Adams was chosen. Of the twenty-four States thirteen voted for Adams, seven for Jackson, and four for Crawford. The vice-president, over whose election there was no dispute, was John C. Calhoun of South Carolina.

The election of 1824–25 had far-reaching consequences. Jackson, while conceding that the result was entirely regular from the point of view of the constitutional requirements, nevertheless insisted that he rather than Adams was the people's choice and that the will of the people had been defeated by the action of the House. Jackson, accordingly, whose personal popularity in the Southwest was very great and whose military exploit in 1815 had earned for him the title of "the hero of New Orleans," was certain to be a formidable candidate for the presidency in 1828, and the legislature of Tennessee shortly nominated him for the office. The renewed candidacy of Clay, who had stood at the bottom of the list in 1824, was less certain, but Clay was already one of the most prominent and influential figures in Congress and the part which he had taken in the House election had shown his power. His acceptance of the office of secretary of state under Adams, on the other hand, lent color to the charge, apparently unfounded, that he had made a "corrupt bargain" with Adams of which the office was the reward, and Jackson industriously spread the charge. The position of Calhoun, also, was peculiar. Some years before, while serving as secretary of war under Monroe, Calhoun had urged the court-martialling of Jackson for the high-handed conduct of the "hero" in invading Florida and summarily hanging two British subjects suspected of treasonable intrigue; but the personal popularity of Jackson had deterred Monroe and the cabinet, and in place of drastic punishment the action of Jackson was sustained. The secret of the cabinet discussions had been well kept and Jackson, who suspected Adams rather than Calhoun of hostility, regarded Calhoun as his friend. Calhoun could not hope to win the presidency in 1828 in the face of Jackson's candidacy, but he might secure a second term as vice-president. On the other hand, if Jackson were chosen president in 1828 he would assuredly be a candidate for re-election in 1832 if he lived, and since a third term as vice-president was hardly to be thought of the prize of the presidency seemed in the way of slipping forever from Calhoun's grasp. The shadows of the election of 1824–25, in other words, darkened the political horizon for at least eight years to come.

A more forcible man than Adams could not have hoped to cope successfully with so complicated a situation. The tide of a new democracy, urged on by the vigorous and unconventional spirit of the West, was flowing strongly, and neither as a politician nor as a statesman was Adams able to stay it or to direct its course. His high sense of public duty would not allow him to use the federal civil service as party spoils, and holders of public office intrigued against him. The comprehensive recommendations of his messages to Congress covered a wider range of important subjects than those of any previous president and showed a statesmanlike grasp of national problems, but the Congress to which they were addressed for the most part passed them by. His broad constitutional views, also, exposed him to attack from the Jackson following. In 1817 Monroe had vetoed on constitutional grounds a bill appropriating money for what were known as internal improvements, a term long used to designate the policy of aiding by federal grants the construction of highways and canals and the improvement of navigable rivers, and for some years after the veto appropriations for those purposes were small. Adams favored internal improvements, and the congressional appropriations for such undertakings amounted by the end of his term to some fourteen million dollars, while expenditures of several times that amount had been forecast by preliminary surveys.

It was clear that the republicanism, if the term might still with propriety be employed, of Adams and his followers resembled far more the theories and practices of the early Federalists than the doctrinal views of Jefferson, and that the new democracy of which Jackson was now the popular embodiment could not at all points claim Jefferson as its author. The Adams following accordingly sought to differentiate themselves from their opponents by taking the name of National Republicans, while the " Jackson men," as they were for some time called, presently took the party name of Democrats. The latter name endured, and the present Democratic party is historically identical, although with varied mutations of principle and fortune, with the new party which took form during the last months of Adams's administration. The National Republicans later took the name of Whigs, and under that name the party continued until the eve of the Civil War, when its remnants gave way to the present Republican party. The broad distinction between a liberal and a strict construction of the Constitution which had divided Federalists from Anti-Federalists was perpetuated in the new party alignment, but the later surrender of the Democrats to the political demands of slavery forced the Democratic party into an extreme State rights position for which the policies of Jefferson and Jackson afforded no sufficient support.

The presidential campaign of 1828, however, was hardly at all a campaign of issues. It was a campaign for the " vindication " of Jackson and the enthronement of " the people," and the campaign slogan " Hurrah for Jackson! " prevailed over any discussion of policy past, present, or future. The election was a Democratic landslide. Jackson received 178 electoral votes in comparison with 83 votes cast for Adams, and the vice-presidential vote for Calhoun was only a trifle less than the electoral vote for Adams. Both branches of Congress had been strongly Republican ever since the Jeffersonian victory of 1800, but the congressional elections of 1828 slightly increased the new Democratic majority in the Senate and added materially to the Democratic strength in the House of Representatives.

The election of Jackson brought to the presidential office the most vivid and emphatic personality that American politics had yet produced. Jackson had little of the imposing dignity of Washington and none of the culture of Jefferson. His experience of public affairs had been limited to a short term as senator from Tennessee and a brief service as governor of that State; his military career, aside from his defeat of the British at New Orleans, had been mainly that of an aggressive fighter of Indians, and his small practice of law had given him neither professional distinction nor a judicial temperament. He was distinctively a product of the frontier West, the idol of a section which cared little for precedent or tradition and still less for the technicalities of constitutional interpretation, but which nevertheless possessed a keen sense of right and wrong and an abiding confidence in the virtue of direct political action. What his policy as president would be no one knew and few of his followers inquired, but there was a general expectation that he would punish his enemies and reward his friends, cleanse the federal government of abuses, and make the national authority respected at home and abroad. Whether or not in the process the requirements of the Constitution would be scrupulously observed none troubled themselves to ask. The Constitution had been made for the nation; it was not the nation that had been made for the Constitution.

A tumultuous inauguration in which crowds of admiring supporters invaded the White House, upset the tubs of punch which had been prepared for their refreshment, and stood with muddy boots upon upholstered furniture, was followed by an unprecedented removal of federal office-holders. Functionaries long in office were arbitrarily dismissed and their places given to clamoring Democrats. The change of personnel was not complete and many political opponents of Jackson contrived to retain their posts throughout his administration, but the wholesale introduction of the spoils system demoralized the federal administrative service as a whole, and established a baneful precedent which continued to be more or less regularly followed until the present civil service law began the substitution of a merit system. Jackson's own position in the matter, however, was entirely clear and his equanimity was not disturbed. In his view government offices belonged to the people, no special experience or skill was necessary in order to perform their duties, and long continuance in office was an evil from which the country should not be asked to suffer.

The eight years of Jackson's presidency were marked by two great controversies which revealed in startling outlines the character and political ideals of Jackson and his aggressive national spirit. Neither controversy could have been avoided, for the seeds of contention were planted in the historical events which ultimately provoked them, but the political significance of the fierce battles which were waged was due in large measure to the personality and methods of Jackson himself.

The first controversy was with the Bank of the United States. The bank had had a prosperous career as a financial institution, its notes circulated throughout the country at par, its services as the fiscal agency, practically the treasury, of the government were efficiently performed, and its paramount influence was sufficient to keep the various State banks in a reasonably satisfactory financial condition. It was, however, a huge financial monopoly, and its capital of $35,000,000, together with its exclusive right to issue a paper currency which the federal government had agreed to accept, made it a powerful factor in national business as well as in national finance. From the date of its incorporation in 1816, accordingly, it had met with opposition, particularly in the southern and western States, where numerous attempts were made to tax the branches of the bank out of existence or otherwise restrict their operations and influence. In 1819 the Supreme Court, in the great case of McCulloch v. Maryland, had upheld the constitutionality of the bank and denied the right of the States to tax its branches, but the decision of Chief Justice Marshall did not end the opposition and the attacks by the States continued.

The attention of Jackson had been attracted to the bank in the campaign of 1828 by the report that the branch of the bank at Portsmouth, New Hampshire, was using its political influence in opposition to his candidacy; but he was already familiar with the hostile state of public opinion regarding the institution in the West, and the Portsmouth incident only confirmed his belief that the bank was dangerous. In a brief reference to the bank at the end of his first annual message he raised the question of monopoly, pointed out that the bank would probably apply for a renewal of its charter which expired in 1836, and suggested that if a bank were looked upon as essential to the financial operations of the government, an institution wholly under government control, and with private profit eliminated, would better serve the purpose than the existing bank. The attack was repeated somewhat more elaborately in his second annual message in 1830, but in each instance the bank was able to obtain from Congress favorable committee reports as to its soundness and efficiency. In 1831, accordingly, with another presidential campaign in prospect for the following year, Jackson contented himself with a brief reiteration of his objections and an ominous reference of the question to the " judgment of the people " and their representatives.

The bank, confident of support from Congress and apparently thinking that the attacks had ended, rashly chose this critical moment to apply for a renewal of its charter. The charter bill was passed by substantial majorities, and Jackson vetoed it. The veto message was a scathing arraignment of the bank and its policies and an excellent campaign document, but it was also a startling revelation of Jackson's constitutional views. Jackson declined to accept the decision of the Supreme Court upholding the constitutionality of the bank as binding upon either the executive or the legislative departments of the government, and insisted that both Congress and the president were at liberty to act in accordance with their own opinions of what was and what was not constitutional so far as the enactment or approval of laws was concerned. Beyond the federal government, moreover, were the States and the people, and the persistent opposition of the States was sufficient to convince Jackson that the people had repudiated the bank. Jackson, in other words, stood forth as the interpreter of the popular mind irrespective of any action which either Congress or the Supreme Court had taken, notwithstanding that the bank question had not as yet been an issue in any national election and the " will of the people " had in no tangible way been expressed. If this novel doctrine were to prevail, government in the United States would cease to be government under a constitution which the Supreme Court was authorized to interpret and to whose provisions, so interpreted, Congress and the executive must conform, and would become a government of presidential intuition. The bank support in Congress, however, was insufficient to pass the bill over the veto and the bank prepared to wind up its affairs.

The veto of the bank bill made the question of the bank one of the pivotal points in the presidential election of 1832, and the overwhelming victory of Jackson was to him sufficient proof that his course was right. A somewhat questionable financial transaction had confirmed his suspicion that the bank was unsound, and he now called upon the secretary of the treasury to remove from the bank the federal funds. Under the law creating the bank the government funds were to be deposited in the bank or its branches unless the secretary of the treasury should otherwise direct, and an order of the secretary was accordingly necessary before the removal could legally take place. In an elaborate paper which was read to the cabinet and given to the press Jackson took pains to disclaim any intention of coercing the secretary of the treasury or of asking that official to do anything which his judgment or conscience disapproved, but he also made clear that the direction of the executive branch of the government was by the Constitution vested in the president and that the opinion of the president upon questions of policy ought in consequence to prevail. Jackson was expounding for the first time the true constitutional theory of the cabinet, for the so-called cabinet officers are not ministers in the European sense of the term, and the policy of an administration is that of the president and not that of president and cabinet combined; but the velvet glove of Jackson's paper only thinly concealed the iron hand.

The secretary of the treasury, McLane, did not feel himself legally justified in removing the deposits. He was accordingly " kicked upstairs " and made secretary of state, and the office of secretary of the treasury was given to Duane. Duane shared the general views of Jackson in regard to the bank, but he could find no legal justification for interfering with the deposits and he was thereupon asked to resign. He refused to resign, and Jackson dismissed him and transferred the treasury portfolio to the attorney general, Roger B. Taney, later chief justice of the Supreme Court, who issued the necessary orders. Arrangements had already been made with a number of State banks to receive the deposits, and the government funds were gradually withdrawn from the Bank of the United States until the accounts were extinguished.

A spectacular episode, but one also of serious constitutional importance, followed. The Senate, which throughout the controversy had been friendly to the bank, called upon Jackson for a copy of the paper which had been read to the cabinet. Although the paper had been published the request for a copy was refused, whereupon the Senate adopted a resolution censuring Jackson for his conduct toward the bank. In an elaborate communication, prepared in the main by Taney, Jackson mercilessly dissected the resolution, defended his course in the bank matter, denied the right of the Senate to censure the president and thereby condemn him publicly without a hearing when the Constitution expressly provides for trial by impeachment if high crimes or misdemeanors are alleged, and requested the Senate to enter the message of protest upon its journal. The Senate, angered at the rebuff, retorted by denying the right of the president to protest and refused to spread the protest upon its records. Thomas H. Benton, senator from Missouri and a warm supporter of Jackson, immediately moved to expunge from the journal the resolution of censure, and when the motion was rejected announced his purpose to introduce a similar resolution at every session of the Senate thereafter until the resolution was adopted or his own senatorial career terminated. With each succeeding session the opposition dwindled, and just before Jackson's administration closed the expunging motion was adopted.   In a melodramatic scene the manuscript journal was solemnly brought into the Senate chamber, black lines were drawn about the offending resolution of censure, and the expunging order was written across its face.   The Bank of the United States, however, had some months before ceased to exist as a government institution and the triumph of Jackson was complete.

There can be no question but that Jackson was in the right in opposing the continuance of the government connection with the bank.   The bank was too powerful a monopoly to be safely tolerated, and its potential political influence, albeit not very aggressively exercised until Jackson began his attack, was a standing menace to popular government.   The methods which Jackson employed, on the other hand, were needlessly violent, and his open denial of the binding force of a decision of the Supreme Court raised a constitutional issue which, if it had become a recognized precedent, would speedily have transformed the government of the United States into an executive autocracy.   The overthrow of the bank undoubtedly gave the federal government a new supremacy, but the problems of democracy took on an unwonted form when a man of Jackson's dominating temper assumed to interpret the people's will.

While the fight with the bank was going on another great controversy, wholly different in character and more immediately threatening the unity of the nation, had been dividing the attention of the country. The enactment of a protective tariff in 1816 had been followed by an extraordinarily rapid growth of manufactures, and the inevitable demand for still further protection, especially strong in New England and Pennsylvania, had been met in 1824 by increased and more comprehensive duties. In the slaveholding South, however, manufactures had no hold, and the argument that protective duties, while of benefit in the first instance to particular States or industries, in fact diffused their benefits throughout the nation and were thus indirectly of advantage to agriculture as well as to manufactures, made no impression upon southern opinion and was viewed with misgivings in parts of the West. To the South in particular, apparently fated by nature to remain a region whose only important industry was the production of a few great agricultural staples through the labor of Negro slaves, a protective tariff was sectional, and sectional legislation, when the protection of slavery was not at stake, was unconstitutional. To be sure, the Constitution empowered Congress to levy taxes, duties, imposts, and excises, but it apparently also restricted the power to the broad national purposes of paying the debt and providing for the common defence and general welfare of the United States; and sectional legislation, it was urged, was not legislation for the general welfare and protective duties were not primarily intended for the payment of the debt.

When, accordingly, in 1828 the tariff duties were again sharply raised, the South, thoroughly committed historically to strict construction habits of thought, vigorously protested. The advent of Jackson, whose opinions on the tariff question were nebulous but who was supposed to be unfriendly to high protection, caused a temporary lull in the controversy. Before many months had passed, however, a violent personal quarrel growing out of the attempt of Jackson to force the social recognition of the wife of the secretary of war disrupted the cabinet, and Calhoun, whose attitude toward Jackson in the Florida episode years before the president had learned, resigned the vice-presidency and became senator from South Carolina. Calhoun had already written an elaborate defence of State rights, although only a few persons knew or suspected his authorship of the document, and the " South Carolina Exposition," as it was called, had been adopted as a report by the South Carolina legislature. The opportunity to put the doctrine of the " Exposition " into practice came in 1832. A new tariff act of that year modified somewhat the tariff duties of 1828, but showed no disposition to abandon the protective principle. South

Carolina accordingly issued an ordinance of nullification declaring the tariff acts of 1824, 1828, and 1832 null and void within the territory of the State, forbidding the collection of the duties, and announcing that any attempt on the part of the federal government to use force would be regarded as incompatible with the longer continuance of South Carolina in the Union. The nullification doctrine of the Kentucky and Virginia resolutions of 1798 had been pushed to its logical consequences, and an open menace of disunion stared the nation in the face.

South Carolina had counted upon the supposed State rights sympathies of Jackson, notwithstanding his vigorous course with the bank, to make its protest and threat effective, and Jackson himself had given much color to the hope. In an acute controversy between the State of Georgia and some Indian tribes whose reservations the State had sought to appropriate the Supreme Court had upheld the title of the Indians to their lands, but Jackson declined to enforce Chief Justice Marshall's decision and did not resent the display of force which Georgia had made, and the Indians were dispossessed. If Georgia could be allowed to accomplish practically by force what it could not accomplish by law or politics, South Carolina might fairly hope for equal tolerance.

Jackson's course with the Georgia Indians hardly admits of explanation on any ground of principle, but the challenge of the South Carolina ordinance of nullification roused to the full his great sense of nationality. He had already quietly made military and naval preparations, and no sooner was the ordinance published than South Carolina found itself confronting a president whom it well knew would not hesitate to act. For some weeks the controversy hung in balance while Congress anxiously sought to frame a compromise which would avert an armed collision.

Under the lead of Clay a compromise tariff, providing for a sliding-scale reduction of duties over a period of years, was enacted and the ordinance of nullification was then withdrawn. Each party could claim to have been victorious, for while the authority of the federal government had been vindicated and the Union had been preserved, the protest of South Carolina had been heeded and the policy of high protection had been abandoned. Clay, who was a protectionist, had yielded to what he regarded as the supreme necessity of saving the Union. Webster, on the other hand, now senator from Massachusetts and the ablest of American constitutional lawyers, would apparently have preferred to see the question settled on its merits, for to his mind the compromise settled no issue of principle regarding the rights of the States and the same question would assuredly arise again. Before another generation had passed the soundness of Webster's judgment was to receive impressive demonstration.

The same rude vigor, the same intuitive perception of what was best or most expedient for the nation characterized Jackson's treatment of lesser issues.

The absence of war and of occasions for extraordinary federal expenditure favored a reduction of the national debt, and by 1835 the debt had been practically discharged. The lavish appropriation of federal funds in aid of internal improvements, many of which were local rather than national undertakings, early encountered the presidential veto, and with some irregular exceptions the States were left to develop their highways and navigable waterways for themselves. The government of France, against which the United States held unpaid claims some of which dated back more than a generation, was brought sharply to book and the claims were paid. Save for the payment of the national debt, on the other hand, the management of federal finances after the separation from the Bank of the United States was disastrous. The State banks which were used as government depositories were ill-regulated and their paper currency, unsupported by any adequate reserve of specie, became dangerously depreciated. A sudden decision in the summer of 1837 to require specie payment in sales of public lands precipitated a wild scramble for specie which demoralized the values of all State bank currency and prepared the way for a financial panic which broke upon the head of Jackson's successor.

Ever since the disruption of the cabinet Jackson had given his confidence increasingly to his first secretary of state, Martin Van Buren of New York. Van Buren was a member of a powerful political organization in New York known as the Albany regency, and the evident purpose of Jackson to make Van Buren his successor in the presidential chair encountered widespread opposition in the Democratic party. In 1832, however, the nomination of Van Buren for the vice-presidency was forced upon the party, and the election of 1836 saw the victory of Jackson's plan. An electoral vote of 170 as against a vote of 73 for the Whig candidate, William Henry Harrison of Ohio, carried Van Buren to the presidency as the residuary legatee of Jackson's prestige. With his political enemies defeated and his political friends rewarded Jackson retired to the Hermitage at Nashville, Tennessee, where he died in the early summer of 1845. He lived long enough to see the great party which he had led hopelessly entangled with slavery, but with Oregon on the point of being added to the Union and plans for the seizure of Mexican territory ready to launch.

Not until Lincoln was there to be another president with so rugged a personality, such clear convictions, or such sheer unhampered courage, nor one who was to leave so deep an impress upon his time. The Democratic party, throughout all its mutations of theory and practice, has continued to join the names of Jackson and Jefferson as those of its two great founders. Yet the contrasts between the two leaders are far more striking than the resemblances. Jackson had none of the fondness for political speculation which characterized Jefferson, and although neither could claim much credit for consistency in moments of crisis, the course of Jackson was more nearly in accord with his public statements than was the course of Jefferson. The guardianship of the doctrine of State rights and strict construction after 1828 belonged logically to Calhoun and his followers rather than to Jackson, notwithstanding that the party of which Jackson was the titular head still held to the doctrine as one of its fundamental tenets. The supreme importance which Jackson attached to the will of the people, and his assumption of a practically exclusive right to interpret that will for himself irrespective of anything that had consciously been voted at any election, was an egotistic pretension for which the American system of government affords no warrant, and if it had continued to have any such force in the hands of succeeding presidents as Jackson gave to it the constitutional character of the federal government would before long have been greatly changed.

The Jackson temperament, in short, was that of an enlightened despot, not that of a constitutional executive, and his liberal interpretation of his powers as president allied him in principle much more closely with the Whigs and later Republicans than with his Democratic supporters. The Jackson régime was a period of vivid personal government little mindful of constitutional restraints, and although Jackson's assertive policy restored to the presidency a prestige which during the preceding twenty years the office had gradually lost, the precedent was hardly one that could be safely followed. It remained to be seen whether the United States, all but alone among the great nations in the possession of a written constitution, was to be governed constitutionally through the harmonious coöperation of executive, legislative, and judicial departments, or whether the magnifying of the presidential office was to enthrone an executive supremacy to which Congress, courts, States, and people would alike be forced to bow.

History goes by stages, however, and the constitutional revolution which the Jackson period threatened to unloose was checked by the contrasted weakness of Van Buren and the development of party organization. The Albany regency had shown the possibilities of political control in a State through the agency of a party machine, and the election of 1832 saw the appearance of national nominating conventions and party platforms. The road was now open for the systematic marshalling of public opinion throughout the country, the selection of presidential candidates through national conventions representing party organizations in the various States, and the framing of platforms whose " planks " should harmonize the divergent views of different sections and conceal the rivalries of factions. The president would still be the most conspicuous representative of his party, but it was evident that candidacy would more and more be the result of compromise and that executive leadership would be shared with party leaders unless the president were a towering personality. Van Buren had no marked personality, and the machine system which he was adept at manipulating prevailed.

Jackson bequeathed to Van Buren the elements of a financial crisis, and in the summer of 1837 the storm broke. The panic of 1837 was not due solely to industrial and financial disorders in the United States, for disturbed conditions in England lent their aid, but it was nevertheless the inevitable outcome of a system under which the federal government, depositing its funds in State banks over whose operations it could exercise no satisfactory control, looked to the banks to provide in their own self-interest a sound currency based upon an adequate specie reserve. Van Buren wisely declined to interfere, rightly judging that the disease had best be left to run its course, but an issue of $10,000,000 of treasury notes was voted by Congress in the hope of relieving the financial strain. Calhoun had secured in 1836 the passage of a law distributing the surplus revenue of the government among the States, and three quarterly instalments had been paid before the panic put an end to the surplus; then distribution ceased and was not resumed. The instalments, which by law were subject to repayment on demand, were not recalled and the amount distributed, about $27,000,000, has never been returned to the treasury. The panic was followed by nearly two years of business depression before the country began slowly to recover. The compromise tariff of 1833 was not interfered with, and the gradual reduction of duties for which the act provided continued to operate for the ten year period which the law established.

In 1840 the first step was taken in the direction of a financial system which should divorce the government from banks of any kind. Jackson in his veto of the bill to recharter the Bank of the United States had suggested the possibility of organizing an institution founded solely upon the credit of the government and its revenues, without authority to engage in private business, and meeting its expenses by selling bills of exchange. The system which was now adopted dispensed entirely with the form of a bank and created instead a national treasury at Washington, with subtreasuries elsewhere, and devolved upon the federal government itself the custody and management of its funds. Political opposition was strong enough to force a repeal of the act within a year, but in 1846 the subtreasury system, as it was called, was re-established and the direct control of federal funds through a federal treasury has continued to the present time. The panic of 1837 drove many State banks into liquidation, and in the period of reorganization which followed a number of the States, notably Massachusetts and New York, undertook to provide better safeguards for deposits and notes; but State bank notes continued to suffer from depreciation and the problem of a national paper currency remained unsolved.

Fortunately for the country the national debt was inappreciable, and not until after the panic did the treasury receipts begin to show a deficit. Population continued to grow by leaps and bounds, rising from 9,300,000 in 1820 to 12,800,000 in 1830 and to more than 17,000,000 in 1840. No modern state had ever shown so marvellous a growth. Foreign immigration was still small, but a modest total of somewhat over 8,000 in 1820 had grown to more than 79,000 in 1837, and in 1842 more than 84,000 immigrants entered the country. The more prosperous immigrants pressed on into the West, attracted by the abundance of low-priced land, but an increasing number of the less resourceful remained in the manufacturing cities and towns of the Atlantic coast region, where they more and more displaced native-born labor in the factories and mills. The presence in some of the larger eastern cities of considerable bodies of foreigners, often ignorant as well as poor, and for whom priests of the Catholic church struggled hard to care, bred an anti-foreigner and an anti-Catholic feeling which took form later in a Native American party and bade fair for a time to become of some permanent importance. Two new States were added to the Union during Jackson's presidency, Michigan in 1836 and Arkansas in 1837, and the early admission of Iowa and Wisconsin, both of which now had territorial organizations, was clearly foreshadowed.

Politically the country was ready for a change. The choice of Van Buren had cost the Democrats the control of the House of Representatives, and the congressional elections of 1838 gave the Whigs a majority in the Senate also.  The Democrats had no outstanding candidate to substitute for Van Buren in 1840 and he was accordingly renominated.  The Whig candidate, on the other hand, General William Henry Harrison, had made a gallant contest for the presidency in 1836, and his record as a fighter of Indians in the Black Hawk war of 1832 gave the party an opportunity to exploit to the full the " hero of Tippecanoe " and the picturesque log cabin life of the West.  With Harrison was associated, as the candidate for the vice-presidency, John Tyler of Virginia, a former State rights Democrat who had broken with his party on the question of the sub-treasury and now regarded himself as a Whig.  It was an unhappy choice as events were to show, but the Whig party had a considerable following in the South and Tyler was a conspicuous representative of his section.

The campaign was picturesque to the last degree. In its lack of issues it resembled the Jackson campaign of 1828 save that the " hero " was not one whose previous defeat was to be avenged.  Open air meetings, torchlight parades, and representations of log cabins with the presidential candidate drinking hard cider took the place of debate, and before the popular enthusiasm the Democracy of Jackson and Van Buren went down to defeat.  Harrison and Tyler each received 234 electoral votes against the meagre sixty which Van Buren secured, and the Whig majority in the House of Representatives was materially increased. For the moment the triumph seemed complete. Old men whose memories went back to the early years of the republic saw in the Whig victory a return to the principles upon which the nation had been founded; younger men saw in it the victory of Whig principles in the West; and even the Democratic South was not disheartened because slavery was secure and new slave territory was on the point of being grasped.

# CHAPTER VII

## A HOUSE DIVIDED AGAINST ITSELF

PRESIDENT HARRISON died exactly one month after his inauguration, and the presidential office passed to the vice-president, Tyler. The situation was fateful for the Whigs. Tyler was sincere and able, but the popular demonstrations of the campaign of 1840 had not been for him, and circumstances rather than political conviction had caused him to be numbered with the Whigs. His strict construction sympathies were not long in showing themselves. No proper system of caring for the government funds existed after the repeal of the short-lived subtreasury act, and the country was threatened with a repetition of the same financial trouble which had helped to bring on the panic of 1837. The Whigs desired a national bank, and Tyler was understood to favor the creation of an institution which, without being open to the criticisms which the second Bank of the United States had invited, would nevertheless serve as the needed fiscal agency of the government. A bill providing for a Fiscal Bank of the United States was accordingly passed, but Tyler's constitutional scruples asserted themselves and the bill was vetoed, the main objection being the permission given to the bank to establish branches without the previous consent of the States. The Whigs in dismay consulted Tyler with a view to ascertaining what kind of an institution he would approve, and another bill conforming to his wishes was presently passed, but again the veto was interposed. The entire cabinet with the exception of Webster, the secretary of state, who was engaged in an important negotiation with Great Britain, immediately resigned, and the Whig leaders, incensed at what they could but regard as an act of bad faith, publicly repudiated the president and thereafter Tyler stood alone. The party which had sung and marched itself to a triumphant victory a few months before was left without an executive head at a moment when one of the gravest national issues which had yet appeared was upon the point of dividing the nation.

The question of Negro slavery had presented itself to the United States in a variety of forms. It was an economic question, not only because staple agriculture based upon slave labor was the only important industry in the South, but also because slave labor and free labor were inherently hostile and free labor would not go where manual work was regarded as dishonorable for whites. From the days when the Constitution was being framed slavery had been also a constitutional question, and the existence of a slave population and of the foreign slave trade had forced the adoption of two of the most important constitutional compromises in the Convention of 1787. It was a political question, committing the South to invincible advocacy of State rights and strict construction for the protection of its labor system, and dividing political parties in their struggles for national support.  It was an international question, for while the African slave trade had been prohibited by law it had not been prohibited in fact, and the abolition of the traffic by European governments left the United States the only power which more or less openly tolerated it.  It was a sectional question, for the ordinance of 1787 had excluded slavery forever from the territory of the United States northwest of the Ohio river, and the Missouri compromise had drawn an east and west line north of which no more slave States were to be erected.  And it was a moral question, for the atrocious conditions under which the African slave trade was carried on, the separation of families in the domestic slave trade or in the settlement of estates, the denial to the slaves of legal rights or assured recognition of the family relation, and the generally ignorant and degraded condition of the slaves throughout the slaveholding area bred a moral revolt against the system among many to whom economic, legal, or constitutional difficulties made no strong appeal.

The moral argument was peculiarly dangerous because it was at once idealistic and uncompromising. Many southern slaveholders regretted the system. Washington was no friend of slavery and Jefferson by his will emancipated his slaves.  Anti-slavery

societies were numerous before 1820, the movement
for voluntary emancipation had support in the South,
and the number of free Negroes, although very small
in the aggregate, tended to increase.  But the emancipation which was freely talked about in public
meetings or discussed in print was too remote
in time to have any practical significance, and the
growth of the cotton industry dulled the consciences
even of moralists to the evils of a system from which
no individual slaveholder could see a practical way
of escape and to which a great section of the nation
obviously owed its prosperity.

It was the work of William Lloyd Garrison to vital-
ize the abolition movement as a moral force.  Garrison had little first-hand acquaintance with slavery,
his personal views were extreme and his language
was often violent and revolutionary, and laws and
Constitution had no sacredness in his eyes when
national sin was to be combated; but the qualities
which made him odious to slaveholders, politicians,
and moderate men generally made him strong with
radical advocates of moral reform, and by 1833 his
writings and addresses, his weekly newspaper " The
Liberator," established at Boston in 1831, and the
American Antislavery Society and other organizations
which he formed or inspired had made abolition a
national question.  When, before long, abolitionists
were mobbed, public meetings broken up, newspapers
seized, and the mails rifled for copies of abolition
publications, the moral revolt against slavery had in-

trenched itself in the conscience of the North too firmly to be thereafter dislodged.

Moral agitation alone, however, could not avail to change an economic system which was imbedded in the fundamental law of the land and inseparably bound up with the political issues over which national parties were contending. There was needed some large political controversy to which the demand for the abolition of slavery could attach itself and whose settlement it might hope in some measure to direct. The opportunity came in the application of the independent state of Texas for admission to the Union. Following the revolt of the Spanish colonies in America which had called forth the declaration of the Monroe doctrine, the Mexican state of Coahuila and Texas had declared its independence, had maintained itself notwithstanding the efforts of Mexico to recover it, and in 1837 had been accorded recognition by the United States as an independent republic. A considerable American population from the South flowed into Texas, drawn by the attraction of rich cotton land as well as by the inherent American spirit of adventure and expansion, and a constitution which recognized and protected slavery was, after some opposition, adopted.

The application of Texas for admission to the Union raised at once the old question of the further extension of slaveholding territory. Texas was nearly four times as large as Missouri, the largest slave State, and the addition to the Union of a region out of which four or five large States might easily be formed would immensely strengthen the representation of slave States in the House of Representatives and destroy, in favor of slavery, the sectional balance in the Senate. The Democrats insisted with much reason that slavery, although not formally mentioned under that name in the federal Constitution, was nevertheless a " domestic " or State institution whose legal existence the federal government had repeatedly recognized and whose rights it was bound to protect, and they accordingly not only championed the demand for the annexation of Texas but further declared that Texas, if it were admitted, was entitled to come into the Union with slavery if its people so desired. Once a member of the Union, Texas, it was generally believed, would consent to be subdivided for the sake of strengthening the slavery cause. The Whigs, on the other hand, were split, the southern Whigs taking in general the same position as the Democrats while the northern Whigs, mindful of the abolition movement, as a rule opposed annexation.

The position of the northern Whigs was an informing indication of the direction which the antislavery movement was taking. The antislavery Whigs were not abolitionists. Their opposition to slavery went no further as yet than the conviction that the institution, while one that must be tolerated and if necessary protected, was nevertheless one whose territorial growth and political influence ought to be restricted. The conclusion was superficial, for if slavery was economically sound and morally defensible there was no good reason why it should not be allowed to spread to any part of the United States in which it would thrive, and no reason at all why a region whose soil and climate were adapted to slave labor should be refused incorporation in the Union unless it would consent to abolish the institution. Neither then nor at any later time, however, was the economic aspect of slavery seriously examined, and the moral argument, forcibly urged only by abolitionists who demanded the extirpation of slavery root and branch, was too radical and unpractical to win general support. The attitude of the antislavery Whigs, in other words, was almost exclusively political, and as usually happens under such circumstances the issue was compromised and the vested rights of slavery prevailed. The handful of devoted abolitionists might proclaim from the housetops the moral doctrine of human freedom and insist that if slavery were not destroyed the Union would perish, but they could not convince the Whigs who walked the streets below that there was any real danger of collapse.

The question was further complicated by a dispute over the boundaries of Texas. The boundary line between the old province of Louisiana and the Spanish possessions in Mexico had never been run, but the territory which France sold to the United States in 1803 under the name of Louisiana was declared by the treaty to be the same as that which the province then had as a French possession and as it had had

when it belonged to Spain.   Each part of the definition was apparently regarded as confirming or ex-
plaining the other, and the boundary which was laid
down by the Spanish treaty of 1819 between American and Spanish territory in the southwest left Texas
a part of Mexico.   In the presidential campaign of
1844, however, the Democrats raised the point that
John Quincy Adams, in negotiating the treaty of 1819
under Monroe, had bargained away, perhaps unwit-
tingly, territory which in fact belonged to the United
States, and that a part of Texas was in law American
soil.   The Democratic platform of that year accordingly demanded the " re-annexation " of Texas.   The
dispute was one in regard to whose merits geographers
are not yet entirely agreed, but the popular appeal of
a demand for re-annexation was obviously very great.

The year 1844 brought the matter to a crisis.   A
treaty of annexation was negotiated, but the antislavery opposition in the Senate was sufficient to prevent ratification and the treaty failed.   Tyler then
took the bold step of sending a copy of the treaty
to the House of Representatives, evidently with the
intention of thereby making the Texas question a
prominent issue in the campaign.   Tyler himself was
not a candidate for re-election, and Clay, the Whig
candidate, had compromised with the Texas issue as
he compromised with most other political questions
throughout his long career.   The sweeping victory of
the Democratic candidate, James K. Polk of Tennessee, who received 170 of the 275 electoral votes, was

partly due to the weakening of the Whigs by a Liberty or abolition party vote in New York, but Tyler rightly interpreted the election as a popular verdict in favor of annexation, and in March, 1845, a joint resolution of Congress provided for the incorporation of Texas within the Union. The terms of the resolution were accepted by Texas in July, and in December Texas was admitted as a State. The ambitious hopes of the slave States, however, were doomed to disappointment. The terms of admission provided that not more than four States, in addition to Texas itself, might with the consent of Texas be formed out of the territory acquired, but no suggestion looking to the subdivision of the State ever found favor once Texas was safely in the Union, and the congressional gains of slavery were limited to two senators and two members of the House of Representatives.

Tyler was fairly entitled to some of the credit for the acquisition of Texas, for while the Whigs had repudiated him, and the Democrats, by their success in the election of 1844, had made annexation a foregone conclusion whether the president wished it or not, the question had come to a head in his administration and had been settled before he retired from office. As with Jefferson and Monroe so with Tyler, the territory of the United States had been enlarged to meet a national emergency and in accord with a natural trend of expansion, and there could be no question but that the people approved. Still another diplomatic success was to be carried to Tyler's ac-

count.  The northeastern boundary of the United
States had long been in dispute, and attempts to run
the line in accordance with the provisions of the peace
treaty of 1783 had encountered obstacles which diplomacy had not been able to overcome.  The British
claim to the extreme northern portion of the State of
Maine had been resisted, and in 1838–39 armed collision along the border seemed imminent.  In 1842
Webster, who by agreement with the Whig leaders
had remained in office as secretary of state after the
other cabinet members resigned, concluded with Lord
Ashburton a treaty which ended the controversy.  A
small section of the northwestern boundary was still
in question, but with that exception all of the dis-
putes to which the treaty of 1783 had given rise had
been disposed of.

Polk had had a comparatively inconspicuous public
career, and his position as speaker of the House of
Representatives had not sufficed to give him much
national prominence.  It was the party and not the
candidate that won the victory of 1844.  Polk was a
consummate politician, however, and the events which
came upon the country were masterfully turned by
him to the advantage of his administration.  He inherited two great issues each of which, although for
different reasons, held a threat of war.  Mexico had
never relinquished its claim to Texas, and the annexation of Texas without the consent of Mexico was
regarded by Mexico as a deliberate violation of international comity.  In the Pacific Northwest the

question of Oregon was nearing its crisis, and the possibility of war with Great Britain had been clearly foreshadowed in 1844 in the campaign slogan of " fifty-four forty or fight."

The claim of the United States to the region known as Oregon or the Oregon country dated back to the end of the eighteenth century, when an American ship captain had discovered the mouth of the Columbia river. The Lewis and Clark expedition had explored the river, and during the war of 1812 an American trading post near the mouth of the river had been captured by the British only to be restored when peace was made. The treaty of 1819 with Spain fixed the northern limit of the Spanish possessions on the Pacific coast at the forty-second parallel, while in 1825 Russia had abandoned its claims to territory on the coast south of the parallel 54° 40'. The Oregon country was the extensive region between these two parallels— between the northern boundary of the present State of California and the southern boundary of Alaska — and from all of the region under the Monroe doctrine foreign colonization was excluded. The British claim, on the other hand, resting in part upon the ancient charter of the Hudson Bay Company and in part upon occupation, was not lightly to be disregarded notwithstanding a considerable American immigration into the Columbia valley, and in 1827 an agreement for the joint occupancy of the region for ten years, subject to renewal, was entered into between the two governments.

The ten-year period had hardly expired when Great Britain was called upon to suppress a rebellion in Canada, and in 1841 eastern Canada was reorganized and responsible government established. Political agitation in Canada evoked a measure of popular sympathy in the United States, especially in New England and New York, and American filibustering raids strained for a time the diplomatic relations of the American and British governments. Negotiations for the settlement of the northern boundary of the United States from Lake Superior westward were long fruitless of results, and the popular demand for " the whole of Oregon or none " was reflected in the demand of the Democratic platform for all of Oregon as far north as the parallel 54° 40′. The possibility of war if Great Britain refused to yield counted for little with the American public, for the fever of expansion had been stirred up by the annexation of Texas and Great Britain was still looked upon more as an ancient enemy than as a continental neighbor.

Fortunately for both nations the quarrel yielded to diplomacy. In 1846 Great Britain, after refusing to accept as the boundary the parallel 49° with the free navigation of the Columbia river, changed its mind and accepted, and a treaty settled the boundary dispute on that basis. Oregon was presently given a territorial organization, and a steady stream of migration across the plains flowed into the fertile valley of the Columbia and prepared the way for statehood thirteen years later. The vague dream of the ancient colonial charters had in part come true, for the United States now extended from sea to sea and the continental pre-eminence of the nation was demonstrated fact.  The first free State west of the Mississippi, Iowa, was admitted to the Union in the same year in which the boundary controversy was settled, Wisconsin was almost ready for admission, and Minnesota had a territorial government.  Only the hold of Spain upon California and the remote Southwest barred the further expansion of the United States to the Pacific.

The war with Mexico was on the part of the United States essentially a war of aggression, and not the less so because Polk manipulated the situation with skill in order to make it appear that Mexico was the offender.  The refusal of Mexico from the beginning to consent to the withdrawal of Texas had irritated American public opinion, and the uncertainty regarding the boundary between Texas and Mexico afforded an excuse for the American occupation of territory, under the guise of protecting Texas from invasion, which Mexico continued to claim as its own. For more than a year after the inauguration of Polk, however, the controversy kept to the field of diplomacy notwithstanding the presence of American troops in the disputed area.  Then, following an attack on April 24, 1846, by a Mexican force upon an American detachment, the news of which was hurried to Washington, Polk framed a message to Congress which reviewed the recent course of events in a way highly prejudicial to Mexico, declared that Mexico had invaded the territory of the United States and "shed American blood upon American soil," and asked for a declaration of war. The message, sent to the houses two days after the news from Mexico was received, was denounced by the northern Whigs as untruthful in fact and a deliberate provocation to war, but the declaration and money were promptly voted and the invasion of Mexico began. That a successful war would mean the further strengthening of the political power of slavery no one doubted, and the opponents of slavery and of territorial expansion never ceased to lay upon the South the responsibility for the war. Outside of New England, however, the war was popular, and the excitement of a military adventure and the prospect of adding still further to American territory quite outweighed the slavery argument.

Ultimate victory for the American armies was not at any time doubtful, but nearly two years of campaigning were necessary before Mexican resistance could be overcome. The first successes were won by General Zachary Taylor, who for months before the declaration of war had occupied the disputed Texas region on the Mexican border, and who on May 8 and 9 defeated the Mexican forces at Palo Alto and Resaca de la Palma in decisive engagements which made him a popular hero. An overland expedition took possession without difficulty of the northern Mexican provinces, now the States of New Mexico and Arizona, pushed on to California, and in coöperation with American land and naval forces which had already been operating there brought California under American control. Polk, who was a confirmed expansionist, decided to keep the northern provinces and California whatever the outcome of the war elsewhere, but to pay Mexico a reasonable price for the territory which it was to be forced to cede. A sum as large as thirty million dollars, twice the amount which Mexico eventually received, was talked of in this connection. The remainder of the war, accordingly, was fought not with a view to further conquest of territory but to prevent Mexico from recovering the northern provinces and to bring it to terms. The central point of attack was the City of Mexico, and with the occupation of the capital in 1847 after a stubborn defence the fighting ceased. General Taylor, who had not enjoyed the full confidence of Polk and who was dissatisfied with the treatment which he had received, had resigned from the army and returned to the United States, and the honors of final victory were gained by General Winfield Scott.

A treaty of peace, concluded on the part of the United States by an American in Mexico, Slidell, without full official authorization, was signed on July 4, 1848, accepted by Polk, and shortly ratified by Congress. The terms were substantially those which Polk had already planned to impose. The boundary between Texas and Mexico was fixed at the Rio Grande river, while west of Texas the boundary continued to the Pacific on a line which left to the

United States the present States of New Mexico, Arizona, California, Nevada, and Utah and a part of Colorado. The area ceded by Mexico embraced over 529,000 square miles, and for this the United States agreed to pay approximately fifteen million dollars. A readjustment of a portion of the boundary in 1853, known as the Gadsden purchase, added about thirty thousand square miles to the original cession. With the exception of the Gadsden purchase and Alaska, the latter not acquired until after the Civil war, the Mexican war left the United States with the same continental area which it now possesses — an area three and one-half times as great as that which the United States possessed at the close of the Revolution and only a little less than that of the vast British possessions to the north. Polk had reason to be proud of his handiwork.

Further than this, however, Polk was not to be allowed to go. The enthusiasm which a successful war had awakened brought him no enduring personal popularity, and although the Democrats still controlled the Senate they had lost in 1846 their majority in the House of Representatives. The Whigs, on the other hand, ready enough to seize party advantage from the war notwithstanding that they had given the war only a divided support, had a popular candidate for the presidency in Taylor, and the election of 1848 was a Whig victory so far as the control of the executive went. The unstable condition of parties was shown by the fact that the Democrats, in spite of the

success of the Whig candidate for the presidency, recovered their control of the House, and Congress and
the president were once more of opposing parties.

The question of slavery could not be kept down.
In 1846, when a preliminary appropriation of money
for the purchase of Mexican territory was asked
for, a Democratic member of the House, David
Wilmot of Pennsylvania, had attempted to attach
to the bill a proviso excluding slavery from any
territory that might be acquired, and the same attempt was again made in 1847. In September, 1848,
gold was discovered in California, and when in a few
months the startling news reached the East one of
the greatest movements of migration that the world
has ever seen began. From all parts of the United
States except the South people flocked to California
in search of gold. Some went by sea by way of the
isthmus of Panama, crowding to repletion the few
steamships that were available; many more made the
long and hazardous journey across the western plains
in wagons drawn by oxen or horses, fighting the
Indians as they went; still others took the long sea
route around Cape Horn. Before the fall of 1849 a
provisional government had been set up, a State constitution prohibiting slavery had been prepared by a
convention, and California applied to Congress for
admission as a free State. The fact that California
had never been a Territory was of no interest to its
people, for they all were familiar with State government in the States from which they came, the popula-

tion was rapidly nearing a hundred thousand, and the pioneers and gold seekers who were building a commonwealth saw no reason why they should not have statehood at once; but it must be statehood without slavery.

The admission of California alone, however, would destroy the sectional balance of States which the South must if possible continue to preserve. The admission of Florida and Texas in 1845 had been followed by the admission of Iowa in 1846 and of Wisconsin in 1848, and the thirty States of which the Union was now composed were equally divided. But where was an offset to California to be found? Texas was unwilling to be subdivided. Less than half of the territory acquired from Mexico outside of California lay to the south of the Missouri compromise line of 36° 30′, and practically the whole of the Mexican acquisition except California was believed to be unfit for agriculture on a large scale. The organization of a territorial government in Oregon merely prepared the way for the formation of another free State. The only apparent solution of the difficulty was to regard the Missouri compromise not as a great national settlement which was to be applied no matter how far westward the territory of the United States might extend, but as a settlement limited to the area which the United States possessed in 1820. In that case the compromise would have no application to the territory acquired from Mexico, and all of that territory except California, which it was agreed would have to be admitted as a free State if it was admitted at all, would be open to slavery if the people so desired. The chance would still be a doubtful one for slavery because of the physical characteristics of the country, but the organization of two Territories, New Mexico and Utah, comprising between them all of the Mexican acquisition except California, held out the possibility of two slave States with which to offset California and Oregon, and the chance must be taken or sectional control of the Senate was lost.

The debate in Congress which attended the framing of what is known as the compromise of 1850 ranged over almost every aspect of the slavery question. To the old arguments which urged the protection of slavery on constitutional grounds, however, was added the new contention that the status of slavery in territory acquired by annexation was properly to be determined only by the people of the region concerned, and that Congress ought neither to legislate slavery into such territory nor prohibit it there, but should leave the people free to choose their " domestic institutions " for themselves. Slave labor, it was urged, was after all primarily a matter of soil, climate, and general circumstances. If nature made slave labor profitable slavery would be established and should be protected. If natural conditions were adverse slavery would not endure even if it were introduced, and no act of Congress would be necessary to legislate it out of a Territory, because it would die of itself. Accordingly the only just policy, if territorial governments were set up for New Mexico and Utah, was to leave the question of slavery to be settled by local option, and to admit the Territories later as States with or without slavery as their constitutions might prescribe at the time of admission.

The plea for local option was difficult to answer notwithstanding that it seemed to cast disturbing doubt upon the constitutionality of such long-established decisions as the ordinance of 1787 and the Missouri compromise. The opponents of slavery extension, on the other hand, strengthened in their faith by the moral opposition to slavery which the abolition movement had kept alive, rightly feared that the supporters of slavery, seeing their control of Congress jeopardized, would leave no stone unturned to force slavery upon the proposed new Territories and thereby succeed in determining in advance the character of the future States as slave or free. Local option, in other words, was a peril rather than a principle. The anti-slavery and free soil forces accordingly insisted that slavery was not a matter in regard to which the people of a Territory should be invited to choose, because the institution itself was bad; that natural law devoted all acquired territory to freedom, and that the whole history of the United States so far as slavery was concerned showed that slavery had always been regarded as something to be restrained in its territorial growth. It had been excluded in 1787 from the territory of the United States northwest of the Ohio river because even at that early date its encroachment had been feared, and the confirmation of the ordinance by the first Congress under the Constitution was a weighty approval of that action. The Missouri compromise further upheld restriction by excluding slavery from most of the Louisiana purchase, although for political reasons it had been necessary to admit Missouri as an exception, and the principle of the Missouri compromise required the extension of the compromise line to the Pacific now that American territory extended so far. It was further urged that Mexico itself had prohibited slavery by law in its northern provinces years before the Mexican war, and that to open the way to the introduction of slavery in the newly-acquired territory would be to re-establish slavery in a region from which it had long been legally excluded.

Two other aspects of slavery, neither of which had as yet been prominent as a political issue, also entered into the great debate. The Constitution provided that no person legally held to service or labor under the laws of any State, if he escaped into another State, should thereby be entitled to freedom from his servitude, but should be given up and returned upon the demand of the person to whom the service or labor was due. The abolitionists had long been active in helping fugitive slaves to find asylum in free States or in Canada, and although the total number of fugitive slaves was small, southern slave owners complained bitterly of the loss of their property, of the difficulties which were met with in obtaining the re-

turn of slaves who were found in free States, and
of the insufficiency of the existing federal laws designed to give effect to the constitutional provision.
The South accordingly demanded the enactment of a
stringent fugitive slave law which would protect them
in their rights. On the other hand many northern
members of Congress had long been hostile to the continuance of slavery and the domestic slave trade in
the District of Columbia, and the distressing scenes
which were frequently to be witnessed in the slave
market at the national capital were a powerful argument for abolition. There was no question of the
authority of Congress over both of these subjects, for
the Constitution expressly provided for the return
of fugitive slaves and gave to Congress complete jurisdiction over the territory occupied as the seat of the
national government.

The death of President Taylor in July, 1850, and
the succession to the presidency of the vice-president,
Millard Fillmore of New York, were without influence
upon the slavery controversy, for the main lines of
compromise, drawn largely under the direction of
Clay, had already been laid down and in a few weeks
settlement was completed. California was admitted
as a State under its free constitution. Two Territories, New Mexico and Utah, were organized with the
promise that when admitted as States they should
be received with or without slavery as their
constitutions might prescribe. A drastic fugitive
slave law was enacted, and the slave trade but not

slavery was prohibited in the District of Columbia.

The compromise of 1850 is a great line of division in the political history of the American nation. It marks the place at which the Democratic party becomes avowedly a proslavery party, committed to the defence of slavery at whatever point the institution might be attacked. The Whig party, on the contrary, was split wide open by the compromise, the southern section siding with the Democrats when slavery was involved, while the northern section, although by no means in favor of abolition, clung to the old policy of restriction. From this time, too, the temper of the slaveholding States underwent a change. Until 1850 the South had been in general willing to admit the weaknesses of slavery as a system, and it had repeatedly apologized for the institution as one which climate and history had together forced it to maintain; but after 1850 apology ceased and slavery was upheld as a worthy system which the South was prepared to support without regard to public opinion elsewhere or to economic or moral argument. Long-established political reputations, too, went by the board, and not even death availed to shield great men from rebuke. Clay's philosophy of compromise had nothing more to offer, and his two-sided attitude toward the greatest of national issues had already put the hoped-for presidency beyond his grasp. Webster, the idol of Massachusetts and the strongest intellectual force among the northern Whigs, turned his back on antislavery and supported the compromise, braved for a few months the contempt and scorn of his constituents and former friends, then died of a broken heart. Calhoun, the shadow of death upon him, was wheeled into the Senate chamber while a colleague read his last plea for slavery and the States, then in a few weeks he too had passed into history. The days of the " great triumvirate " were spent, and the tangled estate which they left was now to be administered by other and stronger minds.

Nevertheless, the conclusion of the compromise of 1850 brought to the country for the moment a great sense of relief. Save in extreme radical circles men affected to believe that the slavery controversy had at last been settled. It was true that the admission of California had destroyed the long-cherished balance between the sections in the House of Representatives and that the outlook for slavery in New Mexico and Utah was dubious, but the willingness of the South to accept the compromise even with these conditions was taken as evidence that the aggressiveness of the slavery supporters had moderated and that sectional strife, if it continued, would now take a different turn. The early demand for abolition, at no time actively championed by either of the dominant parties, had resolved itself into a demand for free soil in new Territories and States; and although it was the free soil Whigs who had forced the fighting in 1850, neither antislavery nor free soil criticism was a serious menace to slavery as such. There was reason for suspecting that slave agriculture was in fact already on the decline, and that another generation or two might see its virtual disappearance because it was unprofitable. If the "peculiar institution" was doomed to early death by natural economic laws there was less need of bitter and distracting controversies to hasten its end.

The hoped-for peace was of short duration, for in a few months the enforcement of the fugitive slave law was driving the North to exasperation. Agents of southern slave owners, armed with legal authority as the law provided, scoured the North in search of runaway Negroes, demanded the arrest of the alleged fugitives by local or State officials, pushed through before federal commissioners a form of judicial hearing in which the fugitive was debarred by law from testifying in his own behalf, and returned the fugitives under federal protection to the States from which they had fled. In the face of an invasion which was always offensive and sometimes brutal moderate antislavery opinions tended rapidly to give way, and throughout the North prominent citizens joined in resisting the arrests and deportations. South Carolina had openly proclaimed tariff laws to be null and void within its borders, only to find its nullification doctrine repudiated by the rest of the country and the federal executive ready if necessary to use force, but half a score of northern States now nullified the fugitive slave law either by overlooking the organized resistance of their citizens or by extending to fugitives the protection of State courts. Fillmore's temper was not that of Jackson, and where Jackson had deployed the army and navy Fillmore could only issue a proclamation. Webster had advised Fillmore that the fugitive slave law was constitutional, and the president was perhaps to be excused for signing the bill, but even Webster's authority had no weight with a North which regarded the law as immoral. Ralph Waldo Emerson, addressing his fellow-townsmen at Concord, Massachusetts, denounced the law as one which no person could enforce or help to enforce without loss of self-respect and the name of a gentleman, and the pithy phrase expressed the judgment of the people.

The law gave the final blow to the tottering Whig party. Weakened by hopeless division into two sectional groups and with no programme save one of compromise, its listless defence of the legislation of 1850 only hastened its end. Even its soldier candidate, General Scott, the "hero of Chapultepec," could not save it in the presidential contest of 1856; and although the Democratic candidate, Franklin Pierce of New Hampshire, was of far less importance than Scott, the Democratic victory was complete. Before another election came round the Whig party had disappeared as a national organization and a new Republican party was ready to take its place.

Even without the odious fugitive slave law, however, the issue of slavery could not have been kept out of politics, for the compromise itself contained the germ of further dissension. The compromise measures had established the principle of local option

regarding slavery in federal territory to which the
Missouri compromise did not apply, but it had not
repealed the earlier compromise or interfered with its
operation. The treatment of the same subject by
two entirely different and inherently opposed methods
in different parts of the United States was an illogical
procedure not likely long to endure, since the arguments which supported the one method could readily
be turned against the other. In less than three years
after the last step in the compromise of 1850 had
been taken the whole question of slavery was torn
open by the demand in Congress for the organization
of a Kansas Territory west of the Missouri river and
the application to the new Territory of the principle
of local option. The region involved, comprising in
general the area of the present States of Kansas and
Nebraska and westward to the Rocky mountains
watershed, had been left without political organization
when Missouri was admitted as a State, but the
slavery prohibition of the Missouri compromise applied to it because it lay north of the compromise line
of 36° 30′ and it had not been affected by the
measures of 1850.

Stephen A. Douglas, a Democratic senator from
Illinois, who had taken a prominent part in framing
the legislation of 1850, championed the demand of
the South for the organization of Kansas Territory
with the local option principle on the ground that
that principle, being inconsistent with the principle of
absolute prohibition of slavery which the Missouri

compromise embodied, had superseded the earlier principle and was now the recognized national policy. The debate which the Kansas proposal unloosed shook the country as no political debate on any subject had ever shaken it. Northern members of Congress, among them numerous Democrats, their repugnance to slavery intensified by the operation of the fugitive slave law, accused the South of deliberately tearing up a national agreement to which the good faith of the nation was solemnly pledged. The South, convinced now that slavery would not be successfully established in either New Mexico or Utah, defiantly insisted upon a new trial of strength in Kansas, and under the leadership of Douglas the South won. The original proposal was modified to the extent of providing for the organization of two Territories, Kansas and Nebraska, instead of one, with some changes of boundary, but not only was the principle of the compromise of 1850 applied to both Territories but the slavery prohibition of the Missouri compromise was specifically repealed.

The passage of the Kansas-Nebraska act in May, 1854, was the last effort of slavery to maintain itself by territorial compromise. With all of the remaining unorganized domain of the United States now by implication open to slavery, the domestic institution which had long been apologized for had become a national institution to be protected and defended like any other. The Union was divided, half free and half slave, but the slave section for the moment was in control. There remained for it the task of establishing slavery firmly in one or the other of the two new Territories and bringing either Kansas or Nebraska into the Union as a slave State. If the South failed in that undertaking and the sectional struggle continued, there was nothing left for the slave States to do but to withdraw, for the days of compromise were over.

# CHAPTER VIII

## THE TRIUMPH OF NATIONALITY

THE struggle for the establishment of slavery in Kansas Territory has been aptly called the prelude to the Civil War. The armed conflict which for two years went on in Kansas was a warning that the time for argument had passed, and that the political claims of slavery would now be upheld by force if they met with opposition. There was little disposition in the South to leave the question of slavery in Kansas to be settled by the natural course of events; on the contrary slavery was if possible to be forced upon Kansas, lawfully if that were practicable, lawlessly if that seemed necessary. The future of slavery hung upon the outcome, for no other region remained in which slavery could hope to exist even if it were introduced. Kansas was in the same latitude as southern Missouri, and while two-thirds at least of the Territory was believed to be sterile the eastern portion was undoubtedly fit for agriculture. Nebraska accordingly dropped for the time being out of sight and Kansas became the battle ground.

The drama unfolded rapidly. The Kansas-Nebraska act became law on May 30, 1854. Within a month a considerable number of Missourians had moved across the border and taken possession of some of the best land. The newcomers were soon followed by parties of emigrants from New England and other northern States, and the New England Emigrant Aid Society undertook to plant in the Territory a preponderant population of free State men and women. The territorial election of 1855 was carried by the proslavery faction by open fraud, armed parties from Missouri entering the Territory on the morning of election day, taking possession of the polling places, stuffing the ballot boxes, and furnishing three-fourths of the total vote returned. The territorial governor was able to set aside the returns on technical grounds in a few districts only, and the proslavery legislature which had been elected hastened to enact the Missouri code of laws for Kansas with the addition of stringent provisions for the protection of slavery. The free State party, which had repudiated the election, organized a free State legislature and elected a delegate to the House of Representatives at Washington as the proslavery legislature had done. With rival governments struggling for control Kansas passed into a period of border warfare having all the characteristics of civil war, and for nearly two years raids, burnings, and armed encounters were the normal order of the day.

Both of the territorial delegates who had been chosen were rejected by the House of Representatives, but an investigation in 1856 by a committee of the House produced only majority and minority reports each of which flatly contradicted the findings of the other. President Pierce gave his support to the proslavery faction and under his orders a free State convention at Topeka was dispersed by federal troops, but a free State constitution was nevertheless drawn up and application made to Congress for the admission of Kansas as a free State. The proslavery party retorted by drafting the Lecompton constitution recognizing slavery, and submitted the constitution for popular approval under conditions by which, if the constitution were rejected, the future growth of slavery would be restricted but the slaves already in Kansas would continue to be held. The free State men denounced the Lecompton constitution as a fraud and stayed away from the polls, with the result that the constitution was adopted by an overwhelming majority.

The Kansas controversy was at its height when the election of 1856 came on. A new Republican party, based upon broad construction principles and calling for a protective tariff and the exclusion of slavery from the Territories, had entered the field and was drawing into its ranks both antislavery Whigs and antislavery Democrats. Public opinion, already excited and embittered by the extraordinary events in Kansas, was further outraged by a brutal assault in the Senate chamber upon Charles Sumner, senator from Massachusetts, a determined opponent of slavery and a brilliant but vituperative orator. The Republican candidate for the presidency, however, John C. Fremont of

California, was known to the country only as a western explorer, and although the Republican popular vote reached the large figure of more than 1,390,000, the Democratic candidate, James Buchanan of Pennsylvania, was elected. An American party, with strict naturalization laws and the exclusion of all but native-born citizens from office as its distinctive tenets, also entered the contest, but its candidate, former President Fillmore, received only a few electoral votes. The congressional elections of 1854 had already overturned the Democratic majority in the House of Representatives, and the combined Republican and American membership controlled the House in 1856.

The antislavery forces in Congress were not strong enough to admit Kansas with its free State constitution, but the rejection of the Lecompton constitution when a vote without conditions was presently taken ended the effort of the South to capture Kansas for slavery. Kansas remained a Territory until 1861, but by 1858 the free State population was in control and the battle for freedom had been won.

On March 6, 1857, two days after the inauguration of Buchanan, the Supreme Court of the United States announced its decision in the famous case of Dred Scott. A decision had actually been reached late in the previous year and Buchanan was aware of its import, but the announcement was held back for political effect until the new administration had taken office. The case, long and carefully prepared, was ideally adapted to secure from the court what the South had long desired, namely, an authoritative judicial decision regarding the status of the Negro and the constitutionality of acts of Congress excluding slavery from parts of the United States. Dred Scott was a Negro whose ancestors had been imported into the United States from Africa and held and sold as slaves. He had lived with his owner, an army surgeon, in Illinois, a State in which slavery was prohibited by the ordinance of 1787; in a part of the Louisiana purchase from which slavery was excluded by the Missouri compromise and where, with the consent of his owner, he had married; and finally in Missouri, a slave State. Following the death of his former owner Scott became the property of one Sandford, a citizen of New York. The case came to the Supreme Court from the federal district court for Missouri, where Scott had brought suit to establish his claim to freedom on the ground of previous residence in free territory and to secure damages for the alleged illegal detention of himself and his family as slaves. Counsel for Sandford had argued that Scott, being a Negro and a slave, was not a citizen within the meaning of the federal Constitution and hence was not entitled to sue in a federal court, but the district court decided in favor of Scott and the case was then carried to the Supreme Court on appeal.

In an elaborate opinion in which a majority of the eight associate justices concurred, Chief Justice Taney denied the claim of Scott to citizenship. The whole history of slavery in the United States, Taney declared, showed that the Negro had always been regarded as of an inferior race whose members certain States had deemed it proper to hold in servitude and to class as property; and while a State might if it chose make a Negro a citizen of the State, such citizenship did not make him also a citizen of the United States or confer upon him the right to sue in a federal court. The importance of Taney's decision at this point will be understood by recalling that the Constitution at that time did not define citizenship, and the Dred Scott case brought out the first authoritative judicial ruling that citizenship of a State was not the same thing as citizenship of the United States.

Here Taney should have stopped. If Dred Scott was not a citizen and had no right to sue in a federal court, the court obviously had no jurisdiction of his plea, and the decision of the federal district court for Missouri sustaining his claim should have been reversed by the customary procedure. Taney was thinking of politics as well as of law, however, and he accordingly went on to consider whether or not Scott was entitled to his freedom by reason of his previous residence in territory from which slavery had been excluded by law. A long examination of the history of the Missouri compromise and of the legal points which it involved failed to show any constitutional warrant for excluding from any part of the territory of the United States anything which any State recognized as property, and the Missouri compromise was accordingly pronounced unconstitutional and void. Associate Justice Curtis, in a powerful dissenting opinion, exposed the inaccuracy of some of Taney's historical statements and the fallacies of his reasoning in regard to the citizenship of Negroes, and sustained the claim of Scott and the constitutionality of the compromise, but the decision of the majority was the decision of the court. The Dred Scott decision upheld with judicial finality virtually every claim of right or privilege that slavery had ever made, and left the Negro without hope even if he were freed.

The legal doctrines of the decision were at least open to debate, and the ruling with respect to citizenship was probably good law. The decision was instantly repudiated, however, by Republicans and antislavery Democrats as immoral, and the obloquy which befell the court for its uncalled-for attempt to settle a purely political question was a blow to its prestige from which it required years to recover. A series of political debates in Illinois in 1858, where a comparatively unknown lawyer, Abraham Lincoln, contested unsuccessfully the seat of Douglas in the Senate, discussed in all its phases the Dred Scott decision and strengthened the Republican opposition. Yet the North as a whole still hoped for peace. Lincoln's pointed assertion that the Union could not continue half slave and half free, but must become wholly one thing or the other, while it expressed a conviction to which the more radical antislavery sentiment of the country was rapidly being driven, did not as yet voice the opinion of the free States as a whole. The long years of compromise had had their effect, and the North still looked for a settlement without the dreaded intervention of force. When in October, 1859, John Brown made a spectacular attempt to free the slaves in Virginia his raid awakened only sporadic sympathy in the North, although it was of Brown that Union soldiers were singing less than two years later.

The presidential election of 1860 was the crucial test. The Republicans were confident, but they were not strong enough to win on the slavery issue alone, and accordingly their platform, while vigorously denouncing the Dred Scott decision and demanding freedom in the Territories, gave a prominent place to the demand for a protective tariff, internal improvements, and a railway to the Pacific. The obvious Republican candidate was William H. Seward, an able antislavery leader who had been governor of New York and United States senator. Seward's firmness on the slavery question in the form which the question had now taken was in doubt, however, and the choice of the convention fell upon Lincoln, whose speeches in the Illinois debates and elsewhere had made him one of the leading exponents of Republican antislavery opinion. With Lincoln was associated as vice-presidential candidate Hannibal Hamlin of Maine. The selection of both candidates from northern States not only emphasized the sectional character of the party, but offered also a bold challenge to the disunionists to show their hand.

The Democrats were divided. The majority, staunchly supporting slavery but as staunchly opposed to disunion, nominated Douglas, while the disunion minority in a separate convention nominated J. C. Breckinridge of Kentucky. A remnant of the old Whigs, taking the name of the Constitutional Union party, held a convention and nominated John Bell of Tennessee on a platform which called for nothing more specific than the Constitution of the country, the union of the States, and the observance of the laws, to none of which demands had any party thus far been opposed. Of the 303 electoral votes 180 were given for Lincoln and Hamlin, all of the northern States except New Jersey supporting the Republican candidates, but it was the popular vote that showed the mind of the nation. In a total vote of 4,675,853 Lincoln received 1,866,352, or considerably less than one-half; Douglas, the Democratic Union candidate, received 1,375,157; and Bell, the candidate of the Constitutional Unionists, received 589,581. The combined vote of the union candidates was thus over 3,830,000, while the vote for Breckinridge, the only candidate who stood upon a disunion platform, was only 845,763. It was clear that disunion as a campaign issue had extremely small support in the country at the same time that the Republicans, notwithstanding an overwhelming majority in both houses of the new Congress, were hardly strong enough with the people to pursue an aggressive policy unless the South forced the issue.

But the South did not hesitate, and again it was South Carolina that led. The day following the election every federal office holder in South Carolina resigned, and on December 20 an ordinance of secession, carefully framed to avoid every constitutional difficulty, declared the State to be independent. Similar action was soon taken in Virginia, Georgia, Florida, Alabama, Mississippi, and Louisiana. Southern senators and representatives in Congress gave up their seats, federal officers in the seceded States surrendered their offices, and federal property, including the mint at New Orleans, was seized. In February, 1861, a convention of seven States met at Montgomery, Alabama, and drew up a constitution for the Confederate States of America, and in March the new government, to which North Carolina and Texas adhered, went into operation with Jefferson Davis of Mississippi as president. Of the five border States of Maryland, Kentucky, Tennessee, Missouri, and Arkansas only Tennessee and Arkansas formally seceded; in the others the disunion movement was frustrated by political dissensions or by the quick action of Union supporters. Delaware, hitherto counted as a slave State, suffered from disaffection but remained in the Union.

President Buchanan was a State rights strict construction Democrat of the old school who had no sympathy with secession, but he could see no legal way of preventing a State from withdrawing from the Union save by resort to coercion, and for coercion the

Constitution afforded no clear authority. The South, accordingly, was practically assured of a free hand throughout the whole interval between the election in November and the inauguration of Lincoln in the following March. Congress, apparently only half realizing the significance of what was taking place, took no important steps to strengthen the resources of the federal government, wasted time in the discussion of further compromises, and actually framed and submitted to the States a proposed constitutional amendment which would have deprived the United States forever of power to interfere with slavery. Lincoln, meantime, remained quietly at his home in Illinois, expressing on occasion his hope for a peaceable adjustment but giving no indication of his plans. Then on the fourth of March, 1861, the unhonored administration of Buchanan passed into history and Lincoln took up the mighty task of preserving the nation from disunion.

Lincoln's inaugural address was conciliatory, but councils of peace were not to prevail. On April 12 Fort Sumter in Charleston harbor, one of the forts which the Confederates had not seized, was fired upon by Confederate batteries and the next day surrendered, and the great Civil war had begun. The Federal army was insignificant and nearly one-half of the force had been lost when Texas seceded, but in response to Lincoln's call for volunteers the North, its party differences forgotten now that the Union had been assailed, sprang instantly to arms. Thanks to the patriotic foresight of Governor Andrew of Massachusetts the Old Bay State was ready, and the Sixth Massachusetts regiment, the first of the hundreds of Union regiments to be in the field, fought its way through the streets of Baltimore *en route* to Washington, where it was quickly joined by the Seventh New York. In a few weeks an assembled army, largely undisciplined and poorly equipped but abounding in spirit, had insured the safety of the national capital. But nation and army demanded haste, and haste brought disaster. On July 21 the Federal and Confederate forces met at Bull Run, and when the beaten and demoralized Federal army poured back to Washington in disorderly retreat the dream of an easy victory over the Confederacy had vanished and the North sternly settled down to war.

From a military point of view the position of the Confederacy had some elements of strength. The seceded States could rest upon the defensive and thereby throw upon the North the burden of attack. Their white population was homogeneous, and the assurance of a food supply through slave labor freed most of the adult male population for fighting. The seizure of federal forts, arsenals, and other property gave the Confederacy an initial advantage in the possession of military supplies, and many officers of the regular army " went with their State " when the States seceded and entered the Confederate service. Moreover, the cause for which the South fought was in form that of independence, the right to live its own

life in its own way, and to that cause all save an insignificant fraction of the people were devoted.  Yet
the elements of weakness were far more important
than the elements of strength.  Of the population of
slightly more than 12,300,000 in the South in 1860, a
number equal to about two-fifths of the total population of the country, 3,500,000 were slaves.  The South
was not a manufacturing region, and unless factories
were established with amazing rapidity the needed
supplies of arms, munitions, and manufactured com-
modities generally could be obtained only through im-
portation from abroad.  A blockade of the coast, on
the other hand, would destroy Confederate commerce,
cotton could not be sold, manufactured goods of all
kinds would before long disappear, and the collapse of
the Confederacy would then be only a matter of time.
The Mississippi river, cutting the Confederacy in two,
was a menace to unity, and unless the lower course of
the river could be held Louisiana, Arkansas, and
Texas could be cut off and the western border of
Mississippi would be open to attack; while the great
length of the northern border, open to simultaneous
attack at a number of points, made the Confederate
frontier hard to defend.

Before the close of Buchanan's administration the
withdrawal of southern members of Congress had
made possible the admission of Kansas as a State, and
with the beginning of hostilities the Democrats, while
retaining their separate party organization, joined
loyally with the Republicans in the work of putting

the North on a war basis.  A long list of statutes provided for the increase of the army and navy and the
enrolment of volunteers, railway and telegraph lines
passed under the control of the military authorities,
the Union Pacific Railway was projected, and factories and mills worked day and night at the fabrica-
tion of military equipment.   The establishment of
the present national banking system in 1863 was followed by the issuance of a series of huge loans for
whose repayment the faith of the nation was expressly
pledged, and by large emissions of paper currency.
Foreign governments were early warned that the war
was regarded by the federal government as a rebellion for whose suppression the army and navy must
be employed, but that the right of the Confederate
States to secede from the Union could not be admitted
and that foreign intervention in aid of the Confederate cause would be looked upon as an unfriendly act.
A federal blockade tightened its hold upon the Confederate coast, and although a certain amount of lucrative blockade-running went on throughout the war,
and Confederate cruisers and privateers dealt hard
blows to American commerce, southern commerce of
every kind was before long practically cut off and
Confederate armed vessels were relentlessly pursued,
captured, or destroyed in every sea.

Lincoln had early meditated the emancipation of
the slaves, rightly holding that slavery was the underlying foundation upon which the Confederate demand
for independence was built.   But the war was a war

for union, not a war for emancipation, and the freeing of the slaves, if it were to take place while the war was going on, would be the act of the president as commander-in-chief of the national military forces and justifiable only as a military measure under the recognized laws of war. In the summer of 1862 Lincoln read to his cabinet the draft of an emancipation proclamation, but the lack as yet of any marked victory of the Federal armies would, it was thought, weaken the moral effect of the proclamation if it were issued then, and it was accordingly withheld. The long-looked-for victory came at Antietam, and on September 22 a preliminary proclamation, announcing that on January 1, 1863, the slaves would be freed in all of the States which had not by that time laid down their arms, was published. The Confederate resistance did not cease, and on January 1 emancipation was proclaimed. The proclamation did not abolish slavery as an institution, that step being one which only a constitutional amendment could achieve, and the act of emancipation applied to those States only in which armed resistance to the federal authority was still going on, but it was nevertheless a death blow to the system and to the Confederacy as well.

The blow was timely, for the North was showing signs of reaction. The unexpectedly long continuance of the war, the heavy loss of life, the repeated calls for volunteers, the arbitrary arrest of thousands of suspected persons and their confinement for long periods without a trial, and the imposition of a draft

system when voluntary enlistment failed, all combined to dampen the enthusiasm with which the North
had rushed to arms and to create an ominous volume
of discontent.  There was a feeling in many quarters
that the war had changed its original character, and
that the destruction of slavery and the supremacy of
the Republican party rather than the saving of the
Union had become the main objective.  In July, 1863,
the enforcement of the draft provoked a formidable
outbreak of mob violence in New York and Brooklyn,
and order was restored only with the aid of Federal
troops hurriedly brought from the front.  The mob
outburst was the more significant because only two
weeks before, on July 1–3, a mighty effort of the Confederacy to invade the North had been defeated at
Gettysburg, Pennsylvania, and although the Federal
victory was not promptly followed up it was clear
to military men that the power of the Confederacy
had passed its zenith and was on the decline.  The
British government, too, strangely misconceiving the
nature of the conflict, had from the beginning been
friendly to the South, and had not only permitted
Confederate cruisers and privateers to be built and
outfitted in British ports, but was apparently willing
to join with other European powers in some kind of
intervention had not France and Russia refused.  The
irritation toward Great Britain did not subside until
in 1870 an arbitration tribunal at Geneva awarded to
the United States substantial damages for the losses
to American commerce which the unneutral conduct

of the British government was held to have caused.

The Republicans, however, were not disturbed notwithstanding significant Democratic gains in the congressional elections of 1862, and in 1864 they renominated Lincoln on a platform which boldly championed all that the party and the president had done in the prosecution of the war and called for the continuance of the war until the Confederate resistance should be crushed. To encourage the growing union sentiment in the South and at the same time emphasize the national character of the party as they had not been able to emphasize it in 1860, the nomination for the vice-presidency was given to Andrew Johnson of Tennessee, a State which had seceded but which the Federal armies had recovered. The Democrats, ready now that the slaves had been emancipated to oppose the continuance of the war, nominated a former Union general, George B. McClellan, on a platform which denounced the conduct of the war as a failure. McClellan had no reason to love the Republicans, for while he had performed praiseworthy service at the beginning of the war he had later been sharply criticized for lack of energy and had eventually retired from the army; but he knew as a soldier that the war had not failed and he accepted the nomination at the same time that he rejected the platform. The election gave Lincoln 212 electoral votes and McClellan 21, while the popular majority for Lincoln was more than 400,000. The Republican policy had been endorsed by the people and the war was to go on.

The force of the Confederacy was nearly spent. The Mississippi had been wrested from Confederate control, and the area of military operations had dwindled until only Virginia and parts of the Carolinas and Georgia offered strong resistance. In Virginia the hammering tactics of Grant, wasteful as they were of human life, were beating down the Confederate strongholds despite the able generalship of Lee. A desolating raid from Atlanta to the sea by Sherman's army showed the hollowness of Confederate power, and hunger, privation, and lack of men for recruits marked the beginning of the end. On April 9, 1865, Lee surrendered to Grant at Appomattox and the great war was practically over. Grant's terms were generous and the demoralized and prostrate South, conscious that Lincoln had never felt for it ill-will, had no reason to anticipate vengeance from the nation whose unity it had failed to break. But the healing task of restoration was not for Lincoln to perform. Five days after Lee's surrender the president was shot in Ford's theatre at Washington and in a few hours was dead. The whole nation mourned his going, for his simple life, his staunch courage, and his steadfast faith had been the people's inspiration, but the South had more reason than the North to regret his passing, for without his moderating influence the future spelled despair.

The victory of the North was a victory of superior numbers, superior wealth, and a superior industrial and commercial resource. Between the two sections no comparison in any of these respects could profitably be made, for the disparity was overwhelming. That the South was able to hold out so long was due to the superb devotion which it exhibited to the cause for which it fought, its skillful utilization of the meagre resources at its command, and the military genius of Lee. Yet the moral issues which the war involved were more significant than the arrays of money and men. In spite of the criticisms which the conduct of the war called out the North never lost sight of the principle of national unity which secession had challenged, and the destruction of slavery and of the political power of slaveholding States was only an incident in comparison with the preservation of the Union. The independence for which the South contended had no such broad moral basis as the demand for American independence had presented in the eighteenth century Revolution, because there was no moral grievance. The economic system which the South sought to uphold was unsound in theory and antiquated in practice, and it was for the good of the South that the system should disappear. The development of the American nation as a modern state demanded free labor and free men, and when at the end of 1865 the Thirteenth Amendment swept American slavery out of existence the nation itself was free.

The problem of restoring normal conditions in the South and of bringing the late seceded States back into their proper constitutional relations with the Union was one of infinite complexity. For more than

four years the Confederate States had maintained a
separate political existence.  They had taken a col-
lective name; they had adopted a constitution with
executive, legislative, and judicial departments;  they
had enacted laws, levied taxes, and issued a paper
currency;  they had sent diplomatic agents abroad
and had sold Confederate bonds to foreign pur-
chasers; and they had carried on war by land and
sea.  During the four years they had distinctly and
in terms repudiated the authority of the United
States, and no federal authority had in fact been exercised in any part of the Confederacy save where
the federal military forces had established themselves.
If, notwithstanding the ultimate failure, secession
had nevertheless been for a time an accomplished
fact, then the Union had been broken, the Confederate States had withdrawn, and their status now was
analogous to that of conquered provinces which the
federal government was free to deal with as it chose.
On the other hand, if secession had never been legally
accomplished and the Confederate States had merely
carried on a prolonged but unsuccessful rebellion,
punishment for treason or rebellion might indeed be
meted out to individuals, but the States as such had
not ceased to be States and were apparently entitled
to be again represented in Congress, to take part in
national elections, and to enjoy the benefit of federal
laws.  Their relative weight in the House of Representatives would of course be reduced, because there
were no longer slaves to be counted as part of their

population and emancipation had not made the Negro a citizen, but they would still enjoy equal representation in the Senate.

The gravity of the constitutional issue, likely at any moment to be raised before the Supreme Court, had been early perceived both by Congress and by the president, and preparations had been made to meet it. The numerous acts and resolutions which were passed during the war and the presidential proclamations which were issued carefully avoided recognizing the Confederate government as in any sense a legal government, and consistently referred to the war as a rebellion or insurrection and to those who aided it as rebels or insurgents. The great collection of Civil War documents published by the government years after the war had ended bears the title " War of the Rebellion: Official Records." The question of how the seceded States were to be restored to their former position in the Union, however, was one upon which Congress and the president differed widely. Lincoln, far less concerned about the constitutional aspects of the case than with the practical necessity of ending the war and restoring peace as quickly and easily as possible, was ready to recognize any Union government which had the support of loyal citizens equal in number to ten per cent. of those who were legally qualified to vote under the laws of the State in 1860, and he was prepared if necessary to uphold such a government by military force; but it was of course understood that the admission of senators and representatives from such a reconstructed State would still rest with Congress. A loyal government which was presently established in Louisiana under this plan was recognized, as was a Union government differently constituted in Tennessee, and both States voted for the Republican candidates in the presidential election of 1864; but although the Republican convention had found no difficulty in selecting its vice-presidential candidate from Tennessee, the electoral votes of both States were rejected by Congress and senators and representatives were refused seats.

Congress was much more concerned than was Lincoln about constitutional procedure and very much less disposed than he to be generous with the South. The congressional opposition to the Lincoln programme rested mainly upon two grounds. The first was the feeling that a number of loyal citizens equal to only ten per cent. of the number of qualified voters in 1860 was too slender a basis upon which to establish a reconstructed State government, and that such a government would not be able to protect the Negroes in their newly-acquired freedom. The other was the conviction that the political restoration of the seceded States properly belonged to Congress rather than to the president; and although there was no serious thought of reducing the States to the position of Territories or holding them indefinitely as conquered provinces, the conviction was strong that unless the process of restoration were carefully guarded and all of its steps firmly controlled the moral fruits of victory would be endangered, those who had led the South to secession would again take control of the State governments, and " rebel brigadiers " would reappear as members of the Senate and House of Representatives. So long as Lincoln lived, however, the congressional policy was of necessity held in abeyance, but the refusal of Congress to seat representatives or senators or to count electoral votes from States which Lincoln had recognized rendered the executive programme practically sterile of results.

The succession of Andrew Johnson as president darkened the prospect of a generous or amicable solution of the reconstruction problem. Johnson was an able man, but he was of coarse fibre. He belonged to the class of southern whites which had held few or no slaves and which despised the planter aristocracy, and his violent temper and objectionable personal habits alienated supporters to whom his political and constitutional ideas might otherwise have appealed. The bitter controversy with Congress which continued throughout Johnson's administration, and which culminated in the attempt of Congress to impeach him and remove him from office, was attended with discreditable incidents which reflected upon both parties and make the period of reconstruction a dark page in American political annals, but the conflict was inevitable because the executive and congressional views as to how reconstruction should be carried out were inherently antagonistic and compromise was impossible. It is obvious now, as it was all but apparent at the time, that the Republican leaders were influenced more and more by their determination to make their party supreme for years to come, but the fear that the president, if his policy were allowed to prevail, would undo much of the work of the war, and that Negro servitude would replace Negro slavery, also weighed heavily in the scale.

The congressional plan as elaborated finally in March, 1867, divided the late seceded States into districts, and placed in immediate charge of each district a military commander intrusted with the supervision of the reconstruction process. Under the direction of the military commander the voters of the States, purged of disloyalty by the administration of a stringent oath which few Confederates could take, were to call conventions which should draw up new State constitutions. The constitutions were to repudiate the secession debts, give the suffrage and equal political and legal rights to Negroes, and exclude from voting and office holding former supporters of the Confederacy who declined to take a prescribed form of oath or who did not receive the benefit of amnesty. In the popular vote which was to be taken on the Constitution Negroes as well as whites were to participate, the Negroes thus voting on the question of the rights which under the Constitution were to be accorded to them; and if the Constitution, after having been approved by this extraordinary body of voters, was also approved by Congress the State might choose its quota of federal senators and representatives and take part in presidential elections. Until the act of Congress had been fully complied with and the States formally recognized, the control of the military commanders was to continue.

Hardly any of the steps which the acts of Congress prescribed would bear scrutiny from the point of view of the Constitution, and the decision to thrust the suffrage upon the Negroes called out widespread dissent. The great mass of the former slaves were ignorant as well as illiterate, and the economic transition from slavery to a wages system had only just begun. The southern whites, however sincerely they might have been disposed to accept the abolition of slavery, could not by any possibility be expected to regard the former slaves as political equals and racial antagonism and social animosity were certain to show themselves in politics. The United States had laid down slavery only to take up the race problem, and the latter problem was more difficult and dangerous than the former. On the other hand the Republicans, while fully expecting that the Negroes would everywhere support the Republican candidates out of gratitude to the party which had given them their freedom, insisted that freedom without suffrage would be an impossible anomaly, and that unless the Negroes could defend themselves at the polls their freedom would not long endure. A number of southern States had already enacted laws which created a virtual condition of Negro servitude under the guise of preventing vagrancy, and it was believed that other

States would not be long in following the example if Congress did not interpose.

Johnson in able messages vetoed the reconstruction acts, but the bills were at once passed over the veto and Congress went steadily on with its programme. A Fourteenth Amendment, setting aside the doctrine of the Dred Scott decision by declaring all persons born or naturalized in the United States and subject to its jurisdiction to be citizens of the United States and of the State in which they reside, prohibiting any State from denying to any citizen of the United States the equal protection of the laws, and penalizing by a reduction of its representation in the House of Representatives any State which denied the right to vote to any person save on account of participation in rebellion or other crime, became a part of the Constitution in 1868. The presence of federal troops insured the carrying out of the congressional policy, and by the end of 1868 most of the southern States had been reconstructed and their representatives had been admitted to the Senate and House.

The grave step of impeaching the president was clearly foreshadowed once the implacable hostility of the president to the congressional policy became apparent, and both Congress and the president hastened the climax. Johnson had not failed to put the reconstruction acts into operation, but fear lest he might use his authority as head of the army to embarrass if not defeat the measures led to an unwarranted invasion of his constitutional power as commander-in-chief by an act which partially removed from his control the commanding general of the army. Johnson on his part, in a series of public addresses at Chicago, St. Louis, and elsewhere, violently attacked Congress and some of its members. In 1868, accordingly, articles of impeachment were voted by the House of Representatives and the trial began before the Senate, the chief justice of the United States presiding. The articles charged the president with high crimes and misdemeanors in that he had interfered with the operation of various acts of Congress, but for popular effect some scandalous passages from his public addresses were also cited. Johnson, who did not appear in person, was defended by able counsel, bore himself with great dignity throughout the proceedings, and by a close vote was acquitted. The impeachment trial marked the extreme height of Republican aggressiveness, but the power of the president had already been broken and the final attack added no weight to his defeat.

The anger of the South at its subjection to military government in time of peace and the extension of the suffrage to the Negroes caused systematic efforts to be made to defeat the evident purpose of the Fourteenth Amendment and prevent Negroes from voting. A Fifteenth Amendment, prohibiting any State from denying or abridging the right of any citizen to vote because of race, color, or previous condition of servitude, was accordingly framed and in 1870 was accepted by the necessary number of State legislatures.

The Supreme Court later decided that the Fifteenth Amendment did not confer the right to vote upon anyone, but merely stated certain grounds upon which the right to vote should not be denied; and for many years the southern States continued to apply restrictions, such as property qualifications or laws limiting the suffrage to those persons and their descendants who possessed the right before the war, in order to eliminate the Negro vote. By 1870, however, the last of the States had been reconstructed and the Union was again whole.

The years of political reconstruction are a period which the thoughtful American can recall only with regret. The problems that had to be solved were without doubt extremely difficult and complex, and the enmities and suspicions which the war had developed created a political atmosphere in which moderation and clear thinking were hard to obtain. The South itself was far from blameless, and the long agony which it suffered was in no small part due to its own shortsightedness and misconduct. But the arrogance of the Republican leaders, flushed with victory and bent upon insuring party control in the South by means of the Negro vote, led them into excesses which many years were needed to redress and some of whose traces still survive. There can be no question but that much of the legislation of the reconstruction period was unwarranted by the Constitution, that the Supreme Court bent before the demands of politics, and that the moral tone of political discussion was seriously lowered. Only in law, moreover, was the attempt to give the ballot to the Negro successful, and Negro suffrage is not yet a fully accomplished fact in any southern State. The penalty which the Fourteenth Amendment provides for States in which the equal right of citizens to vote is denied was practically of no importance and its application has never been seriously contemplated. No effort of any consequence was ever made by the federal government to educate the Negroes whom it had freed, or to help the southern States to bridge the gulf which separated the old régime of slavery from the new régime of free labor. The South, which had been beaten to its knees in war, was crushed politically by reconstruction, and for more than thirty years the Republican party stood with the flag upon the ruins and called it peace.

But the Union had been preserved. The herculean effort to detach a group of important States and form an independent confederation had failed, and the old doctrines of State rights and strict construction which for seventy years had clogged the wheels of national progress had been hurled into oblivion. Yet the fruits of victory, when weighed and measured, were more important for the South than for the North. To the victorious North the downfall of the South meant the triumph of political ideas in which the North had always more or less firmly believed and without which it was difficult to think of the United States as a nation at all. No new political or social vistas of striking color or imposing outline were opened to the North by the surrender of Lee; the progress of the future was to be along lines already marked out and now happily cleared of embarrassing obstructions.  To the South, on the other hand, defeat meant the dawning of a new day, the opening of a new period of social outlook and industrial and agricultural expansion incomparably larger and more fruitful than the years of provincial backwardness which had gone before; and in spite of the losses of war and the political distresses of reconstruction the South had been enriched with a new opportunity and a new hope.  The appeal of the " lost cause " still touches the hearts of a generation to which the war is now only a story which the fathers told, but the appeal of union and nationality knows today neither North nor South, but only a common country, a common allegiance, and an undivided national spirit.

# CHAPTER IX

## THE POLITICS OF INDUSTRY AND POWER

THE twenty years during which slavery, civil strife, and reconstruction absorbed the political attention of the United States were a period of extraordinary economic development as well. For a decade before the war, industry, commerce, and agriculture had been rapidly expanding, and the artificial stimulus which the war gave to agriculture and manufactures continued to show its effects long after the war had ceased. The use of southern cotton, temporarily checked by the war, was quickly resumed when southern markets were again open, but the production of woolen and linen textiles which the lack of cotton had encouraged was by that time firmly established and continued to grow. Food crops in the North and West were large during the war, and the shortage of farm labor which the heavy demands for volunteers occasioned was largely made good by the increased use of farm machinery and by the labor of women. Imports and exports, on the other hand, declined, partly because the export of cotton practically ceased and partly because exceptional war demands absorbed much of the surplus of food and manufactured goods which previously had been exported. The decline was temporary and domestic and foreign exports, which had fallen from about $333,500,000 in 1860 to $158,000,000 in 1864, rose in 1866 to $348,000,000 and by 1874 had reached $586,000,000; and although fluctuations during these years showed that the United States was not yet an exporting country in the sense of producing regularly large quantities of goods intended for sale abroad, American business found compensation in the fact that the extraordinary growth of population, rising from 23,000,000 in 1850 to more than 38,500,000 in 1870, created a demand for food products and manufactures which absorbed far the larger part of what the country was able to produce.

The phenomenon of western development continued to show itself on an imposing scale. Before the war the frontier line of continuous settlement had reached the Mississippi and was extending irregularly into the broad area between the river and the Rocky mountains. Kansas, admitted as a State in 1861, was followed by Nevada in 1864 and by Nebraska in 1867. With Minnesota and Oregon, which had been admitted in 1858 and 1859, and West Virginia, set off from Virginia in 1863 as a reward of loyalty, the Union by 1870 numbered thirty-six States besides the organized Territories. East of the Mississippi a network of railways, built in the case of many of the western lines with the aid of federal land grants and State and local financial help, bound the States together, and the Union Pacific Railway, projected in

1863 but not opened until after the war, brought California and the central Pacific coast for the first time into easy communication with the rest of the country. In 1850, 178,672 miles of postal route served 18,417 post offices; in 1870 the mails were carried over 231,-232 miles of established routes and 28,492 post offices were in operation. The purchase of Alaska from Russia in 1867 did not for many years appreciably influence the course of western settlement, for it was long before the great mineral wealth of the region was known, but the acquisition was politically important because it removed another European power from the continent.

The national debt, which had been practically extinguished in Jackson's time, had been increased by the Mexican war and the purchase of territory from Mexico, and in 1860 stood at about $60,000,000. The Civil war swelled the interest-bearing debt to over $2,200,000,000, to which is of course to be added, in estimating the aggregate cost of the war, the debts of the States and of local communities, the annual interest charge, and the ultimate cost of pensions for Union soldiers and sailors and their dependents. As late as 1921 nearly half a million Civil war pensions were still being paid. The Confederate debt, including the debts of the several States of the Confederacy, was a total loss, the Fourteenth Amendment expressly prohibiting the payment of any public debts incurred in aid of secession or on account of the emancipation of slaves; but the cost of freeing the slaves in the District of Columbia, emancipated by law in 1862, was met by the United States and the war expenses of the loyal States were eventually reimbursed. Extravagant expenditures by some of the reconstruction governments during the years when northern political adventurers, familiarly known as " carpet-baggers," and Negro politicians were in control added some $275,000,000 to the debts of the southern States, the larger part of which was legally valid.

The sudden and extraordinary demand for revenue at the outbreak of the war speedily drained the federal treasury, drove specie out of circulation, and forced resort to heavy taxation, extensive borrowing through issues of bonds, and the issuance of paper currency. Tariff duties were raised, internal revenue taxes reached out to almost every taxable commodity or business transaction and to numerous occupations, and an income tax was imposed. The receipts of the federal treasury, which had amounted to only a little more than $56,000,000 in 1860, rose by 1865 to more than $322,000,000. It was a defect of the congressional policy, however, that while it imposed heavy taxes in many directions the amount raised by taxation was much less than the country was both able and willing to pay, and the large issues of government bonds shifted to a later generation a financial burden a considerable part of which could without great difficulty have been borne while the war was going on. The continuance of heavy taxation after the war, moreover, partly with a view to the reduction of the debt but also, in the case of the tariff duties, because of the firm hold which the protective policy had obtained, produced in a few years a surplus revenue which was a temptation to extravagance, and the problem of bringing the country back to a specie basis was not finally solved until 1879.

The national banking system established in 1863 was an ingenious expedient for securing at one and the same time a paper currency and a market for government bonds, the issuance of national bank notes being based upon the security of bonds which the banks were required to purchase. The huge issues of bonds, however, exceeded the quantity which the banks could absorb, and the need of further currency was accordingly met by the issuance of treasury notes of various kinds and of unsecured and irredeemable paper money commonly known, from the color of the notes, as greenbacks. The constitutionality of so much of the greenback law as made the notes a legal tender in payment of private debts was more than doubtful, and in 1869 the Supreme Court gave an adverse decision which, if it had been adhered to, would have overthrown the greenback policy and greatly embarrassed the government. The occurrence of vacancies, however, shortly gave Grant an opportunity to reconstitute the court, and in 1870 the former decision was reversed and the legal tender provision of the law was upheld. The court had already in Johnson's administration refused to pass upon the constitutionality of the reconstruction acts in a case which the State of Georgia had sought to raise, properly holding that the question was political and not judicial, and the reversal of its decision in the legal tender cases, although generally regarded as a surrender to the political views of Congress, nevertheless freed the hands of the federal government in the difficult matter of the currency and the national debt.

Not for some years was the Republican hold upon Congress or the country seriously endangered. The Democratic party, discredited in the North and West by its old identification with slavery and its sympathy for the South during the period of reconstruction, only slowly recovered prestige, and so long as federal troops were at hand to support the reconstructed State governments the southern States could regularly be counted in the Republican column. The presidential election of 1868, however, while a sweeping victory for Grant, the Republican candidate, so far as the electoral vote was concerned, showed that public opinion was turning. The electoral vote for Grant was 213 in comparison with 80 for Horatio Seymour of New York, the Democratic candidate, but the Republican popular majority was only a little over three hundred thousand in a total vote of more than five and one-half million. The administration of Grant and the Republican Congress increased rather than lessened the growing discontent. Notwithstanding the fact that all of the southern States had by 1870 been restored to their former political rights as members of the Union, the employment of federal troops for political purposes continued; and the attempt of Congress to suppress the Ku Klux Klan and other secret societies which had been formed in the South with the object of regaining the control of State and local government for the whites and preventing the Negroes from voting, joined to an ill-advised effort to take over the supervision of federal elections, had no other effect than to emphasize the partisan policy of Congress, increase the public criticism of the president, and strengthen the Democratic opposition.

The election of 1872 brought into the field no less than eight candidates for the presidency and eleven for the vice-presidency. A Liberal Republican movement, organized by independent and reform Republicans who were willing to support a Democratic candidate as a rebuke to the party in power, had for a year been gathering headway in the East, and a temperance party had been organized. The Republicans profited by factional divisions in the Democratic ranks and by the general unfitness of the leading opposition candidate, Horace Greeley, long an influential Republican and famous the country over as the editor of the New York "Tribune," to whom the Liberal Republicans gave their support; and Grant was again elected with a largely increased electoral and popular vote.

The pressing question was that of the currency.

The disappearance of specie from circulation early in the war and the long-continued use of national bank notes, treasury notes, and greenbacks, none of which were at par in gold, had been accompanied by a marked rise of prices, and although the level of prices had declined somewhat after the war and the paper money was rising in value the currency problem as a whole remained. A wide difference of opinion prevailed regarding the policy that should be pursued. Banking and business interests desired an early return to the gold standard, but in the West, particularly among the farmers, the demand was growing for the continued use of greenbacks and the increased coinage of silver. There was a vague feeling that gold had in some way appreciated in value, and that a gold standard meant " dear money " and the continuance of inflated prices. In 1873, however, when the coinage laws were revised, the coinage of the standard silver dollar was discontinued. The silver dollar had never been a popular coin in the eastern part of the country, but its omission from the list of coins was popularly interpreted as meaning that silver, the cheaper metal, was to be demonetized, and the action presently began to be denounced as the " crime of 1873." A disastrous financial crisis the same year confirmed the popular impression that the financial system was bad, and the burden of responsibility was thrown upon the Republicans, who in general favored the gold standard. The congressional elections of 1874 were a tidal victory for the

Democrats in the House of Representatives, a Republican majority of 110 being replaced by a Democratic majority of 74.  In 1875, however, provision
was made by law for the resumption of specie payment on the first of January, 1879, and a bill to
inflate the currency was vetoed by Grant.

Both of the great parties looked forward with
apprehension to the presidential campaign of 1876.
The discovery of serious financial and political scandals, some of them involving high officials of the
government, was a telling popular argument in favor
of a party change.  Two new parties had in the
meantime arisen.  The Greenback party, an outgrowth in part of the political activities of farmer
organizations known as Patrons of Husbandry, or
Granges, and the forerunner in its financial views of
the later People's or Populist party, opposed the
resumption of specie payment and demanded the
continued use of greenbacks and the enlarged coinage
of silver.  The Prohibition party, the successor of
the temperance party of 1872, called for the prohibition of the manufacture and sale of intoxicating
liquors, a policy which had already been adopted in
a few States.  Neither of these minor parties, however, was likely to be very important except in close
States, and the national contest was between the
Republicans and the now reunited Democrats.  The
Republicans nominated Rutherford B. Hayes, formerly governor of Ohio and a general in the Union
army during the Civil War.  The Democratic can-

didate was Samuel J. Tilden, an able lawyer and prominent party leader who had been governor of New York. The Republican candidate, who had also been a member of Congress, had not shown offensive partisanship in his support of reconstruction, and his nomination was skilfully planned to allay discontent and to win back the Liberal Republicans whose support had been lost in 1872.

The result of the electoral vote showed an unprecedented complication. In South Carolina, Florida, Louisiana, and Oregon there were double returns each certified to as the true vote of the State. In the case of Oregon the dispute involved the legal right of a postmaster to act as a presidential elector, the Constitution prohibiting the appointment as elector of any person holding an office of trust or profit under the United States. In the case of the three southern States the double returns came from rival bodies known as returning boards, each of which represented a government claiming to be the only lawful government of the State. If all of the contested votes were counted for the Republican candidate, Hayes would be elected by a majority of one vote, while the loss of a single vote would give the election to the Democrats.

The excitement throughout the country was intense. The Republican leaders immediately decided to " claim everything," while the Democrats, aware of the disadvantage which they were under in dealing with the contested votes from the South, sought diligently to find a Republican elector who might be bribed. There was loose talk of seating Tilden by force in case the election went against him, but no Democratic president was likely to be seated by force with Grant in the presidential chair. A study of the Constitution only added to the difficulty. The Constitution provides that the certified returns of the electoral votes, transmitted sealed to the president of the Senate, shall be opened by him in the presence of the two houses and that "the votes shall then be counted," but on the question of who shall count the votes or how disputed returns are to be dealt with the Constitution is silent. The Senate was Republican, the House of Representatives was Democratic, and the president of the Senate let it be known that while he was prepared to open the certificates as the Constitution required he would take no responsibility of deciding which returns were lawful or of counting the votes.

There being apparently no constitutional way out of the dilemma an extra-constitutional method was finally devised. The decision of the legal questions involved in the counting of the returns was referred to an electoral commission composed of seven members of the Senate, seven members of the House of Representatives, and a justice of the Supreme Court, and it was agreed that the decisions of the commission should be final unless both houses concurred in rejecting them. The Republican Senate chose four Republicans and three Democrats, the Democratic

House chose four Democrats and three Republicans. With the fourteen congressional members of the commission equally divided politically the momentous responsibility of decision virtually rested with the member chosen by the Supreme Court.   The fundamental legal question which the commission felt called upon to decide was that of determining where, in a presidential election, the authority of a State ends and the authority of the United States begins. The Supreme Court member, Associate Justice Bradley of Massachusetts, had been a Republican, and by a party majority the commission decided that Congress, in counting the electoral vote, could not " go behind the returns," and that the certificate of the recognized government of a State as to what electors had been chosen must be accepted.   The application of this ruling gave all the votes in dispute to Hayes, and he was accordingly declared to have been elected.   Tilden accepted the result without reproaches, but Hayes had to bear throughout the rest of his life the abusive attacks of Democrats who insisted that he had obtained the presidential office by fraud.

Most of the federal troops had been withdrawn from the South before Hayes took office, and Hayes presently withdrew the few that were left.   The reconstructed Republican governments, which only the presence of soldiers or the fear of their employment had sustained, quickly gave way to Democratic governments from which Negroes and northern adventurers were excluded, and from that day until this no southern State except Tennessee has given its electoral votes to a Republican candidate for the presidency, and the vote of Tennessee was given only as late as 1920. Republican reconstruction had created a solid Democratic South. By one device or another the larger part of the Negro vote was eliminated, and for nearly a generation Republicans were only rarely to be found in either State or local offices.

The dignity with which Hayes met the difficult situation in which the disputed election had placed him gradually won the respect of the country, and by the close of his administration the partisan bitterness of feeling in regard to him had largely disappeared. The Civil War was over, and while among the older generation its memories and hates survived, a new generation was addressing itself to new problems. Disastrous strikes and lockouts in 1877, attended in some instances with destructive riots, testified to the existence of a labor situation with which the federal government would sooner or later have to deal. In 1878 the demand for a bimetallic coinage, championed by a National party which had replaced the Greenback organization, was strong enough to force the passage of the so-called Bland-Allison law providing for the compulsory purchase and coinage of two million dollars' worth of silver monthly and restoring the standard silver dollar to the list of coins. Colorado had been admitted as a State in 1876, and the owners of the Colorado silver mines could now make their voices heard in Congress.

Hayes was not a candidate for re-election, and the Republican choice devolved upon James A. Garfield of Ohio, a former member of Congress and like Hayes a Union soldier. The electoral vote again showed a large Republican majority, but the popular vote for Garfield exceeded by only seven thousand the vote for General Winfield S. Hancock, the Democratic candidate, and of the total popular vote Garfield received less than one-half. The outlook for the Republicans was not encouraging. The National or Greenback party, which had polled 81,000 votes in 1876, polled more than 307,000 votes in 1880. The border States of Maryland, Kentucky, Tennessee, and Missouri were Democratic as was also the Civil war State of West Virginia, and the popular vote in California showed a slight Democratic plurality. The Greenback vote, significant of a political revolution which was already threatening the integrity of both the Republican and the Democratic parties, was especially strong in Illinois, Indiana, Michigan, Iowa, Kansas, Missouri, and Texas, and attained figures of more than twelve thousand in New York and more than twenty thousand in Pennsylvania. The meaning of the figures was clear: a new economic sectionalism was emerging in national politics in addition to the political sectionalism of the reconstructed South.

Garfield had earned some credit for independence in 1873 when as a member of the House of Representatives he refused to accept an inordinate increase of salary which Congress had voted to its members,

and early in his administration he freed himself from
subserviency to a group of New York Republicans
familiarly known as " Stalwarts," led by the two
New York senators, Roscoe Conkling and Thomas C.
Platt.   But he was not long to enjoy the honor which
his party had bestowed upon him.   On July 2, 1881,
he was shot by an irresponsible office seeker in a railway station at Washington, and on September 19,
after a lingering and painful illness, died at Long
Branch, New Jersey.   For the second time a president had been assassinated, but the sickness and
death of Garfield raised a question which the death
of Lincoln had not presented.   The vice-president,
Chester A. Arthur of New York, declined to assume
the duties of the presidential office so long as Garfield lived, and as Garfield was wholly incapacitated
from the time of the assault upon him until his death
the executive branch of the government was for two
and a half months practically without a head.   An
old law provided that the presidency, in the event
of the death, removal, or disability of both the president and the vice-president, should devolve upon the
speaker of the House of Representatives or the presiding officer of the Senate.   The new Congress, however, did not assemble until several weeks after
Garfield's death, and the death or disability of Arthur,
if either had occurred during the interval, would have
left the United States without a president and with
no provision for choosing one.   Not until 1886 was
a new law enacted devolving the succession, in case

a vice-president is lacking, upon the members of the cabinet in order beginning with the secretary of state. Even then the question of what, under the Constitution, constitutes disability was left open, to reappear, again without settlement, in the second administration of Woodrow Wilson.

Arthur had an embarrassing record as a New York politician, but his conduct as president was as a whole both dignified and honorable, and his old associations with machine politics had comparatively little influence upon his course as chief executive. His detachment in this respect was the more praiseworthy because the Republican party had for some years been subjected to severe criticism at the hands of reformers for its open support of the spoils system. The partisan theory that " to the victors belong the spoils of office " dated back at least as far as the time of Jackson, but the exclusion of Democrats from office and the use of the federal civil service to reward party workers had been a settled Republican policy ever since the Civil War had made necessary a wholesale removal of disloyal office holders. In 1883 a civil service system was established under which appointments to the larger number of departmental offices were to be made only in accordance with the results of examinations for fitness, and removals for political reasons were forbidden. The new system was long, however, in winning more than formal and halfhearted support from either of the two leading parties, and more than twenty years elapsed before the civil service regulations were allowed to work substantially as they were intended to work.

So far as the personal quality of the presidents went the series from Lincoln to Arthur formed a descending scale. Neither Hayes, Garfield, nor Arthur were strong men, and the forceful executive leadership which the country expected of a president was lacking. The feeling was widespread that the Republicans, notwithstanding their distinguished successes, had been too long in power, that the party leadership was corrupt, and that the welfare of the nation would be served by a change. In 1884 the Democrats, reinforced by the support of large numbers of Independents or "Mugwumps" who had forsaken the Republican party because of its identification with the spoils system and other abuses, found their candidate in Grover Cleveland, an independent and courageous Democrat who in 1882 had been elected governor of New York by an immense majority and had made a commendable record as a reformer. The Republicans nominated James G. Blaine of Maine, a brilliant politician of magnetic personality who had long been a member and for some time speaker of the House of Representatives. The campaign was embittered by the circulation of charges affecting the personal character of the candidates, but the real issues were the protective tariff policy of which Blaine was a staunch supporter, the solid South, and the Republican record as contrasted with Democratic promises of reform. The election was a substantial victory for the Democrats, but the popular plurality for Cleveland was only a little over 62,000 in a total vote of more than ten million, and again less than a majority of the total vote polled. The National or Greenback party vote fell abruptly to less than half the vote that had been secured in the previous elections, but the Prohibition party, whose vote had dwindled in 1880 to ten thousand, polled over 151,000 votes in 1884. The Republicans had lost the control of the Senate in 1880, and had regained control in 1882 only to suffer large losses in the House of Representatives. The election of 1884 strengthened the Republican following in the Senate and somewhat reduced the Democratic majority in the House. The outlook for the new Democratic administration, accordingly, was not reassuring, especially if the tariff issue were raised, for the Republican Senate could be counted upon to oppose to the last any attack upon the cardinal Republican doctrine of protection.

Cleveland possessed abounding courage, and he did not hesitate. A rapidly increasing treasury surplus, due in large part to the continuance of high protective duties notwithstanding a large reduction of the national debt, was an obvious menace to business as well as to politics, for the accumulating revenue represented money withdrawn from circulation and business uses at the same time that it offered a strong temptation to wasteful or unnecessary appropriations. On the other hand the readjusted duties of the tariff

of 1883, the first thoroughgoing revision of the
schedules which had been made since the Civil war,
had refined and perfected the protective system, and
tariff protection as a national political and economic
policy irrespective of the amount of revenue produced, as against any kind of tariff framed primarily
for revenue purposes, was now widely advocated by
manufacturers in all parts of the country, by the wool
growers of Ohio and other western States, and by an
appreciable number of farmers.

In his first and second annual messages to Congress,
in 1885 and 1886, Cleveland called attention pointedly
to the condition of the treasury and the dangers of the
surplus and urged a reduction of duties. But the
Democratic leadership in the House of Representatives
was weak, the Senate was hostile, and nothing was
done. Cleveland then took the bold step of devoting
his third annual message in 1887 solely to the tariff.
He denounced the tariff as a " vicious source " of unnecessary revenue and declared that " a condition
and not a theory " confronted the nation. The surplus in the treasury, it was estimated, would amount
to $140,000,000 by the end of the fiscal year. A re-
vised tariff bill, known as the Mills bill from its
official sponsor, was passed by the House, but the
Senate framed a substitute measure, and as neither
house would accept the proposals of the other the
session ended without action.

Cleveland had staked his chances of a re-election
upon the success of his tariff policy, and the lament-

able failure of his party to support him marked both president and party for defeat. In other respects than the tariff the record of the administration was one of lights and shades. Long-standing complaints, especially outspoken in the central West, of the political influence of the railways and of gross discriminations in transportation rates between localities and shippers were met by the creation, in 1887, of an Interstate Commerce Commission charged with the general supervision of railway rates, and by the prohibition of numerous objectionable practices such as the lavish issuance of free transportation. A law punishing polygamy, aimed especially at the Mormon sect in Utah, and a law prohibiting for ten years the immigration of Chinese laborers, were also passed. The civil service policy of the president, on the other hand, was sharply attacked. Cleveland was pledged to support the new civil service reform, but his application of its principles was by no means nonpartisan and many of the Independents who had voted for him felt that they had been both deceived and betrayed. The veto of numerous private pension bills intended to benefit by special laws veterans of the Civil war, while a courageous effort to check a notorious abuse, aroused the unrestrained anger of the " old soldier " vote.

Cleveland, in short, was in the unfortunate position of being the titular head of a party which he could not control. Little as the Democratic leaders cared for him, however, it would have been party suicide not to have renominated him, and his popular vote in 1888 exceeded by 98,000 that of his Republican opponent, Benjamin Harrison of Indiana. The Democratic electoral vote, on the other hand, was only 168 while that of the Republicans was 233, and the Republicans were once more in control. The political overturn extended to Congress as well as to the presidency, both Senate and House being now Republican. In the enthusiasm of victory small attention was paid to the significant fact that the Prohibition party had increased its popular vote by nearly a hundred thousand and that a new United Labor party had polled more than 148,000 votes.

The Republican leaders in Congress immediately turned their attention to the tariff. It was realized that the duties must be revised and the accumulation of a surplus revenue stopped, but the Republicans chose to interpret the election of 1888 as a national endorsement of the protective system and a condemnation of what was misleadingly called free trade. Under the leadership of William McKinley, a member of the House of Representatives from Ohio, a tariff bill was accordingly prepared and in October, 1890, became law. The McKinley tariff marked a distinct advance over all previous tariffs in its scientific adjustment of duties with a view to protecting American industry against foreign competition. A considerable body of Republican opinion, however, of which Blaine, who had been appointed secretary of state under Harrison, was the mouthpiece, objected that the new tariff, while it might effectually exclude foreign goods and stimulate American manufactures, would not open any foreign markets to American agricultural staples, and that a policy of reciprocity under which the duties might be reduced in return for tariff concessions abroad ought to be included. Provision was accordingly made for the negotiation of reciprocity treaties, and a considerable number of such agreements were presently concluded under Blaine's direction. The interest in reciprocity, however, was of short duration and the results of the policy were not important, and in the course of a few years treaties and policy alike disappeared.

The passage in 1890 of the Sherman anti-trust act prohibiting trusts or combinations in restraint of trade or commerce was a serious attempt to curb the industrial and commercial trusts which had been formed by the hundred during the previous decade; and the repeal of the Bland-Allison act of 1878 with its compulsory coinage of standard silver dollars, and the substitution of the Sherman act under which silver purchases, while still compulsory to the amount of 4,500,000 ounces per month, were to be represented in part by the issuance of silver certificates, was a step away from a bimetallic standard for the national coinage. But the McKinley tariff, the repeal of the Bland-Allison act, and the passage of a dependent pension law which nearly doubled the number of federal pensioners was too great a load for the Republicans to carry, and in the congressional elections of

1890 they met catastrophe. A Republican majority of eight in the fifty-first Congress (1889–1891) gave way to a Democratic majority of 147 in the fifty-second Congress (1891–1893), and the Republican majority in the Senate was also reduced. It was the worst defeat that any American party had ever sustained. The predominant sentiment of the country undoubtedly favored a policy of protection, but the demand for a tariff which should be framed primarily for revenue rather than for protection, and whose protective character, in consequence, should be incidental rather than deliberate had for a long time been growing apace; and the wide popular conviction that the elaborate and complicated McKinley tariff not only gave unnecessary and extravagant protection to certain industries which possessed large political influence and made substantial contributions to campaign funds, but also increased the cost of living more than it increased wages or opportunities for industrial employment, reacted upon the Congress which had supported the measure. Foreign immigration, amounting on the average in the decade from 1880 to 1890 to half a million immigrants a year, had enabled many protected employers to replace native-born workers with low-paid foreign labor, and resentment was easily stirred up against a tariff policy which, it was widely believed, benefited employers and investors at the expense of the living standards of wage earners.

The multiplication of so-called third parties was

symptomatic not only of the increasing dissatisfaction with Republican policy and Democratic inefficiency, but also of the development of issues with which neither of the two great parties seemed able or willing to deal. None of the third parties which had appeared since the Civil War had been able to win any electoral votes except in 1872, but the popular vote of these dissenting groups was of some importance in critical States and an appreciable number of third party candidates had from time to time been elected to seats in the Senate and House of Representatives. The Independent Republican movement of the seventies had been in fact a spasm of liberalism within the Republican party, and most of the Independents who had supported Cleveland in 1884 had returned to the Republican fold by 1888. In each of the two leading parties, however, was to be found a growing body of thoughtful voters who felt no invincible attachment to any party and who cast their ballots for Republican, Democratic, or third party candidates according as the candidates or policies of one party or the other seemed to them most worthy of support; and while the hold of the great historical parties was strong and Republicans and Democrats were born whereas independents and liberals were made, the disintegrating work of dissent continued.

Of the third party movements that had yet appeared the most formidable was that of the People's or Populist party. In part an outgrowth of the grange movement among the farmers of the central

West and inheriting also some of the financial tenets of Greenbackism, Populism represented a new demand for federal aid to agriculture, federal regulation of railway rates and service, and " cheap " money based upon government credit rather than upon gold. The apparent disposition of the Republicans to adhere to the gold standard made the Populists fervent advocates of the silver dollar, and a demand for the free and unlimited coinage of silver became also an important element in the party creed. In the election of 1892, the first presidential election in which the new party appeared, the Populist candidate, James B. Weaver of Iowa, polled over a million votes and secured twenty-two electoral votes, all of the latter in the West. The election, however, went to the Democrats, who had again nominated Cleveland, but the popular vote showed that the People's Party support had been drawn largely from the Republicans and Independents. It had been the hope of political liberalism to hold the balance of power even though it could not elect a president or capture either house of Congress, but the long-established precedent of two parties dividing between them all but an insignificant fraction of the popular vote seemed at last upon the point of being broken, not by the efforts of those who called themselves Independents but by the sudden rise of a veritable new party with its stronghold in the West.

Cleveland was even less than formerly the master of his party, and his second administration encountered

strong Democratic opposition in Congress at the same
time that events were discrediting both the president
and the party in the country.  The Wilson tariff bill,
a Democratic measure in its origin, was so changed
in the course of its passage through Congress that
Cleveland declined to approve it and allowed the bill
to become a law without his signature.  An income
tax provision which the law embodied was presently
adjudged unconstitutional by the Supreme Court, and
it was not until 1913 that the adoption of the Sixteenth Amendment made the imposition of a federal
income tax possible.  A treaty for the annexation of
the Hawaiian islands, negotiated under the Harrison
administration, was withdrawn from the Senate by
the president because of charges that Hawaii had been
coerced, and the annexation of the islands was not
finally achieved until 1897.  A severe financial crisis
in 1893, followed by a long period of business depression, called attention sharply to the dangerous condition of the treasury gold reserve.  Silver certificates
issued against the silver purchased under the Sherman
law were used to withdraw gold from the treasury,
and repeated sales of bonds failed to maintain the
gold reserve at the one hundred million dollars which
by custom had been regarded as the minimum of
safety.  In February, 1894, a bill for the further
coinage of silver failed only through the president's
veto, and in 1896 a bill for the free coinage of silver
passed the Senate but was fortunately rejected by
the House.  The one bright spot so far as Cleveland's

personal popularity was concerned was his vigorous intervention in a boundary dispute in which Great Britain and Venezuela were involved, and his successful though brusque insistence that the question should be referred to arbitration.

The presidential campaign of 1896 revolved about a single issue, that of the free coinage of silver at the ratio of sixteen to one for gold. The Democratic national convention, carried off its feet by a brilliant speech of William J. Bryan, a delegate from Nebraska, adopted a free silver platform and made Mr. Bryan the party nominee; and as Mr. Bryan received also the Populist party nomination the free silver forces seemed for the moment able to sweep the country. The Republicans, opposed to free coinage but unwilling to come out for the gold standard without equivocation because of the uncertain strength of the free silver movement, put their trust in McKinley, whose record on the tariff had made him the leading spokesman of the protected interests and whose financial views were regarded as safe. The campaign was one of popular economic education, and every phase of the intricate and technical subject of coinage and money values was eagerly and voluminously discussed. The resounding victory of the Republicans ended the importance of silver and free coinage as national issues. A popular plurality of more than six hundred thousand for McKinley was matched by an electoral vote of 271 in comparison with 178 votes given for Mr. Bryan, and the business interests of the country took new courage with the realization that a threatened financial calamity had been averted.

There was scanty time for rejoicing over the past, however, for a future of unprecedented greatness was already dawning. The political situation in Cuba had for years been an occasion of anxiety and irritation to the United States. The Spanish colonial administration had been unable to suppress successive revolts which its own corruption and inefficiency had provoked, a war for independence which had begun in 1895 was still going on, and the island itself was being devastated. The natural American sympathy for a people that was oppressed was crossed by the popular feeling that Cuba belonged geographically to the United States and that possession of the island would add to the safety of Florida and the gulf coast States in the event of war, but there can be no question that humanitarian considerations far outweighed any popular desire in the United States for annexation.

The harsh measures, increasing in severity, which were resorted to by the Spanish authorities for the subjugation of Cuba excited general indignation in the United States, but the protests of the American government, although politely received, in the main went unheeded. Fuel was added to the flame when, on February 15, 1898, the American battleship " Maine " was destroyed by an explosion in the harbor of Havana. McKinley was patient but firm, and at the last moment, after a prolonged diplomatic correspondence, the reforms which he had demanded out of regard to American interests and safety as well as out of concern for the welfare of the Cuban people were in terms conceded. But Spanish evasion and delay had destroyed confidence in the good faith of the Spanish government, the country was in a mood for war, and on April 21 war with Spain was declared. The American army was scandalously unprepared, but Spanish resistance was hopeless, and with the battles of San Juan and El Caney and the destruction of a Spanish squadron at Santiago in July the fighting was over and Spain sued for peace. An American squadron under Commodore Dewey, which had been obliged to leave Hongkong because of British neutrality, had in the meantime taken Manila. Preliminaries of peace were signed on August 12, and on December 10 the treaty of Paris recognized the independence of Cuba and transferred to the United States Porto Rico, the Philippine archipelago, and a number of small islands in the Pacific. The United States paid to Spain $20,000,000 but the treaty carefully refrained from making the payment a return for the cession of territory.

The rapidity with which the international stage setting had been shifted was startling. The war had hardly begun when it was over. Within a few months the time-honored American policy of non-interference with the affairs of European governments had been thrown to the winds, and Spain had not only been ordered to withdraw from Cuba but the colonial possessions of Spain in the Pacific, none of which had been in any way concerned in the Cuban dispute, had been seized and their cession to the United States exacted.  With electrifying suddenness and without premeditation America had become a world power, and the old issues which had divided parties and threatened to create a new sectionalism faded into insignificance before the new vision of world responsibilities and world prestige.  The Monroe doctrine and historical isolation still remained to trouble the minds of purists, but with the overwhelming mass of the American people the day of nationalistic contentment passed when the Spanish possessions in the Pacific were surrendered, and an unwonted imperial spirit began to look out upon the world.

# CHAPTER X

## AMERICA AND A NEW WORLD

THE acquisition of the Philippines was not the first appearance of the United States as a Pacific power. The purchase of Alaska had given the United States a longer coast line on the Pacific than any other country possessed, and San Francisco bay and Puget sound afforded superb facilities for commerce with Asia. As far back as 1854 Commodore Perry had opened the door to commercial intercourse with Japan, and while the immigration of Chinese laborers had been prohibited as a concession to white labor in California, political relations with both China and Japan continued to be friendly. By the Berlin treaty of 1890 the United States had shared with Germany and Great Britain a protectorate over the Samoan islands, and when in 1900 the triple agreement was terminated the island of Tutuila with its important harbor of Pago-Pago passed to the United States. A sharp controversy with Great Britain over the seal fisheries in Bering sea had been settled by arbitration in 1893 favorably to the United States. The annexation of Hawaii in 1897 gave the United States a coaling and naval station in the strategic centre of the north Pacific. The conquest of the Philippines, accordingly, was geographically only the further extension of American control in an ocean where the United States had long been firmly established.

It was inevitable that the territorial results and implications of the war with Spain, coming as they did at a time when party dissent and independent voting were manifesting themselves in all parts of the country, should encounter opposition in quarters where colonies and dependencies were regarded as little more than areas for economic exploitation and political oppression. Shortly after the preliminaries of peace with Spain were signed a vigorous anti-imperialist agitation, chiefly supported in New England and Illinois, was organized to oppose the retention of the Philippines. The seizure of an archipelago of some two thousand islands in the remote south Pacific because of Spanish misconduct in Cuba was denounced as an act of wanton spoilation, and the policy of holding the islands as a dependency was declared to be contrary to the spirit of American institutions, a violation of the Constitution, and a dangerous infraction of the Monroe doctrine. When, in spite of the opposition, the treaty of Paris was ratified the anti-imperialists continued to insist that the people of the Philippines, who had organized a revolutionary government which was in control of most of the archipelago except Manila, Cavite, and a few other points, were entitled to their independence, and that the United States ought to announce its purpose to go no further than to aid in the establishment of a permanent government and protect the islands against foreign interference. The discussion of imperial and colonial problems which went on rivalled the days of the free silver movement in its educational character, but the anti-imperialist agitation attracted neither a considerable nor an important following and McKinley refused to turn from his course. The military conquest of the Philippines was systematically pushed, and the capture of Aguinaldo, the Filipino leader, early in 1901 virtually ended the rebellion. The next year a temporary civil administration which had been set up was replaced by a government under a commission some of whose members were Filipinos, and under this commission government the Philippines continued until 1916, when the present form of representative government was established. The provisions of the federal Constitution were not fully extended to the islands, however, because of racial and other conditions, and the inhabitants are " citizens of the Philippine islands " rather than, in the usual sense, citizens of the United States. The settlement never gave satisfaction to those who continued to share the early anti-imperialist views of national policy, and the demand for political independence has been increasingly urged by the Filipinos themselves.

The United States had pledged itself to give independence to Cuba, and with the inauguration of a Cuban republic in 1902 the American troops were withdrawn. A virtual protectorate, however, continued to be exercised over the island and its affairs, and intervention has several times been deemed necessary to restore order or settle election troubles. Porto Rico, which was included in the Spanish cession, received a provisional government which was replaced by a permanent government only in 1917.

Thanks to departmental reforms and a programme of naval construction initiated under the second Cleveland administration and continued under McKinley the war found the American navy ready, but the unpreparedness of the army, political influence in appointments and promotions, and grave scandals which developed in connection with the supply of food and clothing for the troops, called forth a storm of popular criticism to which no effective rejoinder could be made. But the robe of victory and world power went far to cover weaknesses and defects, and the election of 1900 was a complete indorsement of McKinley and his policies. Both the popular and the electoral vote showed a large increase over 1896, and the Republican control of both branches of Congress was unshaken. The enactment of a law definitively establishing the gold standard had eliminated the currency issue from politics, and the Democrats, who again nominated Mr. Bryan, had nothing to offer that the country preferred to the Republican programme. But the imperial work which McKinley had seen begun he was not long to oversee. On September 6, 1901, the president was shot while attending an exposition at Buffalo, and on the fourteenth died. The public mourning for his death recalled the scenes which had followed the assassination of Lincoln, and enemies and friends joined in tributes to a president under whom the nation had seen new visions of power and taken up new and weighty responsibilities.

No personal contrast could well have been greater than that which McKinley and the vice-president, Theodore Roosevelt of New York, presented. McKinley, although deeply versed in the economics of tariff-making, was not in other respects a man of marked intellectual or social interests, and a simple but somewhat old-fashioned dignity which attached to him kept him from emotional enthusiasm or bold outspokenness either in public or in private. The temper of the reformer was alien to him, and the great steps of his administration, so far as they were within his control, were taken only after reflection and always with an obvious regard to their party bearing. He was, in short, a high-minded and consummate politician whom great events had elevated to statesmanship. Roosevelt, on the other hand, although by birth and education a product of aristocratic circles in New York and Massachusetts, had early imbibed to the full the unconventional and aggressive spirit of the far West, and he retained throughout the larger part of his nearly eight years of office the devoted regard of a region whose history and ways he knew and whose temper he loved. His first irruption into politics as a member of the New York assembly had been in the rôle of a reformer, and his subsequent career as a police commissioner in the city of New York, chairman of the federal Civil Service Commission, assistant secretary of the navy, commander of a troop of Rough Riders in the war with Spain, and governor of New York had marked him as a man of outspoken independence and determined enmity to inefficiency and political corruption. A boundless physical energy and love of sports endeared him to young men, while a genuine concern for everyday human welfare and a veritable passion for social justice made him the ardent champion of an endless variety of good causes. No president with such encyclopædic interests or such phenomenal energy had ever filled the executive office, and the Republican leaders who had sought to curb his growing popularity with the masses by relegating him to the unimportant place of vice-president looked forward with apprehension to the years in which he should now be the nation's head.

It was Roosevelt's fortune to succeed to the presidency just at a time when, the responsibilities of colonial power having been accepted, concern for social and economic reform had taken hold of the national mind and was beginning to trouble the national conscience. In place of the constitutional and sectional issues which for generations had predominated in American politics, popular interest was turning to the more immediate and vital questions of trusts, strikes and labor disturbances, foreign immigration, wages and working conditions in factories and mines, and the conduct of business generally. There was a widespread feeling that social and economic conditions in the United States were acutely in need of betterment, that the States were not strong enough to remedy abuses even if they were disposed to make the effort, and that only the power and resources of the federal government could avail to cope with a situation in which vast aggregations of capital acting without regard to State lines seemed to dominate the life of the people as a whole and to threaten the independence of government itself.

Roosevelt's primary sympathies were with causes in which the element of moral appeal was strong, and he was a masterful politician as well as a reformer. He was fully aware that he had not been the choice of his party for president, and the circumstances under which he took office as well as sound political wisdom dictated the carrying on, for the time being at least, of the policies for which McKinley and the Republican party had stood. Until the latter part of his first term as president, accordingly, his course was somewhat restrained. But his overwhelming election to succeed himself in 1904 left him free to follow his bent, and the amazing energy with which he threw himself into the fight against abuses has no parallel in American annals. A rapid succession of messages and addresses, eagerly read by all classes and acclaimed by the people as an inspiring gospel of practical social righteousness, set forth in vigorous and epigrammatic language the evils of " predatory wealth," pleaded the cause of labor and the virtues of an ennobling citizenship, and called for reforms as bewildering in number and variety as they were far-reaching in scope. The tone was often that of the preacher and the concrete results were disappointing, but when powerful trusts were haled into court and " malefactors of great wealth " were pilloried before the country, when a great coal strike was settled through a federal commission which the president had appointed and pure food laws put the shocking practices of certain great food industries under the ban, and when subjects as far removed from ordinary politics as race suicide, college athletics, and reformed spelling came within the president's ken, no one could fail to see that executive influence had taken a new extension, and that even if less was accomplished than was proposed the new vantage ground of presidential power would never be relinquished.

Yet the limitations of Roosevelt were as striking as his powers. With all his hatred of injustice and eagerness for reform his temper was emotional and moralistic rather than positive and constructive. His political philosophy savored at times of the school to which truth is that aspect of a subject which is most vividly perceived, and the fact that he was more often than not on the right side of the economic and social issues in which he interested himself did not make his reasoning always profound, nor did it prevent him from neglecting other matters regarding which there was loud complaint or from acting on occasion in a high-handed fashion hardly susceptible of moral defence. He manifested no special interest in the tariff question, for example, notwithstanding that the Dingley tariff of 1897, imposing still higher protective duties than those of 1890, was denounced by tariff reformers as gross favoritism to the protected industries and an impediment to American business and foreign trade. The war with Spain made inevitable the construction of the Panama canal by the United States and its control as an American waterway, and in November, 1903, the United States acquired by agreement with Panama a perpetual right to the occupancy and use of a canal zone across the isthmus; but when a cession of the zone in full sovereignty could not be obtained by diplomacy a revolution was stirred up with the knowledge of the president, American armed forces intervened, and the desired treaty of cession was extorted. Not until 1921 was the wrong done to Colombia repaired by an agreement to pay for the sovereignty which had been ceded.

The wholesale attacks which Roosevelt made upon abuses of all kinds, joined to the forcible language in which his allegations and proposals were often couched, caused him to be widely regarded in business circles as a dangerous radical of socialistic views. The characterization was only in very small degree merited. Roosevelt was throughout the larger part of his public life a partisan Republican, and the reform which he labored strenuously to obtain was reform within and through the Republican party. He had no sympathy with socialism, and the only political activity of organized labor which for a long time he was able to approve was that which kept within the established party lines. Only when he became convinced that reform through the agency of the Republican party was not to be hoped for and that the party organization no longer represented the progressive sentiment of the country did he abandon his lifelong associations.

Roosevelt might well have been pardoned if, as he retired from office, he believed that he could before long successfully lead a great movement of revolt, for he had become, next perhaps to the emperor of Germany, the most conspicuous and most talked-of political figure in the world. His popular plurality of over two and a half million votes in 1904 was four times as great as the plurality of McKinley in 1900, and although by 1908 his popularity had waned the magnetism of his personality was still an immense political force. He had intervened with a tender of good offices in the Russo-Japanese war and in September, 1905, had had the satisfaction of seeing the war ended by a treaty signed at Portsmouth, New Hampshire. In 1906 he intervened by force in Cuba and established a provisional government, and in 1907 concluded a treaty with Santo Domingo by which the customs administration and the debt of the country were taken under American control. The glamour of his name enhanced respect for the United

States in every quarter of the globe, and his books stood high in the list of " best sellers." No nation except France had ever produced so extraordinary a leader of men, and the bitterest enemies of the American Napoleon could not but admire even while they feared.

Roosevelt had never been bound by precedents or restrained by dread of inconsistency, and he would apparently have been glad to hold the presidential office for a third term. The suggestion met with general disfavor, however, and in 1908 his influence secured the Republican nomination for William H. Taft, who had been governor of the Philippines and later secretary of war. Mr. Bryan, again the Democratic candidate, was still formidable and the popular plurality for Mr. Taft was only about one-half that which Roosevelt had received in the memorable election of 1904, but the party victory was nevertheless emphatic.

The inevitable reaction against the Roosevelt policies, however, and even more against the Roosevelt methods was flowing strongly. The country was tired of exhortation. " Big business," which for a time had walked warily, was recovering its courage, and the convictions of trusts and other offenders were less numerous than the number of prosecutions had threatened. The Republican majority in the House of Representatives had declined since 1904, and in the congressional elections of 1910 Democratic control of the House was re-established with a strong

party majority.  Oklahoma, admitted as a State in
1907, was Democratic, and the two remaining Territories of New Mexico and Arizona were in Democratic hands.  Throughout the country, but particularly in the West and on the Pacific coast, a so-called
Progressive movement was disintegrating the Republican party and vigorously fighting the old party
leadership, and an aggressive group .of " insurgent "
senators and representatives aided the movement in
Congress.  Of the new Progressive movement Roosevelt presently became the leader, and his desertion
of the president whom his influence had placed in
office created a breach between the two men which,
if it did not add to Mr. Taft's political strength, increased distrust of Roosevelt's political sincerity.  In
the cities and industrial centres and to a significant
extent in intellectual circles radical political doctrines
were spreading, and the Socialist party, which had
polled more than a quarter of a million votes in
1908, was preparing to make a great fight for its
popular candidate, Eugene V. Debs, in 1912.  The
submission to the States in May, 1912, of a Seventeenth Amendment of the Constitution, providing for
the election of United States senators by popular vote,
was a step in the direction of increased popular control of Congress, but the opposition was strong, and
although in 1913 the amendment was adopted twelve
States failed to ratify it.

Mr. Taft had none of the crusading zeal which
animated Roosevelt, and his general sympathy with

the old school Republicanism identified him in the popular mind with the party machine against which the Progressive movement was openly arrayed. A stronger man than he, however, would have had difficulty, even without Roosevelt's opposition, in leading the Republicans to victory in 1912, for the country was yielding to the spell of another great personality, that of Woodrow Wilson, Democratic governor of New Jersey. Mr. Wilson's approach to the presidency was unique. By birth a Virginian and by early professional training a lawyer, he had been for the larger part of his life a college professor, had passed from a professorship to the presidency of Princeton University, and from the latter office had entered State politics as a Democrat. Before his political career began he had won wide repute as a brilliant writer and able speaker, and his governorship of New Jersey had revealed him to the country as a masterful politician and a determined foe of political corruption. Cold and reserved, save to his few intimate friends, where Roosevelt was warm and ebullient, and with his intellectual interests centered in politics, his earnest and rhetorically vivid appeals for the recognition of democratic principles in the conduct of national affairs had caught the imagination of liberals everywhere; and while it seemed unlikely that he could draw to his support such of the Progressives as felt for Roosevelt a strong personal devotion, no other Democrat was so well fitted to strengthen the lines of the Democratic party or to profit by the schism in the Republican ranks.

The election of 1912, accordingly, saw three well-known candidates besides Mr. Debs in the field. The regular Republican candidate was Mr. Taft. The Progressives, repudiating his candidacy as representing most of the things to which they were opposed, held a separate convention and nominated Roosevelt, and the Democrats nominated Mr. Wilson. The popular vote for Mr. Wilson was considerably less than half of the total number of votes recorded, but the Democratic electoral vote was colossal. Of the 531 electoral votes Mr. Taft received only eight and Roosevelt eighty-eight; the remainder were given to Mr. Wilson. The admission of New Mexico and Arizona in 1912 had brought the number of States to forty-eight, and of these all but eight were in the Democratic column. Only Utah and Vermont voted for Mr. Taft, and only Pennsylvania, Michigan, Minnesota, South Dakota, Washington, and California voted for Roosevelt. The Progressive vote, drawn mainly from former Republicans, had given the election to the Democrats, and the popular support for Mr. Taft was less than that for either of the other two leading candidates. The Socialist party, although it polled over 900,000 votes, did not succeed in winning any electoral votes. The Democratic tide swept away the Republican majority in the Senate and both branches of Congress were strongly Democratic, although the Progressives won eighteen seats in the House of Representatives.

" This is not a day of triumph," declared Mr. Wilson as he closed his inaugural address, " it is a day of dedication. Here muster, not the forces of party, but the forces of humanity." The evils which he particularly singled out for remedy included " a tariff which cuts us off from our proper part in the commerce of the world, violates the just principles of taxation, and makes the government a facile instrument in the hands of private interests; a banking and currency system based upon the necessity of the government to sell its bonds fifty years ago and perfectly adapted to concentrating cash and restricting credits; an industrial system which, take it on all its sides, financial as well as administrative, holds capital in leading strings, restricts the liberties and limits the opportunities of labor, and exploits without renewing or conserving the natural resources of the country "; an unbusinesslike and unscientific agriculture bereft of suitable facilities of credit; " watercourses undeveloped, waste places unreclaimed, forests untended fast disappearing without plan or prospect of renewal, unregarded waste heaps at every mine "; and disregard of sanitary and pure food laws and of laws regulating the conditions of labor. No Roosevelt programme had been more sweeping, no Progressive demands were more radical.

So far as the president was concerned the execution of the new programme began at once. Congress was called to meet early instead of in December, and on April 8, 1913, Mr. Wilson, brushing aside the established precedent of more than a century, revived the practice of Washington and read his message in person to the two houses. The message itself was devoted to the tariff, and called for a thoroughgoing revision of the schedules in a way to " abolish everything that bears even the semblance of privilege or of any kind of artificial advantage," and the substitution of duties designed to encourage effective competition in business with the rest of the world. The Underwood tariff which was shortly enacted made drastic reductions in the rates which had been fixed by the Payne-Aldrich tariff of 1909, and the protection which it accorded was in general incidental to its revenue purpose.

Mr. Wilson's conception of federal powers was large, and had world affairs continued to run their normal course it is probable that the great movement of reform which Roosevelt had vitalized would have continued with equal, if less spectacular, energy under the new Democratic administration. The first six months of 1914 had scarcely passed, however, when questions of domestic policy were swept into the background by the bursting tempest of the great war. On June 28 the Archduke of Austria was assassinated at Sarajevo, and the long-smoldering rivalries and animosities of the European powers were soon aflame. A few weeks of negotiation and intrigue followed, then on August 1 Germany declared war upon Russia. Hardly had the news been printed when the German armies invaded Belgium and France, and the war which was eventually to involve Europe, Asia, Africa, and America was in full swing. The swift advance of the German forces threatened the obliteration of Belgium and France, and although Great Britain quickly threw its army and navy into the scale on the side of the invaded countries, there seemed small reason to hope that the desolating German rush which was already turning parts of France and Belgium into a desert could in the end be stayed.

The United States had no direct interest in the causes of the war, and its policy of neutrality was in accord with its tradition. But the position of the United States was difficult. Officially the government was neutral, but popular sympathy for Belgium and France was immediate and widespread and the action of Germany in deliberately provoking war was outspokenly condemned. On the question of American intervention, however, public opinion was divided, and it was not clear that Mr. Wilson would have had the country with him had he called early for active participation in the struggle. For more than two and a half years, accordingly, he waited for the logic of events to do their work. In February, 1915, Germany by proclamation established a war zone about the British Isles into which no neutral vessel might enter without being liable to seizure, but the protest of the United States against this interference with neutral rights brought only an unsatisfactory response, and the issue was complicated by a controversy with Great Britain over the use of the American

flag by British merchant vessels and by the refusal
of both Great Britain and France to relinquish the
right to seize neutral vessels carrying enemy goods.
The sinking of the transatlantic steamship "Lusitania"
on May 7 led only to a warning that further attacks
upon merchant vessels would be regarded by the
United States as " deliberately unfriendly." In September the recall of two German attachés who had
been guilty of political intrigue was requested and
before long the Austrian ambassador was dismissed,
but diplomatic relations with Germany and Austria
continued. In March, 1916, the sinking of the
steamer " Sussex " in the English Channel and the loss
of American citizens called out from Mr. Wilson
nothing stronger than a warning that a severance of
diplomatic relations was threatened. Not until February 3, 1917, were diplomatic relations with Germany broken off, only on April 6 did the United
States finally declare war, and the declaration of war
against Austria was postponed until December 7.

The long and irritating diplomatic correspondence
with Germany was viewed with increasing impatience
and hostility by the country and by Congress, and
the more because of public statements which led to
the suspicion that Mr. Wilson was either an invincible
pacifist or else a lukewarm friend of the allies. A
circular letter to the powers, for example, issued in
December, 1916, pointed out that the war aims of
each side, " as stated in general terms to their people
and to the world," were " virtually the same," and a

clear statement of the objects for which the parties were contending was invited. The statement, its qualifying phrase ignored, was bitterly assailed as putting the war aims of Germany and the allies on the same moral plane. The disposition to accept German assurances regarding the conduct of submarine warfare, and the insistence that the allies as well as Germany should respect American neutral rights, were hailed as evidence of sympathy for Germany and of an unwillingness to hold the Berlin government to account. Mr. Wilson stood his ground, however, until the American case was unassailable, and when on April 2, 1917, before a Congress which had met in extra session, he reviewed the course of the conflict and called for a declaration of war, his stern arraignment of the German government and his ringing assertion that " the world must be made safe for democracy " threw the nation into a delirium of praise, and from that moment until the war had ended the American people were as clay in his hands. He had waited for the psychological moment, and when the moment came he seized it with a master hand.

The stupendous energy with which the United States went into the war was an impressive example of what a great democracy could do once its enthusiasm was aroused and its course was clear. A draft law called for the registration of all men of military age, huge appropriations and loans hastened the training and equipment of troops and their dispatch over seas, and transportation, food supply and distribution, and war manufactures were taken under federal control. Enormous shipments of supplies for armies and civilians were poured into Europe, and loans aggregating more than ten billion dollars were advanced to the allied governments. Opposition to the war, both public and private, was ruthlessly suppressed, newspapers and mails passed under a censorship, enemy property was sequestrated, and German sympathizers and pacifists were effectually cowed. The stimulation of industry was unparalleled and wages, prices, and profits rose by leaps and bounds. The adherence of the United States to the allied cause made certain the defeat of Germany, and although none of the great battles of the war were won by American forces alone, it was the overwhelming aid of the United States which made possible the final victory.

In an address to the Senate on January 22, 1917, more than two months before the American declaration of war, Mr. Wilson, looking forward to the time when peace must be made, had declared that it must be a " peace without victory." The statement, although carefully explained and guarded in the address itself, gave deep offence to the growing war sentiment of the country. A review of the president's war utterances, however, makes it clear that Mr. Wilson, while at no time fundamentally sympathetic with Germany but rather the reverse, nevertheless feared that the allies, if victorious at arms, might impose upon Germany a peace so severe as to constitute in itself a provocation to further war, and he accordingly set himself to elaborate the bases of a peace which to him seemed just. His second inaugural address in March, 1917, outlined the principles which such a peace should embody, and in January, 1918, in an address to Congress, he propounded fourteen points as a scheme of political and territorial settlement. The proposals were not new, for all of them had been advanced at one time or another in the speeches or notes of allied statesmen, but Mr. Wilson brought them together and gave them the status of a programme. One of the fourteen points called for the creation of a league of nations, and to the establishment of such a league as the only security against war Mr. Wilson thenceforth devoted himself. The fourteen points, which contained no reference to reparations or indemnities, were accepted by Germany, practically accepted by Great Britain, acclaimed with approval by some of the lesser European States and by racial minority groups which hoped for independent recognition, and were not rejected by France.

On November 11, 1918, the armistice was signed, and on December 2, in his address to Congress, Mr. Wilson announced his intention of going to Paris and of personally taking part in the work of the peace conference. The reception which was accorded to him in Europe was wholly extraordinary. The high ethical tone of his writings and state papers with their brilliant pleas for equality and fraternity among nations, his winning appeals for a moral treatment of all political questions, the sharp distinction which he had drawn between the German people and the German imperial government in apportioning responsibility for the war, his demand for a just peace and for the recognition of the right of every people to live under a government of its own choosing, and the practical programme of the fourteen points of which he was popularly regarded as the sole author, all combined to make him the idol of the masses, the hope of every unfree or oppressed minority, and the embodiment of the democratic ideals which the forthcoming settlement was to consecrate. Back of the American president was the American nation whose boundless resources, thrown into the war only after every effort to maintain neutrality had failed, had determined the outcome of the struggle, but which nevertheless, alone among the powers that would meet at the peace table, asked for itself neither indemnities nor territory nor political advantage of any kind. If peace could be made on the lines which Mr. Wilson had drawn, and American help could be continued in the great task of social and political reconstruction, the name of the president and of the nation which he represented would be held in enduring and untarnished honor by the peoples of the world.

It was not so to be. Mr. Wilson had called for freedom of the seas alike in peace and in war, but

the demand was surrendered before the peace negotiations were begun.  He had denounced the evils of
secret diplomacy and called for " open covenants of
peace openly arrived at," but the peace of Versailles
was framed in secret and the history of the proceedings is not yet fully known.  He had championed the
rights of peoples to self-determination, but few of
the smaller nationalities whose immediate destinies
the peace conference controlled were consulted save
as a matter of form, and minority groups were refused
a hearing.  He had insisted that in disposing of
colonies the wishes of the inhabitants as well as those
of the controlling government should be taken into
the account, but the German colonies were apportioned without even a pretence of consulting the
colonial populations.  The fourteen points had called
for the removal of economic barriers between nations
and the establishment of an equality of trade conditions, but no steps in that direction were taken by
the Paris negotiators.

Mr. Wilson did not attempt to defend himself
against the torrent of criticism which his course at
Paris unloosed, and one may not venture to say with
positiveness why so much of his announced programme was apparently so easily abandoned.  There
is reason for thinking, however, that the programme
of the fourteen points was not so much a minimum
upon which Mr. Wilson intended to insist as a maximum which he would be glad to obtain, that the
complicated economic adjustments which a return

to peace involved were regarded by him as matters for later rather than immediate settlement, and that he looked to the League of Nations, the creation of which outweighed in his thought all other considerations, to adjust the conflicts which the practical application of the peace terms might develop. The territorial dispositions which were made conformed in general to his original proposals, and with these and the League of Nations assured the remainder of his programme was apparently looked upon as incidental.

The treaty of Versailles, the first of the peace treaties which the Paris conference concluded, was signed on June 28, 1919. Although hundreds of printed copies of the treaty had been privately circulated at Paris and unofficial texts were promptly published, Mr. Wilson refused to make public the text of the treaty in the United States or to lay before the Senate the records of the negotiations, but demanded the acceptance of the treaty as it stood. The echoes of the long and heated controversy which ensued have not yet died away. The objections of the Senate, accentuated by resentment at the treatment which it had received, centered in Article X of the covenant of the League of Nations, which was interpreted as binding the United States to support, if necessary by force, the territorial arrangements which the treaty embodied, even though the United States had itself no direct or obvious interest in the matter in dispute; and while the majority opinion of the country apparently favored the acceptance of the treaty as an international settlement to which the United States had contributed and in whose enforcement it was honorably bound to aid, the prospect of long-continued involvement in European political arrangements was nevertheless viewed with apprehension. Mr. Wilson, however, refused to assent to any material modification of Article X, and on November 19 the treaty was rejected by the Senate. The rejection was not final and consideration of the treaty was presently resumed, but on March 19, 1920, ratification was again refused.

Mr. Wilson had for some months been suffering from a physical breakdown to which his labors in behalf of the treaty had contributed, and for most of the period during which the controversy in the Senate was raging he was practically incapacitated. It was a melancholy close of a phenomenal career, for in addition to bodily suffering he had seen his world popularity fade and his motives and conduct had been widely assailed, but he bore reproaches and attacks in silence and left to time the justification or condemnation of his course. The congressional elections of 1916 had broken the Democratic control of the House of Representatives, and in 1918 the Republicans were again in a majority in both houses. There was no strong Democratic candidate with whom to replace Mr. Wilson in 1920, and the Republican nominee, Senator Warren G. Harding of Ohio, won an overwhelming victory. A Nineteenth Amendment to the Constitution opening the suffrage to women had been adopted in time to be availed of in the election, and the popular vote for all the presidential candidates reached the enormous total of more than 26,780,000, or about one-fourth of the aggregate population of the country.

The position of the United States toward Europe, however, was anomalous. So far as American ratification was concerned the treaty of Versailles was dead, but the United States was still technically at war with Germany and Austria, American relations with Germany were still governed by the armistice terms of November, 1918, and the peace treaty with Austria which American representatives had signed at Paris had not been presented to the Senate. The League of Nations had been created and Mr. Wilson had issued the call for the first meeting, but the United States was not a member and nowhere in the country was interest in the League strong. A body of American troops continued to be maintained in the occupied part of Germany, and an unofficial American representative sat with the international commission which had been established at Paris to deal with the question of reparations, but the United States was not a signatory party to the peace nor in any way legally responsible for its enforcement. There was a general feeling that a separate peace should be concluded with Germany and Austria which would end the state of war, and that the United States was entitled to claim the advantages which it would have had if the allied treaties with those powers had been ratified, and in October, 1921, peace was made upon that basis. The equivocal position of the United States did not wholly disappear, however, for American troops remained on the Rhine and the reparations commission continued to have an unofficial American member.

The enthusiasm of war had already given way to pronounced reaction among all classes, and reaction brought hesitation and distrust. American public opinion, convinced that European governments and especially the government of France were militaristic, and that swollen military and naval budgets, ill-adjusted taxation, and excessive issues of depreciated paper money were largely responsible for the slow economic recovery of Europe, veered more and more toward the traditional attitude of aloofness from European affairs; and although the Harding administration convened a disarmament conference at Washington in November, 1921, and arranged with Great Britain, France, Italy, and Japan a programme for the limitation of naval construction, it declined to take part in successive international conferences which were held in Europe to consider the problems which peace and reconstruction had raised. The demobilization of American war industry, the treatment of serious questions of disordered business and widespread unemployment, and the safeguarding of American financial interests abroad called for attention such as in the last years of Mr. Wilson's administration they had not received, and for the moment Europe was left to settle its political and economic problems for itself.

Yet the obvious lessons of the great war had not been forgotten. The United States had played too large a part in the world struggle to remain permanently in isolation, and the moral values for which it had contended bound it in obligations which awaited only the favorable moment to be fulfilled. The problem which faced the United States was how the greatest, richest, best organized, and most powerful democracy in the world could preserve its historical independence of action and at the same time serve with all its force the cause of peace. Once that question could be answered the resources of the nation would again be at the service of mankind.

# CHAPTER XI

## POLITICS AND THE AMERICAN MIND

THE forces which through three centuries operated to produce an American social type were many and diverse. The English inheritance of language, law, custom, and intellectual habit, predominant from the beginning in most of the colonies and in New York and Pennsylvania after the first few years, afforded a primary foundation of the utmost importance, but the modifications which were worked by geographical remoteness, the conditions of life in a wilderness continent, and climatic contrasts between the different sections of the country were far-reaching. At no time were the American colonies a reproduction even on a lessened scale of the mother country. English political institutions were from the outset freely adapted to American needs, the religious controversies which racked England in the seventeenth century lost much of their bitterness when transferred over seas, and the daily life of the people was at once freer, healthier, and relatively more prosperous than that which seventeenth or eighteenth century England showed. The struggle for independence, the erection of a novel form of federal government, the romantic conquest of the West and progressive absorption of foreign territory, the effort to control slavery and preserve the Union, the assimilation of a vast and heterogeneous European population, and the phenomenal growth of agriculture, manufactures, mining, and commerce on a continental scale all worked to develop an American character different from any that the old world had produced. The resulting product, too, was composite rather than cosmopolitan, for the various elements were blended, not merely assembled and associated.

Neither in origin nor in circumstances, however, were the English plantings much alike, and the early years of colonization seemed to promise the creation of types rather than a type. The staunch and rigid Puritanism which long dominated Massachusetts and Connecticut gave to the political and social life of those colonies a moral tinge which even today has not been wholly effaced, and Rhode Island still preserves marked traces of the extreme individualism which its dissenting founders cherished; but the Puritan spirit did not spread to other colonies, and sectarian discrimination remained with few exceptions a New England monopoly. New York and New Jersey, given from the start to commercialism and factional politics, had no marked interest in religious questions of any kind, and the tolerant Quakers of Pennsylvania found their peculiar tenets no bar to worldly success or political class control. In the South, on the other hand, where the religious intolerance and thrifty trading spirit of New England were disliked, the planter class, drawing its wealth from a staple agriculture whose products were marketed directly in England or on the continent, reproduced the easy-going but masterful characteristics of the English country gentlemen from whose loins many of them had sprung. Each section lived as suited its environment or its ambition, envious of nothing that the others possessed and stirred by no impulse to change the status in which circumstances and its own free choice had placed it. The union which came later was the fruit of outside happenings, not of inward discontent with lot or place.

Certain intellectual similarities, on the other hand, early developed notwithstanding the differences of physical environment. New England Puritanism, its intellectual interest long centered in theological speculation, produced a mental and moral habit which, if it long resisted the approaches of literature and robbed the lives of children and young people of joy, nevertheless planted a school in every town, founded the colleges of Harvard and Yale, made the weekly sermon an intellectual performance, and enforced public service as a moral and legal obligation. The generation and a half of Dutch proprietorship in New York bore no important intellectual fruit, and the first generation of English occupation was almost equally barren, but prosperous Pennsylvania, once the period of beginnings had been passed, turned with zest to the publication of books and pamphlets in German and English, the development of newspapers, and the establishment of institutions of learning, and before long New York was following in its wake. A seventeenth century Virginia governor could thank God, apparently in all sincerity, that there were no free schools in that colony, but the college of William and Mary had been established before the seventeenth century closed and the English universities and Inns of Court had a regular succession of South Carolinians among their students down to the Revolution.

The widespread interest in law which prevailed in all the colonies was a natural result of the long controversies over charter rights and royal or parliamentary interference which most of the colonies underwent. The political doctrines of State rights and strict construction which played so large a rôle in political discussion in the constitutional period trace back to the time when the colonies, each standing upon independent ground so far as connection with England went, sought to defend themselves against encroachment by appealing to the letter of their charters or by devising reasons for evading or ignoring the laws of parliament relating to colonial affairs. Physical remoteness and practical liberty gendered also freedom and independence of thought, and when by the beginning of the eighteenth century the old notions of the divine right of kings and the sin of resisting the crown gave way in England to the idea of government founded in popular consent as expressed through a representative parliament, the colonies saw in the new philosophy only a confirmation of principles for which in practice they had all along contended. At every point at which liberty was involved the constitutional thought of most colonial lawyers and of an influential minority of the people had far outrun the prevailing constitutional thought of England when the Revolution of 1775 came on, and the political doctrines of the Declaration of Independence, however much they owed to French political speculation, seemed to the average patriot only impressive statements of English political principles which to the colonists had long been self evident and unassailable.

Edmund Burke, turning with scorn in the House of Commons in 1775 to those who insisted that the rebellious colonies had grown through British nurture, declared that they had grown rather through neglect. The assertion was more than a forensic retort. At no time throughout the whole colonial period did the English government exert itself to develop the American colonies. The acts of navigation and trade, while indeed assuring to colonial vessels and colonial products a privileged market in England, were primarily designed to exploit colonial commerce for the benefit of British merchants and ship owners rather than to protect or encourage American industry of any kind. Substantial duties were from time to time imposed upon American commerce, the important tea trade of the East India Company was a monopoly to be avoided only by smuggling, the restriction of the trade in salt bore heavily upon the colonial fisheries, and in the eighteenth century the prohibition of American manufactures was begun. Not until the Seven Years' war was any considerable military or naval force sent to America, and at the close of the war the westward extension of settlement was barred by a royal proclamation forbidding land grants in the Ohio valley. For more than a hundred years the American colonies were left practically to themselves to clear the forests, develop agriculture, fisheries, and commerce, build roads and bridges, establish schools, fight the Indians and the French, and deal with the Negro slaves whom the home government urged upon them.

Yet the colonies might well have been grateful for neglect, for neglect was building better than either they or England knew. The very absence of paternalism favored the development of qualities which were to become of the warp and woof of American character. Initiative, industry, thrift, and inventive genius, perseverance in the face of great natural obstacles, pride in labor and achievement rather than in birth or social place, respect for intellectual attainment in leaders, individual education and skill in the worker, equality of opportunity for all who would work, and contempt for mere precedent as such, all these are qualities which only a people thrown upon its own resources and compelled to make its way by its own effort ever developes on a large scale, and all were recognized American traits when revolution and national independence put them to the test. Equally characteristic in the field of politics was the pervading sense of justice and fair play and a willingness to cut with clean, swift strokes any knot which after long effort refused to be untied.

The generation which carried the colonies through revolution to independence brought to its task an intellectual and moral equipment of a high order, exceptionally high when the isolation of America from general world interests is recalled. The crude barrenness of the days of beginnings had disappeared. Illiteracy was as good as unknown, newspapers had multiplied in every colony, and books on serious subjects were in demand. The classical education of the colonial colleges bore comparison with that which the English public schools and universities afforded, acquaintance with English literature had taken the place of theological and devotional reading, and the political and legal writings of English jurists and publicists were well known. The state papers of the revolutionary period are admirable examples of literary style and logical presentation of arguments, and political oratory was everywhere esteemed. Ethically, too, the standard of social and public conduct was high. No one can read the history of the Revolution without being impressed by the self-restraint which the mass of the people exhibited under provocation, the constant appeal to the moral aspect of questions in controversy, and the comparative absence of lawless excess and personal self-seeking. The persecution of loyalists left no long memory of ill will, and friendly relations with Great Britain were resumed after the separation as soon as Great Britain itself was willing. A grave seriousness attended the proclamation of independence and the prosecution of the war, and the enthusiasm which followed the final victory was the tempered exultation of men who had solemnly essayed a great work and in faith and sacrifice had brought it to success. The struggle for nationality was no light-hearted adventure from which some measure of romantic distinction might be gained whether one lost or won, and shouts and cheers were less in evidence than prayers of thanksgiving when the prize was grasped.

Thereafter, whether the tide ebbed or flowed, the intellectual and moral life of the nation was inseparably bound up with politics: politics of leadership and parties, politics of territorial expansion and wilderness conquest, politics of States in conflict with the federal power, politics of slavery and disunion, politics of industry and economic strength. Naturally, the early stages saw more problems developed than were solved. The struggle for the adoption of the Constitution divided public opinion at the outset into two great camps, soon transformed into two national parties, and from that time onward the two-party system relegated all independent or third party movements to the background and magnified party regularity at the cost of independent political thinking. Only once in American history has the two-party system gone to pieces and only twice have third parties seriously affected a presidential election. The existence of a written Constitution over whose interpretation the two dominant parties differed radically emphasized the merely legal sides of public questions, turned whole masses of voters into amateur lawyers as a presidential election approached, subordinated the consideration of governmental policy to the narrower study of constitutional power, and encouraged technical procedure in the courts. Broadly or strictly interpreted, however, the " worship of the Constitution " which foreigners have often noted kept its hold, and few of the nineteen amendments that have been adopted have affected the foundation lines of the instrument.

How nationality was best to be developed and conserved, on the other hand, was a question in regard to which public opinion was long divided. A strong minority of the nation at all times and a substantial majority for considerable periods looked upon the growth of federal power as a dangerous centralization, and insisted that only by sedulously preserving the rights of the States could federal absolutism be averted. There can be little question but that State rights and strict construction, both as political theories and as party programmes, were a positive hindrance to the growth of a unified national spirit, and that the relegation of great questions of policy like internal improvements to the States, few of which pursued in such matters an enlightened policy and most of which had no policy at all, retarded both social and political progress; but with a Constitution to be obeyed and a federal system to be applied the controversy had to be fought out. The salvation of nationalism came with the opening of the West. Every western State was the direct creation of the federal government, a tangible and grateful embodiment of federal power set in the wilderness to possess the land; and while the bank controversy, the slavery issue, and nullification were every whit as vital to the West as to any other section, regard for the nation and its prestige overshadowed historical precedents and fine-spun constitutional distinctions and gave to the consideration of clearly national questions a distinctively national tone. The West had nothing to defend except its liberty of thought and conduct, no inherited local attachments which held its people from moving forward as the frontier pursued the sun, and liberty within the bonds of national allegiance and affection shackled neither its action nor its mind.

Nevertheless the United States long remained isolated and provincial. The political and social revolutions which swept over Europe in the eighteenth and nineteenth centuries had few marked repercussions in America. The French Revolution made no deep or lasting impression upon American political thought or social habit, partly no doubt because the United States had already put liberty into practice for itself; and the successes of Napoleon inspired in the American people neither fear nor imperial ambition. The conservative reaction against constitutional government which followed the final overthrow of Napoleon had no counterpart in the United States; the warning policy of the Monroe doctrine, so far as popular approval of the doctrine was concerned, voiced an instinctive dread of being disturbed rather than an informed and reasoned fear of political absolutism; and the liberal movements of 1830 and 1848 came and went with no discernible influence upon American politics.

There were reasons why the United States should have been so little moved. The study of modern languages did not begin to displace Greek and Latin in American colleges until after the Civil War, continental literature was little known save through fragmentary translation or occasional critical comment, and foreign travel was too difficult and costly to be widely indulged. A few feeble experiments in communism and co-operation were almost the only public evidences of interest in the theories and schemes of social reorganization which agitated western Europe after the Napoleonic wars, and the political exiles whom the reactionary policy of Metternich and his contemporaries sent to the United States found liberty and opportunity but not a following. It was long the fortune of the United States to receive European social impulses late, months or even years after the movements themselves had spent their initial force, and what was then left of novel thought or programme became the more readily dissipated in the great

American mass. That the result was loss of interest in what was being thought, said, and done in Europe is evident, but the loss was not wholly without compensation, for while intellectual aloofness aided the provincial trend the barriers of time and distance worked for American society more than one happy escape.

It was easier to let Europe go its way, moreover, because contact with European governments and individual Europeans had so often been unfriendly. The interference with American commerce prior to the war of 1812, the long controversies over the northeastern and northwestern boundaries, the neglect of France to pay long-standing claims until payment was energetically demanded, the strained relations with Great Britain over Oregon and the Canadian rebellion and with Russia over Alaska worked in practice to create distrust. The observations of European travellers were often unsympathetic and unintelligent, and although the typical Yankee or western Hoosier whose peculiarities diverted Europe was as infrequent in reality as was the noble savage of Cooper's novels, American temperament was sensitive and the fantastic picture gave pain.

The irritation at foreign criticism, always tending to degenerate into contempt for foreign opinion, was the greater because all the while settlement was growing and a nation was being built. The men and women who pushed the frontier westward, levelled the forests, broke the tough sod of the prairies, opened

roads, built homes, churches, and schools, set up town
and county governments, drafted State constitutions
and codes of law, established factories and mills, set
steamboats and barges afloat on the rivers and the
Great Lakes, founded banks and commercial houses,
and pledged their credit in aid of railways and canals,
were practical idealists with whom political opinion
and the gospel of work went hand in hand; and the
people of the older East, if their life because of age
was less romantic, were not less zealous for the greatness of the nation whose foundations they had laid.
The widespread support for a protective tariff policy
came naturally to a country whose physical resources
were immense but whose money capital for their
development was small, and the lucrative home
market which a rapidly growing population afforded
seemed only a proper reward for American investment.   To produce as much as possible at home and
buy as little as possible abroad, to give preference to
American ships in both domestic and foreign trade,
to pay wages commensurate with the standard of
living of the native born, and to use profits and surplus for the enlargement of industries rather than as
an endowment for leisurely living, became the national
policy; and although precious natural resources were
too often recklessly wasted and small economies were
often despised, the marvellous growth of wealth
through agriculture, manufactures, and trade nevertheless brought the dream of economic conquest to
realization.   It was a practical and immediate con-

ception of greatness because material opportunity abounded and the tangible prizes of success were large, but it was not a selfish ideal, for all who came were welcome to share.

The protracted and intense absorption of the people in the development of economic life goes far to explain the long-continued tolerance of slavery and the efforts to dispose of the slavery question by compromise. Few thoughtful persons outside of the slave-holding States had failed to perceive, long before the threat of secession became an open challenge, that the South was falling behind, that its intellectual growth had been stunted and its planter aristocracy hardened into a caste, and that its political power was being used for obstruction or sectional aggrandizement more than for the well-being of the nation as a whole. The exhilaration of every territorial expansion was appreciably chilled by the reflection that with each new annexation the old straw of the slavery issue must again be threshed. So long, however, as cotton continued to be produced in quantities sufficient for American and foreign demands moral repugnance to slavery was not strong enough to determine northern or western public opinion, for the northern cotton mills were prosperous, the export trade in cotton meant freights and profits for American-built ships, and a South which did not raise its own food was a near-by market for the agricultural products of the central West. Not until the Union was attacked did the rest of the country turn in all its strength upon the institution which had nourished sectionalism and bred secession, and the bitter intensity of the change of front was shown not only in the relentless prosecution of the Civil war and the extirpation of slavery as an institution, but even more in the drastic programme of reconstruction which the dominant Republican party ruthlessly enforced upon the beaten and prostrate South.

That the North and the West, once the unity of the nation was threatened, should launch themselves into the fight with something of the exaltation and intolerance of a crusader finds its explanation also in the forces of religious fervor and humanitarian interest which had long been stirring in northern and western society. The great religious revivals which for a generation before the Civil war repeatedly swept the central West raised whole communities to extraordinary emotional heights, magnified personal confession of sin and profession of faith as social virtues, and made the prevailing Protestantism an effective handmaid of reform. What Methodism and Presbyterianism achieved by sensational methods in the West, Unitarianism accomplished by quieter but more enduring intellectual agitation in New England. Throughout the country was to be seen a phenomenal multiplication of religious sects, often with peculiar tenets or practices, and interest in temperance and prison reform was for a time widespread. Women, although long politically subjected, set the moral tone of every northern community, and conventional standards of personal morals were prevailingly high. Immigrants from Europe were welcomed as to freedom's paradise provided they would work, and the marked emphasis upon party regularity in domestic politics was no bar to the admission of political exiles who fled from persecution at home. The organized hostility to foreigners and Catholics which for a few years thrust itself upon State and national politics was a localized episode due primarily to the economic menace of masses of ignorant immigrants and to the belief that the Catholic church was a political as well as a religious power, and before the Civil war the agitation had disappeared. Every northern and western State had a developed system of free public schools, sectarian colleges dotted the country, and State universities were being established. Against a region whose hard-working pursuit of material wealth was broadly crossed by religious, educational, and philanthropic aspiration the lance of slavery and disunion could be tilted only to be broken.

The nationalizing influence of the youthful literature which flowered rapidly after 1815 has also to be counted. Irving, although a large part of his life was spent abroad, added the "Sketch Book" to the world's classics, fixed for more than a century the popular conception of the social life of Dutch New York, and told in elaborate detail the story of Washington. The vivid imagination of Cooper idealized the Indian in contact with the whites, Longfellow softened and humanized the traits of the Pilgrim fathers and gave to the exiled Acadians of Nova Scotia a pathetic immortality, and Hawthorne flashed the lights and shades of New England Puritanism upon a generation which had almost forgotten its colonial past. Hildreth had published before the Civil War a monumental narrative of American history down to 1820 whose later volumes emphasized the achievements of Federalism, and Parkman's " Oregon Trail " had been written and published before Hildreth's work appeared. The essays of Emerson were a challenge to ethical and speculative thought as well as to religious conservatism, and Story and Kent had written masterly expositions of American law which the courts still cite. The *North American Review* and other magazines had begun to do for American literature what the great English monthlies and quarterlies had long done for literature in England, and a group of great editors in New York were making newspaper editorials a political power. No account of slavery and its overthrow would be complete that did not recognize the modest literary contribution of Mrs. Stowe, for the generation which fought to preserve the Union was the same which had wept over the sufferings of Uncle Tom and cursed the brutal tyranny of Legree.

The Civil war stands in American history as both a culmination and a point of departure. All that the nation possessed of character and material resource went into the war on the one side or on the other, but although slavery was abolished and the Union saved from rupture both victors and vanquished bore scars which the sixty years that have since elapsed have not sufficed wholly to obliterate. Only slowly did the sectional and party animosities which the war had aroused disappear, and long after the formal task of political reconstruction was completed the South was often spoken of with bitterness and its loyalty was held in question. Practical concern for the welfare of the Negro waned rapidly in the North after emancipation, Negro education was left almost wholly to private or sectarian effort, and the barrier of race and color operated not only to prevent social intercourse but also to limit increasingly for Negroes the field of skilled employment. The political temper of the solid South, joined to the disposition of immigrants when naturalized to ally themselves with the Democrats rather than with the Republicans, made membership in the Democratic party long a social stigma in many northern States and cemented the hold of the Republicans upon the business and professional classes. Neither party was much concerned to keep its political methods pure, and the corrupt use of money in national, State, and local elections was an evil common to both; and when the Democrats who had saluted Cleveland as a leader failed to support his recommendations, fought him openly in Congress and in the press, and exhibited in practice no higher moral standards and less capacity for rule than their Republican opponents, reformers and independents found it easy to denounce both parties as offering only a choice of evils and to register a fruitless protest by staying away from the polls.

The American temperament was tolerant of political abuses, but it was not disposed to accept in perpetuity either inefficiency or corruption, and before long the work of reformation began both within and without the party organizations. Men whose business or professional fortunes were still to be made braved social odium and supported Cleveland, and young men who had sneered at politics as " dirty business " laid aside their prejudices and took a hand. Teachers of economics and political science put protection and political corruption on the defensive in colleges and universities, and newspapers found it expedient to drop their party banners and proclaim at least a nominal independence. A powerful weekly press, including denominational journals of wide circulation, came to the aid of civil service reform, tariff revision, and sound money, popular books on political and economic subjects multiplied, and the brush and pencil of the cartoonist exhibited without mercy the foibles and vices of politicians. A new generation in Congress turned from the old and distasteful issues of the war and reconstruction to the more vital problems of trusts, railway regulation, and financial reform, while beyond the Mississippi the opening of transcontinental railway lines and the development of mining, grain growing, and cattle raising were banishing the last remnants of the frontier and forming a prosperous and energetic society ready to follow any leader who could lead with small regard to the party to which he had once belonged.

The war with Spain, bringing together the South, the North, and the West in a brief but exhilarating common effort and opening new vistas of world power, only deepened the national searching of heart, and a veritable mania for investigation and reform prepared the way for the sweeping and fervid exhortations of Roosevelt. A mere enumeration of the things to which the public mind with feverish vigor turned its attention would be bewildering. Scandals were hunted out and probed, administrative practices were overhauled, charges of corruption in elections or in public office were exposed, and State laws undertook to regulate party primaries, punish bribery and fraud, and limit campaign expenditures by candidates. State constitutions were repeatedly revised or amended, associations of lawyers busied themselves with the drafting of model statutes, city government by commission was widely essayed, new political devices of referendum, initiative, and recall were introduced, and suffrage for women was hopefully pressed. The appointment of committees in the House of Representatives was wrested from the control of the speaker and a close oligarchy of party leaders, and public hearings on measures of importance became an established practice. Without essential modification of the Constitution itself the legislative machinery of the federal government was liberalized and executive efficiency enhanced, and government in States and nation became a government of the people and for the people to a greater degree than had ever before been known.

The reconstitution of social life kept pace with the reform of politics. The establishment of an eight-hour day, payment of wages in money instead of in orders for goods, the regulation of the labor of women and children, factory and tenement house inspection and improved building laws, the abolition of the sweat shop, industrial insurance, old age pensions, and accident prevention, stricter regulation of railway transportation, the abatement of immigration abuses, improved housing and municipal sanitation, federal control of public health and epidemic diseases, city planning, open spaces and playgrounds, the extirpation of commercialized vice, rigorous supervision of the liquor traffic clearly foreshadowing ultimate prohibition, free and compulsory education for the masses and State-supported education in universities and professional schools, and a scientific and humanitarian treatment of poverty, crime, and delinquency are only the more striking incidents of a crusade which made social service a passion and broadened the foundations of national happiness. Where public funds failed private generosity came to supplement them, and the millions of accumulated wealth which were poured out in aid of social undertakings made American giving the amazement not only of other peoples but of the nation itself.

Neither politically nor socially, however, did the

American temperament lose its practical and inherently conservative character. No exposure of industrial abuses shook the hold of capitalism upon prevailing economic thought, and the economic teachings of socialism at no time acquired wide popular vogue. Save for the short-lived Progressive movement and the less important Populist agitation, political liberalism never broke completely with old party affiliations and liberal journals lived only by the aid of private subsidies. The unstinted generosity of the rich maintained throughout a predominantly practical interest, and the endowment of scientific research or professional study was more readily obtained than philanthropic support for literature, art, or general public education. The war with Spain bred no aggressive spirit in international relations, and the successful and mighty efforts of the world war left the United States as destitute as ever of militaristic ambition and anxious only for the speedy return of peace. In America as everywhere the overthrow of the Russian imperial government was acclaimed as a great step toward liberty, and the revolutionary movements which succeeded the downfall of the Tsar were watched with sympathetic attention by all classes, but when constitutional revolution gave way to bolshevism official recognition of the novel régime was refused and the propagation of communist doctrine in the United States was ruthlessly repressed. Wherever a European population was starving or pestilence was rampant American financial relief and

scientific skill were ready with their aid, and the huge
war loans to the allies were granted for the asking,
but after the war was over no fervor or subtlety of
petition could induce either government or people to
do for Europe what it was firmly believed Europe
should be left to do for itself. Stirred to the depths
as it easily is by the appeal of great human causes,
gigantic as is the strength which it disposes when it
feels that the time for action has come, the American
mind keeps firm its hold upon reality and trusts to
the perfected working of tried historical processes for
the coming of the social betterment to which the
nation has never ceased to aspire.

The history of American democracy is only in a
special and limited sense a story of material growth.
The subjugation of nature to the service of man has
been cast for the United States upon a continental
scale and the physical fruits of conquest have been
varied and large, but the temper of the conquerors
has been from the beginning the temper of those who,
fixing their eyes upon the future, have thought of themselves as they would like to be. Neither discourage-
ment nor contentment nor illusion has ever dominated
the American spirit for long, and the failures and
successes of yesterday have been only the points of
departure for today. It is the priceless possession of
the American nation that it is still young, that it still
has material battles to fight and conquests of mind
to gain, and that in a world which has not yet found
peace its spirit ranges generous, buoyant, and free.

# BIBLIOGRAPHY

# BIBLIOGRAPHY

## CHAPTER I

### THE CENTURIES OF BEGINNINGS

AUTHORITIES. A considerable number of the most important contemporary accounts have been collected, with editorial notes, in Jameson's *Original Narratives of American History;* Hart's *American History Told by Contemporaries,* covering the whole period until after the Civil War, gives numerous short extracts. The European situation in the period of discovery and early settlement is admirably summarized in Cheyney's *European Background of American History.* The best brief modern account of Spanish exploration and conquest is Bourne's *Spain in America.* For the French achievements Parkman's *Pioneers of France in the New World, The Jesuits in North America, La Salle and the Discovery of the Great West, The Old Régime in Canada, Frontenac and New France, A Half Century of Conflict,* and *Montcalm and Wolfe* still hold their place in scholarship and literary charm; Thwaites's *France in America* is the best brief account. Channing's *History of the United States,* intended to cover the whole period, is a scholarly narrative embodying recent investigations. The fullest account by an English writer is Doyle's *English in America,* but the treatment of colonial affairs in Gardiner's *History of England in the Reigns of Elizabeth and James I,* and the later works by the same author on the Puritan period in England, should not be neglected. See also Eggleston's *Beginners of a Nation,* Fiske's *Dutch and Quaker Colonies,* Andrews's *Colonial Self-Government,* and Greene's *Provincial America.* Selections from charters and other formal documents (to 1898) are in MacDonald's *Documentary Source Book of American History.*

## CHAPTER II

### THROUGH REVOLUTION TO INDEPENDENCE

AUTHORITIES. Of the comprehensive narratives of the Revolutionary period that of Channing, *History of the United States,* is the most scholarly and judicious. Lecky's *History of England in the Eighteenth Century* gives a critical English view. Tyler's *Literary History of the American Revolution* is indispensable for an understanding of the period, and Fisher's *Story of the American Revolution* is often important for details. Burke's speeches on American Taxation and Conciliation with America are the great pleas of a great statesman. The most useful biographies, important also in some cases for the early constitutional period as well, are those of Franklin, Samuel Adams, Patrick Henry, John Adams, Washington, and Jefferson in the *American Statesmen* series, and Sumner's *Robert Morris,* the latter the most elaborate account of Revolutionary finance. There is an admirable brief sketch of the finances of the Revolution in Dewey's *Financial History of the United States,* which work should also be consulted on all later financial topics.

## CHAPTER III

### FRAMING A NATIONAL CONSTITUTION

AUTHORITIES. To Channing's *United States* may now be added McMaster's *History of the People of the United States*, beginning with the close of the Revolution and extending to the Civil War, and rich in social and economic material. Hildreth's *History of the United States*, an older work extending to 1820, is still important. Bancroft's *History of the Formation and Adoption of the Constitution* is a ponderous work not yet wholly superseded, but McLaughlin's *The Confederation and the Constitution* gives in brief compass the essential data. Farrand's edition of the debates in the Federal Convention has displaced all earlier editions. The classical contemporary exposition of the Constitution is *The Federalist*, by Hamilton and others, available in numerous editions. There are useful biographies of Madison and Jay in the *American Statesmen* series.

## CHAPTER IV

### THE ORGANIZATION OF GOVERNMENT AND POLITICS

AUTHORITIES. For the general narrative Channing and McMaster as before, and in addition Schouler's *History of the United States*, an important work extending to 1865. Hildreth, who wrote with a Federalist leaning, should not be passed over. Stanwood's *History of the Presidency* is the authoritative account of the successive presidential elections. Additional biographies in the *American Statesmen* series include those of Marshall, Gallatin, and Monroe. With 1789 begin the regular series of Senate and House journals and other documents, debates in Congress (in successive collections known as *Annals of Congress, Congressional Debates, Congressional Globe,* and *Congressional Record*), the *United States Statutes at Large,* and the decisions of the Supreme and other Federal courts. Richardson's *Messages and Papers of the Presidents* is a standard compilation. There are editions, in some cases several editions, of the collected writings of most of the earlier statesmen of prominence.

## CHAPTER V

### DEMOCRACY AND NATIONALITY

AUTHORITIES. For the period from 1801 to 1817 Henry Adams's *History of the United States* is of marked importance, especially on the diplomatic side. Channing's *Jeffersonian Period* and Turner's *Rise of the New West* are valuable summary accounts. Mahan's *Sea Power in the War of 1812* is a special study of high value. Additional biographical literature includes the lives of Cass, John Quincy Adams, and Jackson in the *American Statesmen* series, and the lives of Jackson by Parton (an old-fashioned work still valuable) and Bassett. The most notable work of reminiscence is the diary of John Quincy Adams, supplemented now by Ford's edition of Adams's writings. Turner's *The Frontier in American History* is an interpretation of the first importance; Roosevelt's *Winning of the West* has scholarly merit as well as literary interest.

## CHAPTER VI

### A NEW PHASE OF DEMOCRATIC CONTROL

AUTHORITIES. To the biographies already referred to, and the diary of John Quincy Adams, should be added the lives of Webster, Calhoun, Benton, and Van Buren in the *American Statesmen* series, Benton's *Thirty Years' View* (1820–1850), Amos Kendall's *Autobiography*, and the diary of Van Buren. Special studies of importance include MacDonald's *Jacksonian Democracy*, Hart's *Slavery and Abolition*, DuBois's *History of the Suppression of the African Slave Trade*, Houston's *Critical Study of Nullification in South Carolina*, Catterall's *History of the Second Bank of the United States*, Taussig's *Tariff History of the United States*, and Bourne's *History of the Surplus Revenue of 1837*.

## CHAPTER VII

### A HOUSE DIVIDED AGAINST ITSELF

AUTHORITIES. Until 1850 the authorities are mainly those already referred to. After 1850 Rhodes's *History of the United States from the Compromise of 1850* is the fullest and most important narrative account. Burgess's *Middle Period* and Garrison's *Westward Extension* are useful shorter studies. The lives of Seward, Sumner, Chase, and Lincoln in the *American Statesmen* series, and the elaborate life of Lincoln by Nicolay and Hay, also deal with the period. For the Mexican war J. H. Smith's *War with Mexico*, Polk's *Diary*, a human document of remarkable interest, and McCormac's *James K. Polk*.

## CHAPTER VIII

### THE TRIUMPH OF NATIONALITY

AUTHORITIES. The monumental history of the abolition movement is W. P. and F. P. Garrison's *William Lloyd Garrison*. Spring's *Kansas* is the best and most picturesque account of the Kansas episode. The best biographies of John Brown are those by Sanborn and Villard. Burgess's *Civil War and the Constitution* is indispensable for the constitutional side of the Civil war, as are the same author's *Reconstruction and the Constitution* and Dunning's *Reconstruction, Political and Economic*, for the reconstruction period; see also the life of Thaddeus Stevens in the *American Statesmen* series. For the position of the South, Davis's *Rise and Fall of the Confederate Government*, Stephens's *War Between the States*, and Pollard's *Lost Cause* are of first-rate importance. For economic conditions in the South during the war, Schwab's *Confederate States of America*. Dewey's *Financial History of the United States*, already referred to, gives an admirable view of Civil war finance. The elaborate government publication known as *War of the Rebellion: Official Records*, is a vast collection of war documents, chiefly military and naval. The documents of the Confederate government, with the exception of the statutes of the Confederate Congress, are still for the most part unpublished. The memoirs of Grant, Sherman, Sheridan, McClellan, and other military leaders have some importance as personal narratives or apologies.

## CHAPTER IX

### THE POLITICS OF INDUSTRY AND POWER

AUTHORITIES. Rhodes's *History of the United States from the Compromise of 1850,* which ends with 1877, is continued by the same author's *History of the United States from Hayes to McKinley.* Sparks's *National Development* and Dewey's *National Problems* are compendious narratives of much usefulness. Problems of tariff and revenue are ably treated in Taussig's *Tariff History* and Dewey's *Financial History,* already referred to; see also Laughlin's *Bimetalism* and Horace White's *Money and Banking.* The collected writings of George William Curtis are especially important for the civil service reform movement. For international questions see Hart's *Foundations of American Foreign Policy,* Moore's *Principles of American Diplomacy,* Fish's *American Diplomacy,* and Latané's *America as a World Power;* with these, for the documents, Moore's monumental *International Law Digest.* Attention should again be called to Stanwood's *History of the Presidency,* containing the texts of party platforms and details of presidential campaigns and electoral votes, and Richardson's *Messages and Papers of the Presidents.*

## CHAPTER X

### AMERICA AND THE NEW WORLD

AUTHORITIES. With the exception of Sparks's *National Development* and Dewey's *National Problems,* already cited, and Paxton's *Recent History of the United States,*

recourse must now be had to the various annual cyclo-
paedias and political almanacs, the *International Year
Book* and *American Year Book* being especially comprehensive. Bishop's *Theodore Roosevelt and his Time* and
Woodrow Wilson's *State Papers and Addresses* are of
fundamental importance. There is as yet no scholarly
account of the world war, and most of the popular sketches
are highly biased; McMaster's *The United States in the
World War,* Crowell and Wilson's *How America went to
War,* and Scott's *Survey of International Relations between the United States and Germany, 1914–1917,* have,
however, some usefulness. The fullest and ablest account
of the negotiations at Paris is Temperley's *History of the
Peace Conference,* with the texts of the various treaties
and numerous documents.

## CHAPTER XI

### POLITICS AND THE AMERICAN MIND

AUTHORITIES. There is no comprehensive work on the
topics treated in this chapter. The following, however,
will be found useful in addition to many of the works
already cited: *The Cambridge History of American Litera-
ture,* Merriam's *American Political Theories,* Bryce's
*American Commonwealth,* De Tocqueville's *Democracy in
America* (for the first half of the 19th century), Hayes's
*American Democracy, its History and Problems,* Croly's
*The Promise of American Life,* Stearns's *Liberalism in
America.*

# CHRONOLOGY

# CHRONOLOGY

## I. Until the Revolution

1492. First voyage of Columbus. Second voyage 1493, third 1498, fourth 1502. Neither voyage extended to the mainland of North America.

1493. A bull of Pope Alexander VI divided America between Spain and Portugal.

1497. Cabot discovered some part of North America, probably Cape Breton or Labrador. The basis of English claims to American territory.

1513. Ponce de Leon explored Florida.

1519. Pineda found the mouth of the Mississippi.

1539-42. De Soto traversed the Gulf coast from Florida to the Mississippi.

1587. Grant of American territory to Raleigh, who named the territory Virginia. A "lost colony" planted in North Carolina.

(1603-25, *reign of James I*.)

1606. First Virginia charter; first settlement 1607.

1609. Second Virginia charter.

1612. Third Virginia charter, revoked by the crown 1624.

1614. John Smith explored the New England coast.

1619. Representative government established in Virginia; first introduction of negro slaves.

1620. Grant of territory to the Council for New England. Settlement of Separatists at Plymouth.

1621.   Charter of Dutch West India Company; 1623,
        first settlement at New Amsterdam (New York).

(1625–49, *reign of Charles I.*)

1628.   Puritan settlement at Salem, Massachusetts.

1629.   First charter of Massachusetts: annulled 1684.
        (Parliament dissolved, no other for eleven years.)

1632.   Charter of Maryland; taken away 1688, restored
        1715; representative government established in
        Massachusetts.

1635.   First English settlement in Connecticut.

1636.   Settlement of Providence, Rhode Island; Harvard
        College established.

1638.   Swedish settlements on the Delaware; passed
        under English jurisdiction 1664; acquired by
        Penn from the Duke of York 1682; Delaware
        a separate colony 1703.

1639.   Fundamental Orders of Connecticut, the first
        frame of government.

1643–84.   New England Confederation.

1644.   Patent for Providence Plantations.

1649.   Maryland Toleration act.

(1649–60, *Commonwealth and Protectorate.*)

1651.   Beginning of series of navigation acts and acts
        of trade, intended to control colonial trade in
        the interest of England; 1660, so-called First
        Navigation act, consolidating and extending
        earlier provisions; numerous later acts to 1696.

(1660–85, *reign of Charles II.*)

1663.   First charter of Carolina; second charter 1665; in
        1729 the two colonies of North and South Caro-
        lina passed under the control of the crown;
        charter of Rhode Island, legally operative, with
        some changes at the time of the Revolution,

until 1843; charter of Connecticut, legally operative, with changes as in Rhode Island, until 1818.

1664. Following war between England and Holland the Dutch possessions in America, which had been taken by the English, were given to the Duke of York (later James II), and the names of New Netherland and New Amsterdam were changed to New York. Grant of New Jersey by the Duke of York to Berkeley and Carteret; in 1674 the colony was divided, and Carteret's rights in East New Jersey were later acquired by Penn and Quaker associates; New Jersey a royal province from 1702.

1681. Charter of Pennsylvania, in force until the Revolution.

1682. La Salle took possession of the Mississippi valley for Louis XIV of France; 1699, first settlements in Louisiana; 1718, New Orleans founded.

1683. Representative government established in New York.

(1685–89, *reign of James II;* 1688–89, *English Revolution.*)

(1689–1702, *reign of William and Mary.*)

1689–97. War between England and France, known in America as King William's war, and involving war between the English and French colonies without change in the territorial status of either.

1691. Second charter of Massachusetts, with Plymouth incorporated; Maine later purchased by Massachusetts from the Gorges claimants.

1693. William and Mary College established.

1701. Cadillac founded Detroit.

(1702–14, *reign of Anne.*)

1702–13.　War of the Spanish Succession, known in America as Queen Anne's war.

(1714–27, *reign of George I.*)

(1727–60, *reign of George II.*)

1733.　Charter of Georgia, limited to 21 years.

1744–48.　War of the Austrian Succession, known in America as King George's war.

1746.　Princeton College founded.

1756–63.　Seven Years' war (fighting in America from 1754).

(1760, *beginning of the reign of George III.*)

1763.　Peace of Paris.


## II.  The Revolution and the Confederation

1763.　Royal proclamation regulating the administration of the territory acquired from France.

1764.　Sugar act, a revival and revision of the Molasses act of 1733, regulating the colonial trade in sugar products.

1765.　Stamp act, repealed 1766 to the accompaniment of a Declaratory act asserting the right of Parliament to tax the colonies; Stamp Act Congress at New York.

1767.　Townshend Revenue acts; modified in 1770 with the retention of a duty on tea.

1768.　British troops sent to Boston.

1770.　March 5, Boston Massacre.

1772.　Committees of Correspondence begin in Massachusetts, later appointed in all the colonies; burning of the *Gaspee* in Narragansett Bay.

1773. December 16, destruction of East India Company tea at Boston.

1774. The "five intolerable acts": (1) closing the port of Boston, (2) altering the Massachusetts charter, (3) providing for the trial in England or in other colonies of persons accused of crime through enforcement of revenue laws, (4) regulating the provision of quarters for troops, (5) relating to the province of Quebec. Sept.–Oct., First Continental Congress, Philadelphia, issued a Declaration of Rights and adopted a non-importation and non-consumption agreement known as "The Association."

1775. April 19, battles of Lexington and Concord; May 10, meeting of Second Continental Congress, in existence until the adoption of the Articles of Confederation, 1781; June 17, battle of Bunker Hill; July, Washington took command of the American army; December, unsuccessful attempt to take Quebec.

1776. March 17, British evacuated Boston; June, unsuccessful attempt of British to take Charleston; July 4, Declaration of Independence; August, battle of Long Island, followed by Washington's retreat across New Jersey; December, battle of Trenton.

1777. January, battle of Princeton; June, Burgoyne's invasion; August, St. Leger defeated at Oriskany; September, Washington defeated at Brandywine Creek; October, Burgoyne surrendered at Saratoga, Washington unsuccessful at Germantown; November, Articles of Confederation adopted by Congress and submitted to the States

1778. February, alliance with France; British abandoned Philadelphia, but occupied Charleston and Savannah; beginning of three years' war in the South; Indian power broken in the Wyoming valley; Kaskaskia and Vincennes taken by Clark.

1779. Naval victories of John Paul Jones.

1781. Articles of Confederation in effect; October, surrender of Cornwallis at Yorktown.

1782. Preliminary treaty of peace.

1783. September 3, definitive treaty of peace.

1784. Jefferson's plan for the organization of the western territory.

1787. May, Federal Convention, Philadelphia; September, Constitution adopted by the convention, transmitted by Congress to the States, and ratified by conventions in eleven States by the end of 1788; Northwest Ordinance, or Ordinance of 1787, adopted by Congress while the Federal Convention was in session.

## III. Constitutional Period

1789–93. *First Washington administration. 1st and 2d Congresses.*

April 30, 1789. Washington inaugurated at New York, the administration dating legally from March 4; Federal capital at New York 1789–91, then at Philadelphia until 1801, then removed to the District of Columbia.

1789. North Carolina ratified the Constitution.

1790. Rhode Island ratified the Constitution; first decennial census.

1791.  First Bank of the United States chartered, the charter expiring by limitation in 1811; Vermont admitted as a State; December, first ten Amendments of the Constitution in force.

1792.  Kentucky admitted as a State.

1793.  Proclamation of American neutrality in war between England and France; Genet episode; cotton gin invented by Eli Whitney.

1793–97.  *Second Washington administration.  3d and 4th Congresses.*

1794.  Whiskey insurrection in Pennsylvania; Jay treaty with England.

1796.  Tennessee admitted as a State.

1797–1801.  *John Adams administration.  5th and 6th Congresses.*

1798.  January 8, Eleventh Amendment in force; X. Y. Z. affair; naval war with France; Alien and Sedition acts; Kentucky and Virginia resolutions.

1801–05.  *First Jefferson administration* (Jefferson chosen by the House of Representatives).  *7th and 8th Congresses.*

1801–02.  War with the Barbary states.

1803.  Ohio admitted as a State; Louisiana purchased from France.

1804.  September 25, Twelfth Amendment in force.

1805–09.  *Second Jefferson administration.  9th and 10th Congresses.*

1806.  Embargo act; the Burr conspiracy.

1809–13.  *First Madison administration.  11th and 12th Congresses.*

1810.  American occupation of Spanish territory east of the Mississippi.

1812. Declaration of war against England; Louisiana admitted as a State.

1813–17. *Second Madison administration. 13th and 14th Congresses.*

1814. August, capitol and other buildings at Washington burned by the British; September, naval battles of Lake Erie and Lake Champlain; October, British and Indians defeated by Harrison at the Thames; December 24, treaty of Ghent.

1815. January, defeat of the British by Jackson at New Orleans.

1816. Protective tariff act; second Bank of the United States chartered (the constitutionality of the bank was upheld by the Supreme Court in 1819, in the case of McCulloch *v.* Maryland; the charter expired by limitation in 1836); Indiana admitted as a State.

1817–21. *First Monroe administration. 15th and 16th Congresses.*

1817. Mississippi admitted as a State.

1818. Jackson invaded Florida; Illinois admitted as a State.

1819. The Floridas acquired from Spain by treaty (ratified by Spain 1821); Alabama admitted as a State.

1820. First Missouri compromise; Maine admitted as a State.

1821. Second Missouri compromise; Missouri admitted as a State.

1821–25. *Second Monroe administration. 17th and 18th Congresses.*

1823. Declaration of the Monroe doctrine.

1824. Protective tariff act.

1825–29. *John Quincy Adams administration* (Adams chosen by the House of Representatives). *19th and 20th Congresses.*

1825. Erie canal completed.

1828. Protective tariff, known as the " tariff of abominations."

1829–33. *First Jackson administration. 21st and 22d Congresses.*

1830. The " great debate " in the Senate between Webster and Hayne; first section of the Baltimore & Ohio Railroad opened.

1831. First national nominating convention, that of the Anti-Masonic party; the " Liberator " founded by William Lloyd Garrison.

1832. Bill to recharter the Bank of the United States vetoed; protective tariff act, modifying the duties of the act of 1828; South Carolina ordinance of nullification; Jackson's proclamation to South Carolina; New England Anti-Slavery Society founded.

1833. Compromise tariff act.

1833–37. *Second Jackson administration. 23d and 24th Congresses.*

1833. Removal of the deposits; Senate resolution censuring Jackson expunged from the journal January, 1837.

1836. Act for the distribution of the surplus revenue among the States; " gag rule " of the House of Representatives against the reception of abolition petitions; Arkansas admitted as a State; Texas declared its independence of Mexico.

1837–41. *Van Buren administration. 25th and 26th Congresses.*

1837.  Michigan admitted as a State; panic of 1837.

1839.  "Aroostook war" over the disputed northern boundary of Maine.

1840.  Independent Treasury act, repealed 1841, system reëstablished 1846.

1841–45.  *Harrison and Tyler administrations* (Harrison died April 4, 1841).  *27th and 28th Congresses.*

1842.  Ashburton treaty settling the northeastern boundary dispute; tariff act.

1844.  Treaty for the annexation of Texas rejected by the Senate.

1845.  Texas annexed by joint resolution, admitted as a State in December; Florida admitted as a State.

1845–49.  *Polk administration.  29th and 30th Congresses.*

1846.  May 8, battle of Palo Alto; May 9, battle of Resaca de la Palma; May 13, declaration of war against Mexico; Wilmot proviso regarding slavery in territory purchased from Mexico; Iowa admitted as a State.

1847.  February, battle of Buena Vista; September, occupation of the city of Mexico.

1848.  February 2, treaty of Guadalupe Hidalgo ending the Mexican war; discovery of gold in California; Wisconsin admitted as a State.

1849–53.  *Taylor and Fillmore administrations* (Taylor died July 9, 1850).  *31st and 32d Congresses.*

1849.  A free State constitution adopted by California.

1850.  Compromise measures; California admitted as a State; Clayton-Bulwer treaty with Great Britain regarding an isthmian canal.

1852.  Publication of "Uncle Tom's Cabin."

1853–57.  *Pierce administration.  33d and 34th Congresses.*

1853. Gadsden purchase of Mexican territory.

1854. Kansas-Nebraska act; Republican party organized in Michigan; Ostend manifesto regarding the annexation of Cuba.

1855–56. Civil war in Kansas.

1857–61. *Buchanan administration. 35th and 36th Congresses.*

1857. Dred Scott decision; panic of 1857.

1858. Lincoln-Douglas debates in Illinois; Minnesota admitted as a State.

1859. John Brown's raid at Harper's Ferry; Oregon admitted as a State.

1860. December 20, South Carolina ordinance of secession.

1861. January, Kansas admitted as a State; February, government of the Confederate States of America formed at Montgomery.

1861–65. *First Lincoln administration. 37th and 38th Congresses.*

1861. April 13, surrender of Fort Sumter; July 21, first battle of Bull Run; the Trent affair.

1862. Union victories at Fort Henry, Fort Donelson, Madrid, and Island No. 10; March, *Monitor-Merrimac* encounter; Lincoln's message recommending compensated emancipation; April, battle of Shiloh; New Orleans taken; June–July, Wilderness campaign; August 29–30, second battle of Bull Run; September, battle of Antietam, followed by the Emancipation Proclamation, effective January 1, 1863; greenback currency introduced; Union Pacific and Central Pacific railways chartered; Homestead act.

1863. July 1–3, battle of Gettysburg; July 4, Vicksburg

taken, completing the opening of the Mississippi; September, battle of Chickamauga; November, battle of Chattanooga; National Bank act; Habeas Corpus act; Draft act, followed by riots in New York; West Virginia admitted as a State.

1864. May, Wilderness battles; June, the *Alabama* sunk by the *Kearsarge;* August, Mobile taken; August-October, Sheridan's Shenandoah valley raid; September, Atlanta taken; December, Savannah and Nashville taken; Nevada admitted as a State.

1865–69. *Lincoln and Johnson administrations* (Lincoln assassinated April 14, died the next day). *39th and 40th Congresses.*

1865. April 9, surrender of Lee; April 26, surrender of Johnston; May 29, Johnson's amnesty proclamation; December 18, Thirteenth Amendment in force.

1866. Freedmen's Bureau act; Civil Rights act; June, Fourteenth Amendment adopted by Congress, in force July 28, 1868; Atlantic cable opened.

1867. Reconstruction acts; Tenure of Office act; impeachment of Johnson; Nebraska admitted as a State; Alaska purchased from Russia; National Grange of the Patrons of Husbandry formed.

1869–73. *First Grant administration. 41st and 42nd Congresses.*

1869. Knights of Labor organized.

1870. Fifteenth Amendment in force.

1870–72. Federal election acts, popularly known as the " force bills."

1871. Treaty of Washington for the arbitration of the

*Alabama* claims and the northwest boundary controversy.

1873–77. *Second Grant Administration. 43d and 44th Congresses.*

1873. A Coinage act, later known as " the crime of 1873," omitted the standard silver dollar from the list of coins; panic of 1873.

1875. Resumption act, providing for the resumption of specie payment January 1, 1879.

1876. Colorado admitted as a State.

1877–81. *Hayes administration* (Hayes chosen in accordance with the decisions of an Electoral Commission). *45th and 46th Congresses.*

1877. Baltimore & Ohio Railway strike.

1878. Bland-Allison Silver Coinage act.

1880. Treaty with China restricting Chinese immigration.

1881–85. *Garfield and Arthur administrations* (Garfield shot July 2, died September 19). *47th and 48th Congresses.*

1881. American Federation of Labor organized.

1882. Act prohibiting for ten years the immigration of Chinese laborers; 1892, act extended for another ten years.

1883. Pendleton Civil Service act; revised protective tariff act.

1884. Revised tariff bill defeated.

1885–89. *First Cleveland administration. 49th and 50th Congresses.*

1887. Cleveland's tariff message; Interstate Commerce act.

1889–93. *Harrison administration. 51st and 52d Congresses.*

1889. North Dakota, South Dakota, Montana, and Washington admitted as States.

1890. McKinley Tariff act; Sherman Anti-Trust act; Sherman Silver Purchase act, repealed 1893; Idaho and Wyoming admitted as States.

1892. Homestead, Pa., strike.

1893. Treaty for the annexation of Hawaii submitted to the Senate, later withdrawn by Cleveland.

1893–97. *Second Cleveland administration. 53rd and 54th Congresses.*

1893. Panic of 1893; Behring Sea arbitration.

1894. Wilson-Gorman tariff act; Chicago railway strike.

1895. Venezuela boundary controversy with Great Britain.

1896. Utah admitted as a State.

1897–1901. *First McKinley administration. 55th and 56th Congresses.*

1897. Dingley protective tariff act.

1898. February 15, Battleship *Maine* destroyed by an explosion at Havana; April 11, McKinley's message on the Cuban crisis; April 19, joint resolution on the independence of Cuba; April 23, declaration of war against Spain; May 1, Dewey's victory at Manila; July 3, destruction of the Spanish fleet at Santiago; August 12, preliminary peace; December 10, definitive treaty of peace (a later cession of islands in the Philippines November 7, 1920); July, Federal Bankruptcy act.

1899. Tripartite treaty (United States, Great Britain, and Germany) partitioning the Samoan Islands; First Hague Conference.

1900. Civil government established in the Philippines.

1901–05. *McKinley and Roosevelt administrations* (McKinley shot September 6, 1901, died September 14). *57th and 58th Congresses.*

1901. Panama Canal treaty with Great Britain replacing the Clayton-Bulwer treaty of 1850; first of several important acts amending the Interstate Commerce act of 1887.

1902. Act for the reclamation of arid lands; anthracite coal strike.

1902. Commission government for the Philippines established; replaced by representative government in 1916.

1903. Isthmian Canal convention.

1904. Panama Canal Zone treaty.

1905–09. *Roosevelt administration. 59th and 60th Congresses.*

1907. Inland Waterways Commission established; Oklahoma admitted as a State.

1908. First conference of governors at Washington.

1909–13. *Taft administration. 61st and 62d Congresses.*

1909. Payne-Aldrich tariff act.

1910. Postal savings banks established.

1910–11. Garment workers' strike, New York and Chicago.

1912. Arizona and New Mexico admitted as States.

1913. February 25, Sixteenth Amendment in force.

1913–17. *First Wilson administration. 63d and 64th Congresses.*

1913. May 31, Seventeenth Amendment in force; Underwood tariff act; Federal Reserve Bank system established.

1914. August, declarations of war in Europe.

1916. Champlain Barge Canal completed.

1917–21. *Second Wilson administration. 65th and 66th Congresses.*

1917. February 5, Immigration Restriction act (further

restrictions by act of June 5, 1920); March 2,
Porto Rico Government act; March 31, Virgin
Islands occupied by the United States under
treaty of purchase with Denmark; April 2, Wilson's war message; April 6, declaration of war
against Germany; December, declaration of war
against Austria.

1918. November 11, armistice; Erie Barge Canal opened.

1919. January 18, Peace Conference opened at Paris;
June 28, treaty of Versailles signed; November
19, treaty rejected by the Senate.

1920. January 16, Eighteenth Amendment in force;
March 19, treaty of Versailles again rejected by
the Senate; April 13, Railway Wage Board
established; June 10, Nineteenth Amendment in
force.

1921– . *Harding administration. 67th Congress.*

1921. May 18, Immigration Restriction act establishing
a quota system, operative until June 30, 1922,
but subsequently extended; May 27, Emergency
Tariff act; June 16, Federal Budget and Accounting act; July 2, joint resolution declaring peace
with Germany and Austria; August 15, Meat
Packers and Stockyards act; August 24, Grain
Exchange Trading act; August 25, treaty of
peace with Germany signed; October 18, peace
treaties with Germany, Austria, and Hungary
ratified by the Senate; treaty with Colombia
paying for the Panama Canal zone; November,
Washington Conference on disarmament; December 13, four-Power treaty (United States,
Great Britain, France, and Japan) regarding the
Pacific.

# INDEX

Date Due